THE ART OF
INSPIRED LIVING

COACHING SERIES

THE ART OF INSPIRED LIVING

Coach Yourself with Positive Psychology

Sarah Corrie

KARNAC

First published in 2009 by
Karnac Books Ltd
118 Finchley Road, London NW3 5HT

British Library Cataloguing in Publication Data

A C.I.P. for this book is available from the British Library

ISBN 978 1 85575 671 7

Edited, designed and produced by The Studio Publishing Services Ltd,
www.studiopublishingservicesuk.co.uk
e-mail: studio@publishingservices.co.uk

Printed in Great Britain

www.karnacbooks.com

CONTENTS

For David.
Thank you.

LIST OF EXERCISES

ABOUT THE AUTHOR

Dr Sarah Corrie is a Chartered Clinical Psychologist who is committed to helping her clients achieve transformational results in their lives. She has extensive experience in both public and private sector services and runs her own practice as well as working as a freelance writer, trainer and lecturer. Sarah is an Accredited Therapist, Supervisor and Trainer with the British Association for Behavioural & Cognitive Psychotherapies, and a Founder Member of the British Psychological Society's Special Group in Coaching Psychology. She is also Deputy Course Director of the Postgraduate Diploma in Cognitive Behavioural Psychotherapy run by Royal Holloway, University of London and Central and North West London Mental Health NHS Foundation Trust. Sarah has a background in the performing arts and is a member of Equity and the Imperial Society of Teachers of Dancing.

ACKNOWLEDGEMENTS AND PERMISSIONS

Many people have contributed to this project and I owe them all a debt of gratitude.

I would particularly like to thank my editor, Professor David Lane, for seeing the potential in the book and for his unfailing support and encouragement at every stage of the process. Without him, there is no doubt that this book would never have been written.

I am also grateful to Robin Linnecar and Claire Palmer for their positive and helpful reviews of the manuscript, and to Oliver Rathbone and all at Karnac who have helped bring the project to completion.

Special thanks go to Peter Hoy for devoting many hours of his free time to proof-reading the manuscript and for detecting the numerous errors that come from knowing the text too well. His support and commitment to the project have helped make me a better writer.

My heartfelt thanks to all at Oakhill Health Centre who make coming to work such an easy and pleasurable experience. Your interest in what I do and your support of my work over many years is more appreciated than you realize.

As always, my gratitude goes to Ian Lacey, who has helped to bring the book into being in many different ways and who, in the past two years, has taken such great strides in following a path of his own choosing. He embodies the art of inspired living on many levels. Your story is in here too.

Finally, I wish to thank all of those people who have so generously allowed me to include their stories in this book. Your experiences inspire me to do better every day. Without you, this book would make no sense.

Permissions

I would like to thank the publishers, organizations and individuals who granted permission to reference, adapt or reprint the cited material:

Harold Ober Associates for permission to quote an extract from *The Patriot* by Pearl S. Buck.

Steve Pavlina, for permission to reproduce a section of his article, 'The meaning of life: from purpose to action' (22 June 2005) at www.StevePavlina.com.

PDF Net and the Professional Development Foundation for permission to adapt their work on areas of learning.

Martin Seligman, for permission to reproduce his work with Christopher Peterson on signature strengths.

The case studies in this book are genuine and based on actual people whom I know personally, or with whom I have worked with professionally. In order to protect confidentiality, some names have been changed and certain stories represent an amalgam of several people.

Foreword: Building your Future through The Art of Inspired Living

For our first book in the Practice section of this series we wanted to create an offer of value to the coach or to anyone using coaching. The aim was to provide ideas and materials that a coach could use to enhance their work with clients. We also wanted to offer a guide to practice written in a way that an individual reader could use the tools to guide their own development, working with a coach or with the help of a constructively critical friend.

We did not want to produce yet another self-help guide which promised untold health, wealth, and happiness by following some prescribed rules to become more authentic and discover your true self. While such books have been found helpful to many, few of them have been based on a solid understanding of psychology and many provide prescriptions that promise far more than they can deliver.

Our aim was to commission a work which took as its starting point modern developments in psychological understanding and written by an author with the credentials to speak to you with confidence and clarity about building your future.

We believe we have succeeded with Sarah Corrie. Her own life experience, as outlined in her letter to her readers, talks of her own period of crisis and change. She uses this to inform the book. However, unlike some texts which try to offer advice based largely on personal experience, Sarah draws upon her extensive practice and writing as a psychologist. As a psychologist she is committed to a scientist–practitioner model – in which evidence informs practice and practice shapes evidence.

She has taken the emerging field of positive psychology and provided the reader with a way to use this to enhance their own approach to meeting their needs. The result is a practical guide to the art of inspired living.

What can you expect from this book?

It provides a learning journey that starts with an inspiration inventory. This invites you to review the core domains of your life. As Sarah says, 'It will help you become clearer about what's working really well, which areas need a little refining, and which need some major attention.'

She then provides a MAP to guide you on your journey. This MAP, derived from research into coaching practice and built on the principles of positive psychology, takes you step by step through the process of building the tools you need to achieve your goals. At each stage those who want to read more of the evidence base behind this work can follow the bibliography to review the literature.

As a coach, it will provide a coherent set of tools and exercises you can use with your clients. If you want to coach yourself, then we suggest recruiting a constructive friend who cares for you, but who can provide an alternative viewpoint to give you a different perspective on yourself. Share your journey with them and reflect upon the work you do in the exercises. The book provides a comprehensive set of ideas and, by working through the MAP, you will build the competence to tackle a range of issues. It is not a self-help guide to therapy, and is certainly not an alternative to therapeutic help. It is a guide to making decisions in key areas of your life that you want to change.

As such, it is, as the title suggests, a guide to the Art of Inspired Living. We wish you well with your journey.

Professor David Lane
The Professional Development Foundation

Introduction: A Letter to the Reader

Dear Reader

There is an old Native American proverb that says, 'You have to live your life from beginning to end; no one else can do it for you'. These words sum up a fundamental truth about our existence. From the moment we are born, to the moment we die, our life is the one thing that we can truly call our own. Certainly, there are many elements that we do not directly control, but at this point in our history, many more of us have greater choice over how our lives unfold than ever before.

But choice also brings with it challenge and responsibility. How exactly do you 'live your life from beginning to end'? How do you work out where you want to be headed – and how do you know when you have got there? What gives you a sense of purpose? What is your contribution to the world? Knowing the answers to these questions does, I believe, lie at the heart of a better and more mature response to the challenges we face, both as individuals and as a society.

This book is about learning to live your life more fully. It doesn't promise you abundant joy, the relationship of your dreams, untold riches, or miracle cures. But what it does promise you is a comprehensive programme of personal development, change, and growth that is highly effective.

This coaching programme has been developed with two audiences in mind. The first comprises those who wish to coach themselves to success and who are confident about achieving positive results once they know the basic framework. The second audience is those who work as coaches and who are looking for new ideas and frameworks that they can build into their existing practice. Whatever has drawn you to this book – whether it is because you feel you have reached a crossroads in your life, because you have a very specific goal in mind, or because you are a coach looking for some fresh ideas – there is something here for you.

As you'll discover, I have a great deal of faith in what psychology has to offer. True, life is hard. There are many questions to which psychology does not have the answer and not everyone is helped by the same things. But both my experience and the research evidence tell me that there is so much we can do to enhance our lives, if we only know how. The Art of Inspired Living is available to us all.

My story

About 20 years ago, I reached a turning point in my life. I had trained to be a classical dancer, completing an arduous, eight-year professional training that equipped me for working with a top ballet company. But, after only a few months of working professionally, I knew something was seriously wrong. At the end of every performance, I would be in intense pain. My joints were getting progressively stiffer and sometimes when I woke up in the morning, I couldn't walk at all.

The X-rays confirmed my suspicions: I needed surgery. On the surface, everything went smoothly. But, well after the anticipated recovery period, the pain had not gone away. If anything, it had got worse. After a year of rehabilitation, I was forced to face the facts; my career was over.

At the time, it felt as though my life had ended. Because my whole world had been organized around being a dancer, it felt as though I had lost my identity. If I could no longer do the one thing I believed I had been put on this earth to do, who was I? I didn't even know how I would earn a living, as I had few academic qualifications and no experience of the job market outside of the theatre. I felt profoundly lost. But even though I couldn't see it at the time, I was at a crossroads and about to take a turning that would change everything.

One cold, rainy afternoon, on my way to meet a friend for coffee, I found myself with an hour or so to spare. With time to kill and no umbrella, I ducked into the nearest bookstore, which I thought would give me a place to warm up and dry off. More by chance than by design, I wandered into the personal development section and, to avoid looking as though I had just walked in to get out of the rain (even though I had), selected a book from the shelves and started to flick through the pages.

That book was to change my life. It was called *Feel the Fear and Do It Anyway* by Susan Jeffers, and for me became a gateway to a new future. I learnt that there were people who felt exactly as I did – full of doubts and fears – and that even highly successful people had these feelings about themselves. I learnt that fear didn't need to hold me back and that, far from being a sign of failure, such feelings were simply part of being human. Suddenly, I saw myself as someone who had choices – and as someone who could succeed. For the first time in a long time, it felt safe to think about a different future.

As I pored over the pages of my new purchase, I also realized something else – that books have the potential to transform people's lives. A good friend and early mentor once told me that reading opens all possibilities, and that afternoon I understood exactly what he had meant. I could see how books could be powerful tools for healing old wounds, identifying and fulfilling untapped potential, and negotiating turning points in our lives. I promised myself that if I ever had anything useful to say, anything that might help other people in the way that this book was helping me, then I, too, would write about it.

But it was to be a number of years before I was able to fulfil that promise. For now, experiencing a glimmer of hope, I decided to train to be a dance teacher and qualified a year later. Although I had loved the training, I was beginning to realize that my real interest lay in helping people manage the psychological consequences of injury and premature retirement. As there wasn't any outlet for this kind of work at that time, I began to look elsewhere. What happens to someone when fundamental life changes force them to reassess who they are, I wondered. What enables them to keep going? How do they go about rebuilding their lives? What are the steps that people need to take?

Pondering these questions and reflecting on my own experiences led me to become a volunteer for my local mental health unit. Here, I had the chance to meet and work with people who were engaging with the challenge of rebuilding their lives each and every day. I felt humbled by the extent of their struggles and eager to learn more. Kind and watchful staff patiently answered my many questions and directed me towards relevant reading (more books!) where I discovered that psychology had some illuminating and helpful things to say. My questions were being answered and my ideas about my own future began to crystallize.

Soon after this, I enrolled on a degree in psychology, and after my first lecture I knew I had found what I had been looking for. Although it would take a further seven years before I qualified as a clinical psychologist, I had taken the first steps towards a new career and a new life.

Be aware of your assets

As a psychologist, I have had the privilege of working with hundreds of people who are committed to fulfilling their potential. Every day, I witness the extraordinary journeys that my clients are willing to undertake in order to understand themselves better, discover new solutions, and even, in some cases, to reclaim their lives. I never cease to be moved by their refusal to be beaten by setbacks, and their determination to build lives that reflect their values and priorities.

And yet, it is these same people who often fail to recognize the strengths and resources that they bring to their journey. Instead of appreciating their individuality and respecting themselves for their courage, they view the challenges they face with shame, criticism, or even contempt. They miss the bigger picture – that the intention to face themselves honestly and discover what they really want is the battle half won, and that the biggest asset they possess is themselves.

In her book about the life and work of Martha Graham, Agnes de Mille quotes the great dancer and choreographer as saying the following:

> There is a vitality, a life force, an energy, a quickening that is trans-
> lated through you into action, and because there is only one of you

in all of time, this expression is unique. And if you block it, it will never exist through any other medium and it will be lost. The world will not have it. It is not your business to determine how good it is nor how valuable nor how it compares with other expressions. It is your business to keep it yours clearly and directly, to keep the channel open. [de Mille, 1952])

There is something in this sentiment that speaks directly to my intention in writing this book. Your story, your choices, and your contribution are unique to you. It is not your business to judge their value relative to those of others. It is your job to know your unique profile of strengths, needs, and contribution so that you can appreciate them as the assets that they are and use them to create a life that inspires you.

How psychology can help

Coaching is one of the most valuable investments a person can make in themselves and their future. It can have a profound and enduring effect and help you achieve results way beyond your expectation. Of course, coaching cannot tell you how to live your life. But it can equip you with ideas, methods, and techniques that will help you build a more rewarding and successful future.

Contemporary studies in psychology can provide a secure foundation for building effective methods for self-coaching, and these provide the foundations for the chapters which follow. Ten years ago, I would not have been able to say this with such confidence. Traditionally, psychology focused almost entirely on problems and how to solve them. Despite monumental leaps in these areas, solving problems is not the same thing as knowing how to fulfil your potential. No matter how many problems you fix, if something deeper needs attending to, your life will not inspire you.

However, the last few years have witnessed an exciting development that promises new insights into how we can discover and develop the best in ourselves: the birth of a discipline called 'positive psychology'. Positive psychology is concerned with identifying the strengths, qualities, and skills that contribute to a meaningful and abundant life. It does not sign up to the naïve notion that we can all be, have, and do anything we want. But by drawing on advances in theory and research, it does identify distinct pathways towards personal growth and self-mastery that can enhance our quality of life in significant ways. Combine this with what psychology already knows about motivation and change and you have a recipe for success. As with all recipes, you may ultimately decide to vary the ingredients a little, but if you have mastered the essentials, you are going to get good results time after time.

Introducing you to The Art of Inspired Living: an overview of this book

The Art of Inspired Living is organized in four parts. In Part I, I introduce you to the fundamentals of successful coaching. We begin with an Inspiration Inventory, so that you can clarify the core areas of your life that are working well and those that need some attention. I then introduce you to a coaching model called 'MAP' that will help you clarify your sense of purpose, your attitudes to life, and the goals that make sense for you. This model is simple to learn and you can use it any time you want to coach yourself to success.

In Part II, we will explore the 12 Principles that make up *The Art of Inspired Living*. By putting these principles into practice, you will be able to celebrate what you already have, build more of what you really want, and nourish your potential.

In Part III we will look at some specific ways in which you can apply these principles to different areas of your life. Although there are a potentially limitless number of areas with which coaching can help, I have chosen those areas for which my clients most commonly request help.

1. How to be inspired at work.
2. How to achieve a healthy work-life balance.
3. How to create healthy self-esteem.
4. How to have a healthy relationship with your body.
5. How to develop and sustain rewarding relationships.

Finally, in Part IV, we pull all the different themes together so that you can develop an action plan for the future.

Getting the most out of this book

The Art of Inspired Living will help you to compile a personal port-folio of knowledge that allows you to achieve your goals, fulfil your potential, and pursue what really matters to you.

My task is to guide you step by step through the different chap-ters. Your task is to transform everything you read into a form that makes sense for you – a personal wisdom that can help you to make informed choices about your life.

So, before you get under way, give some thought to what you might need to support you through the process. First, you will need to invest in a journal or notebook that can become a personal learning log. Your learning log is the place for recording any insights, realizations, thoughts, or questions that occur to you as you go along, and is also where you should complete the exercises that are presented throughout the book. It could be a bound note-book, or a loose-leaf folder – whatever feels right for you. You will probably find it helpful to record in your log the page numbers in the book that relate to the exercises you complete in the log, so that you can easily refer back at a later date.

You will also need a system for recording your gains. At the back of the book you will find a 'Gains Diary' specifically for this purpose. Gains can be tangible outcomes, such as goals achieved, or changes in your thoughts, feelings or behaviour, or they can take the form of key insights or new understandings. Use a separate notebook if you prefer, but however you do it, monitoring your progress is essential to successful coaching, so make sure you have a system in place for recording this part of your learning journey.

I recommend that you resist the temptation to try to absorb the contents of this book all at once. Take time to build a relationship with the ideas presented and to explore how they relate to your life. If it helps, discuss them with family and friends, your coach or therapist, and see how they compare with other methods you have learnt.

At the end of most chapters you will also find relevant bibliog-raphy/resources sections, each of which contains a rich resource of ideas, both academic and practical. Many of the references are rele-vant for other chapters, too. Those books and articles that are marked by an asterisk are particularly applicable if you are looking for practical ideas to help fulfil your potential, or in some cases overcome common problems. Those that have no asterisk are aimed primarily at coaches, psychologists, therapists, and others who offer professional services to clients for the purposes of enhancing well-being and personal development. They will also appeal to readers who would like to learn more about the ideas behind *The Art of Inspired Living* and who would like a more academic foundation upon which to build their own coaching framework.

And finally . . .

Our lives are short and we need to honour them. You are the author, every day creating afresh the vision that manifests as your life. Although you have a story to tell, more importantly you have a story to write – your future. This book is dedicated to the story that is yet to be written and is a calling to fill your world with what has meaning for you. Most of all, it is an invitation to live without apology or excuse, taking full responsibility for what has been given to you and what is yours to change. Welcome to the adventure that is your life.

With best wishes from Sarah Corrie.

Bibliography

*de Mille, A. (1952) *Dance to the Piper*. Boston, MA. Little, Brown.

PART I

CHAPTER ONE

Getting Down to Business with the Inspiration Inventory

What do you want from life? What really matters to you? Where do you want to be five years from now?

Imagine that, having worked through this book, you emerge feeling that something important has changed – and changed for the better. How will you know? What would be a 'big win' for you?

Knowing your answers to these questions is absolutely essential to the journey you are about to undertake. If you are going to coach yourself to success you need to know where your priorities lie and what you hope to get out of the process. You have to know not only what you want but why it matters to you and how it will make a difference to your life when you achieve it. In other words, you need to know your agenda for buying this book in order to make it work for you.

Right now, there may be several areas of your life on which you want to coach yourself. These might include enhancing your self-esteem, achieving a better work–life balance, improving your motivation to follow through on a particular goal or embarking on a new career. Your coaching journey may involve a major rethink of your lifestyle or just a little tweaking at the edges.

To help you think about this, I want to introduce you to a tool called the Inspiration Inventory. The purpose of the Inspiration Inventory is to help you review the core domains of your life. It will help you become clearer about what is working really well, which areas need a little refining, and which need some major attention.

I suggest that you take a photocopy of the inventory, and make it the first page of your learning log. Take your time to think about the core domains listed below and then rate each one from 0–10 according to how satisfied and fulfilled you feel (0 = a total lack of satisfaction and fulfilment; 10 = totally fulfilled and satisfied).

Exercise 1. The Inspiration Inventory

1 **Overall happiness and emotional well-being:**

0   1   2   3   4   5   6   7   8   9   10

Prompt questions: Do you enjoy your life? Are you glad just to be alive? Does your life inspire you or are you often anxious, disillusioned, or unhappy?

2 **Relationship to self:**

0   1   2   3   4   5   6   7   8   9   10

Prompt questions: Do you respect the person that you are? Are you at peace with yourself, confident in your abilities or do you worry about coming up to scratch?

3 **Intimate relationships:**

0   1   2   3   4   5   6   7   8   9   10

Prompt questions: Do you feel loved, appreciated and supported by those that matter to you? Can you express emotional and physical intimacy easily? Can you give and receive love freely?

4 **Friendships and social life:**

0   1   2   3   4   5   6   7   8   9   10

Prompt questions: Do you have good friendships based on mutual respect and trust? Can you be yourself in your friendships or do you feel pressured to be someone you are not?

5 **Health:**

0   1   2   3   4   5   6   7   8   9   10

Prompt questions: Do you have abundant energy? Do you respect and nurture your body? Do you nourish yourself with healthy foods, sufficient sleep, and time to relax and unwind?

6 **Lifestyle and work–life balance:**

0   1   2   3   4   5   6   7   8   9   10

Prompt questions: Does your lifestyle reflect and honour your priorities? Do you have a good work–life balance or often feel exhausted or 'burnt out'?

7 **Career and work:**

0   1   2   3   4   5   6   7   8   9   10

Prompt questions: Do you enjoy your work? Does it inspire you and enrich your life? Does it allow you to express your talents and abilities? Does your work sustain or undermine you?

8 Money and finances:

0   1   2   3   4   5   6   7   8   9   10

Prompt questions: Do you have sufficient money to meet your needs? Are you satisfied with your income? Do you have a system for organizing your finances, including outgoings, savings, and pension?

9 Hobbies and leisure interests:

0   1   2   3   4   5   6   7   8   9   10

Prompt questions: Do you have fulfilling hobbies and interests separate from your work? Do you have sufficient time for this part of your life or is it often eroded by work or other pressures?

10 Values and principles:

0   1   2   3   4   5   6   7   8   9   10

Prompt questions: Are you clear about what you stand for? Are you living life according to your core values? Are there any areas of your life in which you compromise your values?

11 Community and contribution:

0   1   2   3   4   5   6   7   8   9   10

Do you feel you make a difference to the world, even in a small way? Do others benefit from your talents and gifts?

12 Spiritual life:

0   1   2   3   4   5   6   7   8   9   10

Prompt questions: Is there space in your life to develop your potential, your expanded self, and your spiritual self? Do you feel the need to belong to a religious or spiritual community? If so, is this need being met?

13 Any other areas important to you (name them in the space below).

0   1   2   3   4   5   6   7   8   9   10

Prompt questions: What other areas of your life really matter to you that are not included in the above?

Helpful hint. As you go through the Inspiration Inventory, think about where you are now in each of these areas compared with five years ago. Are the results favourable or not? This will help you interpret your scores in the light of your recent life history.

Interpreting your results

Any areas where you scored between 8 and 10 are core domains that are working very well for you and from which you are drawing a sense of fulfilment and inspiration. Write four column headings in your learning log: Fulfilled; Might Need Attention; Need Some Attention; Need Attention Urgently. Then check your responses in the Inventory, and write down each area and your score in the appropriate column, identifying these from the list below.

- 8–10 = a core domain in which you are fulfilled and that probably does not need attention right now.
- 4–7 = a core domain that needs some attention at some point, although it might not be your immediate priority.
- 0–3 = a core domain that requires some urgent attention, so you will probably want to prioritize this. Check back over your responses. In how many areas of your life did you score 0–3?

So how did you do? In which areas did you score the highest? Which were the areas on which you scored the lowest? What do your scores tell you about the quality of your life and what needs to change?

What's working well

Let's start by looking at those areas of your life that are going well – those areas where you gave yourself a rating of 8 or more. These areas give you a clue about the strengths, talents, and resources you already have available to you, the same strengths and resources you will need to bring to those areas you want to change. So, think about the role you have played in creating these results. What skills, talents, attitudes, and outlooks have helped you create these effects for yourself? Record your thoughts in your learning log, under the heading 'The reason my life is working well in these areas is because . . .'.

What might need some attention (at some stage)

Now look at those areas where you scored between 4 and 7. You are experiencing some degree of satisfaction, but not as much as you would like. The chances are that you feel these areas of your life will need attention at some point in the future. See if you can identify what is getting in the way here. What attitudes or beliefs are holding you back? Which of your skills and talents are not being used to their full potential? How are you currently organizing your life that prevents you from giving yourself a rating from 8-10? Write your thoughts in your learning log, under the heading 'The reason why these areas of my life are not working as well as I would like are . . .'.

What definitely needs to change

Consider those areas where you are dissatisfied, unfulfilled, or seriously uninspired (any area where you gave yourself a score between 0 and 3). Just like your strengths, the core areas you have identified contain some important clues about you, your values, and how you have chosen to organize your life. So, see if you can work out why you have struggled in these areas. It may be that you are currently missing some important skills or knowledge, or that old habits of thinking, feeling, and behaving are undermining your attempts to succeed. Make a note of anything that seems relevant in your workbook, taking as your heading 'The reason I am struggling in these areas is because . . .'.

Selecting your core domains for self-coaching

Once you have a clearer picture of the core areas that are working well and those that are not, you are in a stronger position to coach yourself to success. Based on the results of your Inspiration Inventory, what do you think are the most important domains to work on right now? Make a list of these in your learning log.

> **Helpful hint**. You can select as many areas as you like, but, depending on how many core themes you think need attention, you may find it beneficial to select just one or two to begin with.

Once you have identified the core domains for your coaching journey, double-check them against the following questions:

- Six months from now, what would you *most* like to be different?
- What would you like more of in your life?
- What, if anything, would you like less of?
- How will you know when you've achieved the results you are looking for?
  - How will you feel?
  - How will you think about yourself, others and life in general?
  - How will you organize your life differently?

Now pull it all together. If you review all your answers, what is the area (or areas) you are going to focus on right now? Write these in your learning log, beginning with 'The core area/s in which I most want to coach myself is/are . . .'.

If you have worked through the previous exercises, you will now have a clear idea of the key area or areas that are going to be the focus of your self-coaching. In the next chapter, I will show you how you can coach yourself to success, using a model called 'MAP'.

CHAPTER TWO

Developing Your Coaching 'MAP'

Before we look at the principles that make up the art of inspired living, I want to introduce you to a simple but powerful coaching model, called 'MAP' (MAP is based on original work by David Lane and colleagues. For a more detailed overview see Lane and Corrie [2006].) 'MAP' stands for:

Mission: Your sense of purpose, the vision you have for your life, what you are aiming for and why it matters to you.

Attitude: The attitudes, beliefs and perspectives that you bring to your coaching journey, as well as the attitudes and perspectives you need to succeed.

Process: The methods, tools, procedures and techniques you need to get from where you are now, to where you want to be.

Once you know the specifics, you can use the MAP model any time you want to make changes to any area of your life. So let's look at MAP in more detail.

Your Mission: where are you going and why?

If you are going to coach yourself effectively, you need to be clear about where you are headed and why this is important to you. Your Mission is not about what you do – it's about your reason for doing it. Having a vision of your life – who you are and what you stand for – helps you develop your potential by keeping you focused on what really matters. It allows you to distinguish between those things you really want, and those things that are just the stuff of envy or fanciful day-dreams. Being clear about your Mission also helps you stay committed to your goals when the going gets tough. So, if you have a tendency to start things but not follow them through, lose heart easily, or find that your successes have a hollow ring to them, take note! Your mission probably needs some clarification.

In Principles 1–4 we'll explore some powerful methods for discovering your mission so that you can use it as a source of inspiration and make it the basis for your life goals.

Your Attitude: perspectives that will guide you to success

Your Attitude refers to the attitudes, beliefs, and perspectives you hold about yourself, other people and the world around you. It also includes your ideas about success, such as whether or not you believe you are capable of achieving your goals.

The Attitude you bring with you to your coaching journey has been shaped over many years by the knowledge and life experience you have accumulated as well as the beliefs of your family, community, work environment, and society. Many of these beliefs will have served you well, but others may be holding you back. If you want a destination that is truly of your own choosing, you need to disentangle yourself from the web of values in which you are immersed, to identify those that still matter to you, and those you have outgrown. You also need to learn how to cultivate an Attitude that will support you in achieving your mission.

In Principles 5–8 you will discover which type of Attitude you need to coach yourself in for the art of inspired living – one that will enhance your quality of life and that will fast-track you on the route to success and fulfilment.

The Process for success: shaping up your tool kit

Once you are clear about your Mission and Attitude, you can design an action plan that will help you get the results you want. Your Process involves drawing upon all the resources you have available to you – your knowledge, your skills, your relationships and networks; in fact, anything that supports you in translating your cherished dreams into a reality. Your Process is essentially a tool-kit, derived from psychological theory, from which you can select different methods according to the task in hand.

In Principles 9–12 you will discover four essential Processes that will help you decide how to turn your Mission into your reality. We will draw on your existing resources and then expand them by introducing you to some new methods and techniques for fine-tuning your goals and designing your own learning journey.

So now you know the core areas you are going to prioritize, and the template you will be using to design your journey. In the next section, we will look at where you are heading and why – the first stage in your self-coaching, which is understanding your Mission.

Bibliography

*Britten, R. (2004). *Change your Life in 30 Days*. London: Hodder and Stoughton.

*Canfield, J., with Switzer, J. (2005). *The Success Principles. How to get from Where You Are to Where You Want to Be*. London: Element.

Carr, A. (2004). *Positive Psychology. The Science of Happiness and Human Strengths*. Hove: Brunner-Routledge.

Cavanagh, M. J., & Grant, A. M. (2006). Coaching psychology and the scientist–practitioner model. In: D. A. Lane & S. Corrie (Eds.), *The Modern Scientist–Practitioner. A Guide to Practice in Psychology* (pp. 146–157). Hove: Routledge.

*Grant, A., & Greene, J. (2001). *Coach Yourself. It's Your Life. What Are You Going to Do with It?* Harlow: Pearson Education.

*Jeffers, S. (1987). *Feel the Fear and Do It Anyway*. London: Arrow.

Lane, D. A., & Corrie, S. (Eds.) (2006). *The Modern Scientist–Practitioner. A Guide to Practice in Psychology*. Hove: Routledge.

Snyder, C. R., & Lopez, S. J. (Eds.) (2005). *Handbook of Positive Psychology*. New York: Oxford University Press.

*Zander, R. S., & Zander, B. (2000). *The Art of Possibility: Transforming Professional and Personal Life*. Boston, MA: Harvard Business School Press.

PART II

THE 12 PRINCIPLES OF
THE ART OF INSPIRED LIVING

CHAPTER THREE

Introducing Principles 1–4:
Your Mission

Discovering your Mission: knowing
what you're here to do

'There were many ways of breaking a heart. Stories were full of
hearts broken by love, but what really broke a heart was taking away
its dream – whatever that dream might be'

(Pearl S. Buck)

You matter. Fundamentally. Essentially. The world is potentially a
better place because you are in it. You matter not because of what
you can do but because of who you are. You matter not because of
what you have achieved but because there is no one, anywhere in
the world, who is exactly like you.

Your uniqueness is something to treasure and celebrate. It is
your gift to the world. It is also your most powerful resource. But
do you know how to make it work for you?

Knowing your Mission – your sense of purpose, the vision you
have for your life and what your life might be – is the first, vital
step that you can take towards inspired living. Having a clear
Mission speaks to the 'why' of your life: why you get up in the
morning, why you have certain dreams, why you pursue certain
goals and why you persist in the face of defeat. Your sense of
purpose (whether you are aware of it or not) flows through every
nuance of your being.

How knowing your Mission informs
the art of inspired living

When your sense of purpose is clearly defined, life flows more easily. You have more enthusiasm, energy and passion for everything you do, you find that new and exciting opportunities come your way more frequently, and you achieve success more easily. Life opens up to you with a positive sense of inevitability.

The reason for this is not as mysterious as it may sound. When your choices and actions are governed by a clear Mission, you have more enthusiasm and passion because you are devoting your time to what really matters. You have more energy because your resources are strategically focused and you are no longer 'sidetracked' by false goals. You have a greater abundance of opportunities because you are looking out for them and attuning your awareness to what you want, rather than focusing on everything that could go wrong. And because of this, you keep focused and motivated, which makes it more likely that you will succeed.

Because you feel good about yourself and your life, you also radiate positive energy into the world. People experience you as empowering, even inspiring, and so start to gravitate towards you – they want to be around you, work with you, and socialize with you. They want you to be successful, and so start to offer you the very opportunities you need to enrich your life and fulfil your potential. Once you are clear about your Mission, the core areas of your life (remember the Inspiration Inventory in Part I?) start to fall into place.

You are your ultimate creative project

More than any other aspect of 'MAP', your Mission is a reflection of your internal world. It is not so much about changing aspects of your life, but uncovering what is already there – the treasure that lies buried beneath the surface. See it as embarking on an archaeological dig: you will need to prepare the ground, certainly. And as with many artefacts that have been lying underground for so long, the value of your discoveries may not seem immediately obvious. But they are treasure none the less.

You may already have a strong sense of your Mission but if not, don't worry. Discovering your sense of purpose is one of life's more momentous tasks and so it is worth taking your time over it. Principles 1–4 are designed to help you explore your Mission in depth so you can discover what it is, how it is influencing your life already, and how you can build it into your life in a more direct way. For now, all you need to know is that your Mission is made up of four key elements:

Principle No. 1 Your authentic self: the person that you are, were born to be, and that harbours the unique essence of you.
Principle No. 2 Your meaning: what you want your life to stand for and what adds meaning.
Principle No. 3 Your signature strengths: character qualities that are central to who you are and that are the foundation of your values.
Principle No. 4 Your courage: having the courage to embrace change and live your Mission through your choices and actions.

Because uncovering your Mission is essentially an exploratory and creative process, you will find that many of the exercises in Principles 1–4 involve story-telling tasks, rather than learning specific techniques (which we look at more in the Attitude and Process sections of 'MAP'). This is because story-telling is one of the most powerful ways of uncovering aspects of ourselves that have been obscured by the pressures of daily living (including the pressure to be 'grown up', 'realistic', and 'sensible').

Story-telling gives you permission to get around the objections that may be raised by your rational mind ("I could never do this") so that you can start to entertain possibilities for yourself and your life that might otherwise feel overly ambitious or just plain ridiculous. In stories, we enter a world that can be of our own making – an essential starting point for the art of inspired living.

A clear Mission speaks to your authenticity, your integrity, and your creativity. It reflects the very best of you now, and the best of you that is yet to come. Enjoy discovering your uniqueness, your gift to the world, and what it is that makes you the person you are.

CHAPTER FOUR

Principle No. 1: Honouring the Authentic You

'At bottom every man knows well-enough that he is a unique being, only once on this earth; and by no extraordinary chance will such a marvelously picturesque piece of diversity in unity as he is, ever be put together a second time'

(Nietzsche)

Welcome to Principle No. 1: how to honour your authentic self in everything you do. In this chapter, you will discover:

- *what it means to be 'authentic'.*
- *why honouring your authenticity is essential to your sense of purpose.*
- *how to ensure your life choices come from a place of authenticity.*

Who are you, at the very core of your being? What is that 'inner fragrance' that you would define as your true self? Coaching yourself towards the life you want starts with knowledge of your unique contribution to the world, the essence that Nietzsche described as your own 'marvelously picturesque piece of diversity'.

Nina's story

When I first met Nina, she was struggling with symptoms of depression – a label that had been assigned to a series of experiences and difficulties that had left her feeling like a failure. But underlying this was a deeper sense that something was wrong.

A vivacious and intelligent university student, Nina was failing at her studies: she couldn't quite bring herself to attend lectures and seminars, was missing deadlines for course work, and had already failed a year's worth of exams. Having at first put this down to her own inadequacies, depression had given her another explanation. But this clearly was not the whole story.

Nina had a passion for theatre and loved acting. As she explained to me, as soon as she set foot on the stage, she felt at home. What was interesting was that, however crippling her symptoms of depression, she had no difficulty running the busy university theatre company, organizing productions, and learning the lines for her own roles. We began to get curious about what this discrepancy between her university self and theatre self might mean.

After some weeks of our working together, Nina allowed herself to voice what she had never admitted before – even to herself: that above all else, she wanted to be an actor. At university she had never quite managed to apply herself to her studies because, deep down, they reflected her desire to do what she *thought* was right, rather than pursuing what truly *felt* right. Being on the stage felt truly right for Nina and as long as she refused to acknowledge her passion, to herself as well as others, something inside was being crippled. By admitting to herself what it was that she most wanted from life, Nina had begun the process of claiming and honouring her authentic self.

The quest for authenticity

Discovering and honouring the authentic self is a quest that has preoccupied some of the greatest minds in history. From Socrates to Freud, to some of the leading psychologists and coaches of today, knowledge of the self has been considered the gateway to achieving a happy and fulfilling life.

Authenticity is the first of your 12 steps to inspired living for a good reason. Research has shown that honouring our authenticity is associated with a greater abundance of happiness and positive emotions, increased optimism, and enhanced self-respect and self-esteem. It also allows us to be clear about what we stand for, enabling us to align our actions with our choices and values.

People who honour their authenticity are able to:

- live according to a personal definition of integrity;
- decide what matters to them rather than following someone else's definition of success;
- favour self-reliance over pleasing others;
- receive constructive criticism without feeling undermined;
- stand up for what they believe in, even when this means going against the crowd;
- enjoy success without making achievement the basis of self-esteem;
- see problems as challenges rather than personal failures;
- form wise relationships.

In reality, it is probably only a few highly evolved individuals who are capable of achieving these standards all of the time! You probably have certain aspects of your authenticity that you stand by through thick and thin, and other areas in which you compromise all too easily. Perhaps you welcome constructive criticism, but cannot trust your successes. Perhaps you form wise relationships, but feel obliged to follow someone else's formula for how you should live. We each have blind spots that can get in the way of honouring our authenticity. Without awareness of these blind spots, and a willingness to address them we can, just like Nina, get seduced into ways of living that are not a true reflection of who we are.

How and why we betray our authentic self

Living from a place of authenticity enables you to hold in mind the big picture of your life, even when the demands of day-to-day living seem to conspire against you. So why aren't we more authentic, more of the time?

Psychologists have long been fascinated by the question of why we betray our authenticity. Carl Rogers, one of the founders of the humanistic psychology movement, suggested that the answer comes from the rules we learn early on in life. We are each born with a fundamental drive to fulfil our potential, but also need to gain the approval of others so that they will love and protect us. Although securing the good opinion of others enables us to survive (after all, we are totally dependent on our caregivers when we are young), it can also backfire.

For example, if your parents consistently gave you approval for excelling at school, but were critical when your grades were mediocre, you learnt an important lesson: that in order to be valuable in the eyes of those who matter, you needed to achieve certain standards. Or if your parents approved of you for fulfilling their ambitions, but got angry when you expressed a desire to do things 'your way', you learnt that you needed to be someone other than your true self in order to be loved. These standards become what Rogers termed our 'conditions of worth' – and if we fail to meet them, our self-esteem suffers.

As our lives unfold, we are shaped further by our encounters with our peers, our communities, and the world of work, all of which bombard us with subtle (and not so subtle) messages about what is and is not acceptable. We learn that working long hours is good and wasting time is bad; that material wealth is a sign of success or worth; that beauty comes in a certain package, and so on. Over time, we internalize these conditions of worth to the extent that they become the lenses through which we judge ourselves and relate to others.

Of course, finding a way to belong in the world is adaptive and life affirming, and many of the rules we learn from our parents and peer groups are very valuable. The problem only comes when the gap between 'who I am' and 'whom I think I should be' becomes too wide to be sustained. Swallowing society's demands without first digesting their implications, or prioritizing 'fitting in' over an informed understanding of responsibilities to self, family, and community, creates a void between our private and public selves that can become crippling.

There are a number of warning signs that the gap between who you are and who you think you should be is becoming too wide. See if you display the signs by photocopying Exercise 2 below, placing it in your learning log, and ticking the relevant column.

Exercise 2. Warning signs that the false self is running your life

Sign of false self	True of me most of the time	True of me some of the time	Rarely true of me
1. Unable to express your opinions, ideas, and wishes openly and honestly.	☐	☐	☐
2. Compromising your own values and desires to avoid upsetting others.	☐	☐	☐
3. Difficulty 'owning' your successes, dismissing them or attributing them to luck.	☐	☐	☐
4. Feeling as though you are living your life according to someone else's formula.	☐	☐	☐
5. Feeling like an impostor in your own life.	☐	☐	☐
6. Worrying excessively about whether or not others like you.	☐	☐	☐
7. Worrying excessively about others' expectations of you.	☐	☐	☐
8. Not being able to make choices about what you want from your life.	☐	☐	☐

If you ticked 'True of me most of the time' for any of the above, your authenticity needs some attention. You probably know the signs already. You may feel pressured to be someone you are not, find yourself distorting the image you present to others in order to fit in or feel compelled to stick with a particular job, lifestyle, or relationship you have long out-grown. You have probably long since dismissed your most cherished hopes for your life as out of reach. But the good news is that you can start to reclaim your authenticity once again.

Learn to recognize the stories that shape your life

The idea that there exists within each of us a 'true self' waiting to be liberated is an idea that has proved remarkably persistent in the Western world. The flourishing demand for make-overs, plastic surgery, and personal development programmes all bear witness to the idea that we each have a true self that can be rediscovered or (if found wanting) reinvented.

In years gone by, the self was seen as a relatively straightforward entity. A person possessed a single identity through which others could know them as good or bad. In this sense, the self was seen as a stable entity at the core of an individual's personality.

But today, we are confronted with an increasingly complex world in which our identities are no longer clear-cut. We are bombarded with a bewildering array of often contradictory ideas about who we are and how we should live. Technology allows us to communicate with the far side of the world in a matter of seconds, exposing us to versions of reality very different from our own. In our multicultural society, the diverse range of beliefs about the nature of the self are challenging long-established beliefs about what is and is not acceptable; we are having to consider how we negotiate these differences in order to live together harmoniously. All of this creates a plethora of potential selves that would formerly have been unthinkable.

This poses real challenges for the person wanting to pursue authentic living! In an era in which so much is possible, to arrive at an understanding of what it means to be 'authentic' is to be willing to grapple with something far more complex than any popular notion of a 'true self.' So how can you remain true to that inner essence of you and establish an authentic direction for your life in the face of so many options?

The philosopher Michel Foucault believed that, in the modern world, the authentic self is an ongoing creative project that gradually evolves through the stories we construct about ourselves, other people, and the world around us. Many psychologists share this view, claiming that authenticity is achieved when we see ourselves as the authors of our lives, rather than as a character merely acting out the drama of stories constructed by past events. In this sense, the quest for authenticity becomes one of clarifying and, where necessary, redefining your story.

There are three stages to this process of redefinition, listed below.

1. Identifying the stories that make up your limiting view of yourself.
2. Rewriting the stories that have contributed to inauthentic living.
3. Writing new stories that support authentic living.

1. Identifying the stories that make up your limiting view of yourself

The stories you tell yourself and others are not just the outcome of your experiences. They actually *create* who you are by making you feel competent or incompetent, empowered or disempowered, inspired or uninspired, according to the plots they define. This is because at the heart of the stories we tell ourselves lie the fixed beliefs we have about ourselves – what we can do, what we can't do, how we are worthwhile and how we fall short.

For example, if you have constructed a story about yourself as 'stupid', this story will be acted out in your life in a number of ways. You may selectively remember those times when you think you behaved in an unintelligent way and will avoid opportunities to grow and stretch yourself for fear of exposing your inadequacies. Over time, you may indeed begin to act in ways that you or others might label as 'stupid'.

Honouring your authenticity – that inner essence that can guide you wisely through life's journey – involves uncovering those stories that you are performing in your life and which dominate how you see your choices. The following exercise is designed to help you clarify what some of these stories might be. Use your learning log to write down any key points or themes which emerge.

Exercise 3. My story

Find yourself a quiet place where you will not be disturbed. You need to allow yourself about 30 minutes for this exercise, so switch off the phone, make yourself comfortable, and allow yourself to relax. You may find it helpful to close your eyes and take a few slow breaths to relax your mind and give your imagination free rein.

Imagine that a new movie has just been released. It is called 'My Story', and it is about you and your life. What kind of film would it be – an epic drama or a quirky comedy? Is the ending happy or tragic? Who are the main characters? What type of adventures does the hero/heroine (you!) have?

Once you have the details of your movie clearly in your mind, use the following questions to think about how this story has influenced your self-image and the choices you have made in your life:

1. Where does this story come from? Who and what are its major influences?
2. How has this story affected you? In what ways has it:
   - helped and hindered you?
   - inspired you or caused you to lose heart?
3. How has this story influenced your choices?
   - Which goals has it led you to choose?
   - Which goals has it caused you to avoid or abandon?
4. What elements of this story might you now need to discard because they disempower you?

Write a short description of any themes you identify in your learning log. Be sure to include the events that contributed to the development of your story and how you feel about your story now, taking account of your answers to the questions above.

---

2. Rewriting the stories that contribute to inauthentic living

Exercise 3 probably alerted you to a plot that is getting in the way of you fulfilling your potential. It may be a story that you have outgrown, one that represents the unhelpful influence of others, or one that has simply become a habit. In fact, its origins do not matter. What matters is that now you know what the story is, you are in a stronger position to examine it objectively and make changes where changes are required.

If authenticity can be seen as a process of reclaiming authorship of your life, then sacrificing your authenticity can be understood as becoming the victim of stories that do not empower you. Your fate is one of acting out a drama that no longer serves you. This may be because your story lacks flexibility – perhaps you have developed a rigid attachment to an old story that prevents you from seeing yourself as a project in the making. Or it may be because you believe there is only one way to tell your story, and so you find it hard to identify others that might empower you to live differently.

What matters is not so much the content of your stories (we cannot change the past) but the manner in which you tell them. Do you swallow them whole? Or can you suspend judgement long enough to be curious about them, to question them and to consider them from new and more enriching perspectives? As life coach Rhonda Britten points out, we are often highly attached to our stories, and share them with others as though they were true. But a story is just a story.

Exercise 4. Meeting the director of 'My Story'

Imagine you are meeting the director of your film 'My Story'. Like a film director in real life, this part of your self controls not the content of the story, but which aspects of the plot are emphasized and which get downplayed. In other words, the director determines how the story is told in order to create a certain type of impact.

For the purposes of this exercise, the director represents a part of you that is not truly honouring the authentic self – the main character in the film.

As before, find yourself a quiet place where you won't be interrupted. You need to allow about 30 minutes for this exercise. Make yourself comfortable and allow yourself to relax. You may find it helpful to close your eyes and take a few slow breaths to quieten the mind.

When you are ready, imagine that the director of 'My Story' greets you and sits down. Note what the director is wearing, his/her tone of voice and if he/she reminds you of anyone (developing a detailed image that engages all the senses often makes the exercise richer). When you are both comfortable, ask your director the following questions, giving them every opportunity to speak openly.

1. Where does your vision of 'My Story' come from? Who was most important in shaping its development and what experiences or events helped this vision evolve?
2. From what are you trying to protect me, by portraying 'My Story' in this way? In what ways do you believe the main character falls short?
3. What plotlines, beliefs, and values have you uncritically accepted from others? How does this empower and disempower the main character?
4. What is the price that the main character pays for living by this version of 'My Story'?
5. If I remain true to your version of 'My Story' for the rest of my life, how will I feel about its influence on my life and the choices it has encouraged me to make?

After you have given the director an opportunity to speak, identify the most significant themes and write them down in your learning log. What is the story that the director is trying to convey? How has this version of 'My Story' protected the main character (you)? How has it empowered and disempowered you? In what ways does it capture or fail to capture the essence of you? Ask yourself honestly if you want to live the rest of your life through the plot of this particular story and what you stand to gain and lose by your choice.

Be sure to make a note of any key themes and insights.

---

3. Writing new stories that support authentic living.

Being authentic involves recasting yourself as the author and director of your life by deconstructing fixed, outgrown, or unhelpful stories about who you are in favour of stories that are rich in meaning, diversity and choice.

Another, complementary way of expanding our stories has been offered by psychologist Susan Harter, who suggests nurturing 'positive false self attributes'. Positive false self attributes refer to those qualities, choices, and actions that are not currently part of how we define ourselves, but that might equip us with greater story-telling potential. As she explains, pretending can be a form of experimentation that broadens our sense of possibility. New behaviours rarely feel authentic to begin with, but with practice can become so. Through acting in different ways, we can begin to shape new stories that enable us to move between current selves and desirable false selves without compromising our values.

If you review your answers to the previous exercises, which positive false self attributes would it be helpful for you to acquire at this point in your life? What new stories do you need to tell yourself about who you are and who you might become? How could you start to enact some of these stories? Are there any small steps you could take to start extending your range of stories (your answers to Exercise 2 might give you some important clues)?

> **Helpful hint**. The prospect of having multiple authentic selves presents us with a delightful range of possibilities, but don't see this as a chance to slip into the realms of fantasy! As you work through the next exercise check that any new story you construct fits with the values you hold dear and reflects your responsibilities to your family and community.

For the next exercise, identify just one of the stories that you would now like to acquire.

Exercise 5. Reclaiming authorship of your life

Imagine that the movie 'My Story' is being remade. The previous version is now widely recognized as a misguided interpretation of the main character's adventure. The new movie is going to reflect a different angle and has a new director. In this version of the film, an empowering story is told – one that creates new possibilities for how you live your life.

In this interview, you are meeting the new director for the first time. This director represents an authentic part of you – that part which is in tune with your needs, responsibilities, and heartfelt hopes for the future and which is determined to honour this part of you in how your story is told.

The director enters the room, greets you, and sits down. Notice what he/she is wearing, his/her tone of voice and if he/she reminds you of anyone. Then ask this director the following questions:

1. What is your version of 'My Story'?
2. Where does this vision come from? Who has been most instrumental in nurturing its development and what experiences or events helped this version evolve?
3. What kind of person will I become if I allow myself to live this version of 'My Story'?
4. How will this version of 'My Story' enrich my life? How will it make it more challenging?
5. What plotlines, beliefs and values do you encourage me to embrace? How will performing these plots, beliefs and values impact on my life?
6. At the end of a life lived by the story you tell me, how will I feel about your influence on me and the choices you have encouraged me to make?

After you have given your director an opportunity to tell their story, see if you can identify the most significant themes. What is the story that this authentic self is trying to tell you? How will it empower you? In what ways does it capture or fail to capture the essence of you? Ask yourself honestly if you would like to live more of your life through the plot of this particular story and what you stand to gain and lose by your choice.

Write down the director's answers and any thoughts and insights you have.

Take home message

In this chapter you have uncovered the cornerstone of your Mission: identifying and honouring the authentic you. As therapist Michael White explains, we live through and perform our stories. Just like fiction, each of your stories about who you are and who you might become has its own plot that contributes something important to how you live your life, for good or ill. So if your stories are not inspiring you, change them!

Of course, I am not suggesting that honouring our authenticity is a simple matter of choice. Our stories become woven into the fabric of our being, including our biology, in complex ways, so we do not discard them lightly. None the less, by becoming aware of limiting stories and contemplating ourselves as the authors of our lives, new possibilities can begin to emerge. Honouring your authenticity is a lifelong project, a commitment to a vision of who you are and who you might become – and, as with all commitments, it is one that needs to be renewed over and over again.

Authenticity is like a diamond. Each diamond is unique, possessing its own molecular structure. But when you examine the diamond under different conditions, it reflects the light as different colours. If you examine the diamond from one perspective, it radiates emerald green. Look at it from another angle and the colour becomes flame red. Another position still will reveal a vibrant purple. All of the shades are equally 'authentic', but the angle at which the diamond is held and the light conditions in which it is examined determine which colour will reveal itself on which occasion. Within the molecular structure that is embedded in your genes and developed through your personal history and the stories you tell about it, you have the capacity to cultivate and radiate a spectrum of selves. Enjoy exploring and expanding the many shades of you!

Honouring the Authentic You

One thing I will take away from this chapter is: . . . (write your answer in your learning log).
One thing I will do differently as a result of this chapter is: . . . (write your answer in your learning log).

Bibliography

Bruner, J. (1986). *Actual Minds, Possible Worlds*. Cambridge, MA: Harvard University Press.

Foucault, M., & Rabinow, P. (1991). *The Foucault Reader. An Introduction to Foucault's Thought*. London: Penguin.

Harter, S. (1999). *The Construction of the Self. A Developmental Perspective*. New York: Guilford.

Harter, S. (2005). Authenticity. In: C. R. Snyder & S. J. Lopez (Eds.), *Handbook of Positive Psychology* (pp. 382–394). New York: Oxford University Press.

Pinkola Estes, C. (1992). *Women who Run with the Wolves*. London: Rider.

*Rogers, C. (1961). *On Becoming A Person*. New York: Houghton Mifflin.

Rosenwald, G. C., & Ochberg, R. L. (Eds.) (1992). *Storied Lives. The Cultural Politics of Self-Understanding*. New Haven, CT: Yale University Press.

White, M. H. (1980). The value of narrativity in the representation of reality. *Critical Inquiry*, 7: 5–28.

White, M. H., & Epston, D. (1990). *Narrative Means to Therapeutic Ends*. New York: Norton.

*Young, J. E., & Klosko, J. S. (1994). *Reinventing Your Life*. New York: Plume.

CHAPTER FIVE

Principle No 2: Meaning Matters

> 'He who has a "why" to live for can bear with
> almost any "how"'
>
> (Viktor Frankl)

Welcome to Principle No. 2: discovering the meaning of your life. In this chapter you will learn:

- *what it means to live according to a well-defined sense of meaning.*
- *how to discover and nurture what makes life meaningful for you.*
- *how living from a place of personally defined meaning will benefit your life.*

Outside the Royal Festival Hall in London is a statue of Nelson Mandela. Beneath the bronze there is an inscription that reads, "The struggle is my life". This statement sums up something about the essence of meaning that I want to explore with you in this chapter – namely, that neither abundant opportunity nor the absence of struggle is essential to what matters most. What matters above everything is knowing what you stand for.

In my work as a psychologist I have noticed that the people who seek out my services tend to fall into two categories: those whose lives are underpinned by a clear sense of meaning and those whose lives are not. These people are not distinguishable in terms of the difficulties they have or indeed the levels of distress that they are experiencing. However, each group brings a decidedly different set of attitudes and expectations and a very different set of resources.

When I first met Jill she had recently been diagnosed as depressed following a series of traumatic life events that included the serious illness of her partner. But despite struggling with her mood, motivation, and concentration (symptoms common to depression), her vibrancy shone through. Granted, she could not see this when we first started working together, but it was an energy that was ever-present. It seemed that however difficult things were and however low her mood became, there was a life force that refused to be extinguished.

Early in our work together I ask people what makes their life meaningful. For those who have a sense of this, my question ignites a spark of recognition. It is as though these people have a deep well inside them that, no matter how difficult things get, they know is still there. My question becomes an invitation to plumb the depths of that well and to hook out what might lie neglected at the bottom. When I see a spark of recognition, I know that we will do good work together, for they have a deeper sense of meaning that can sustain them when all else seems lost.

What makes life meaningful?

It is easy to assume that the quest for meaning is some esoteric enquiry that has nothing to do with the realities of day-to-day living. And yet, contemplating the meaning of life is something most of us do from time to time. There is probably a good reason for this.

Knowing what makes life meaningful provides a sense of direction that helps you navigate life's ups and downs, affirms your sense of identity, and can even increase your sense of self-worth. Indeed, the quest for meaning is so important that most of us would be prepared to sacrifice a good deal for what we believe in. Mahatma Gandhi, Martin Luther King, and Nelson Mandela are iconic examples of just how far human beings are prepared to go to pursue what has meaning, but many of us would similarly sacrifice our happiness, well-being, and even our lives for those people and causes that we hold dear.

So what makes life 'meaningful'? Throughout history there has been no shortage of people offering opinions on precisely this subject. However, a particularly useful approach is that of Martin Seligman, one of the world's leading researchers on happiness. He proposes that a sense of meaning is to be found when we have a sense of joining with something larger and more significant than our small, individual selves. This 'something larger' may involve a sense of being totally alive to the experience of living, such that our experiences resonate with our innermost reality, as mythologist Joseph Campbell suggests. Or it might relate to devoting oneself to a project or cause.

One of the most powerful examples of this I have ever witnessed occurred while I was watching a television news report about the shortage of medication for people in India suffering with AIDS-related illnesses. The reporter interviewed a young woman who had declined antiviral drugs in order to allow someone else the opportunity to receive treatment. Knowing that without them she would die, she none the less reported a profound sense of peace. She had chosen a path that allowed someone else to live and this selflessness in the face of great suffering gave this young woman a sense of meaning.

Psychiatrist and author Viktor Frankl suggests that there are three very powerful means of creating meaning in our lives:

1. Undertaking a project, doing good work or carrying out some action that has a positive impact on others or the world around us.
2. Encountering something or someone who has a significant impact, such as witnessing the magnificence of nature or connecting with another human being at a 'soul level'.
3. By the attitude we take toward unavoidable suffering and seeing its effects as having significance for our lives and how we live them.

Do any of these definitions of what makes life meaningful ring true for you? Think about your own experiences. When have you felt most alive? Does this coincide with the times when your life seemed to be most meaningful? Or does it relate to having had a very specific cause to which you are dedicating your time and energy? Write your thoughts in your learning log, under the heading 'What makes my life meaningful'.

Know your basic framework

Author Steve Pavlina suggests that the way we answer questions about the meaning of our life provides the basic framework for everything else we do.

To take an extreme example, if your basic framework is organized around protecting the natural environment and endangered species and you are committed to preserving the rights of all living beings, you are likely to be strongly opposed to vivisection. You might campaign against animal cruelty, be vegetarian, join organizations such as Greenpeace, and act in ways that you believe minimize harm to the natural world.

Conversely, if your basic framework centres around reducing human suffering and you are strongly committed to finding a cure for a fatal disease, you might support animal experimentation. You might conclude that this is an unfortunate but acceptable approach to finding a solution, viewing animal experiments as a necessary sacrifice for a greater cause. In light of this, you may then decide to make financial donations to institutions that are conducting animal research in order to find answers that will reduce human suffering.

These examples may seem poles apart in terms of their ethical perspectives. However, both outlooks are driven by a basic framework of meaning that determines subsequent choices and actions. Similarly, your sense of meaning and the causes to which you are committed will represent a vital organizing framework for selecting meaningful goals, making life-affirming choices, and aligning your behaviour with what you want.

How would you define the meaning of your life, in the sense of what drives you and what matters most? What would you see as your 'basic framework' and how does this operate in your life? Write your thoughts in your log, under the heading 'The primary meaning of my life'.

This is your life: the very practical task of meaning-making

In the cult comedy *Hitchhiker's Guide to the Galaxy*, the answer to the meaning of life became famous: 42. The answer was simple enough, but the exact question remained a mystery. This highlights something important about the quest for meaning – if you are to have an answer that has implications for your life, you must first ask yourself the right kind of questions!

Trying to work out the meaning of life in the abstract is a bit like searching for the pot of gold at the end of the rainbow: a waste of time. The idea that there is some universal, abstract meaning to life misses the point. The problem is that it implies that meaning is pre-destined – something that is universally assigned rather than personally defined and something that we find out, as opposed to something that we create.

Many psychologists would argue that our meaning is unique and specific – something that can be fulfilled by us alone. But it does not follow that we each have one meaning that, if discovered, can fulfil us for all time. In fact, the meaning we seek needs to evolve as we do. What made your life meaningful at ten years old will not be the same thing that makes it meaningful at 50 years old.

Psychologists working in the field of positive psychology tend to agree. Roy Baumeister and Kathleen Vohs, for example, highlight how our lives typically draw meaning from a wide range of sources including family, work, and spirituality, as well as various projects and the accomplishment of our goals. Rather than getting hung up on the notion that we each have a destination waiting for us, we can consider the range of destinations that might be possible and the range of activities, commitments, and relationships through which we draw meaning. Our lives are, as a Buddhist teacher once told me, many possibilities. Our task is simply to allow the possibility of our lives to unfold.

Wake up to your life – it isn't forever

Some years ago, when I was on retreat, our teacher encouraged us to spend time walking around the cemetery adjacent to the retreat centre, noting the names of the people buried there and the tributes lovingly engraved on the tombstones. For a society that is so fearful of death, and that goes to such lengths to avoid thinking about it, this may sound like a strange strategy. But the point of the exercise was not to elicit existential angst. It was about discovering how facing up to the reality of death – even the death of someone you never knew – can unclutter the mind remarkably quickly. Once you clear out the clutter, what is left is what really matters. And there lies the secret to what has true, personal significance.

It was one of the most helpful pieces of advice I have ever been given. Even now, whenever I have a big decision to make, am facing a problem that seems insurmountable, or need to clarify my sense of direction, I will take myself off to a churchyard and just sit quietly for a while. It is not that I am expecting a visitor from another dimension, or sudden insights to fall Eureka-style from the heavens. It is just that looking at the names on the tombstones somehow creates a space inside of me to reconnect with what is most important in my life. After all, this – one day – will be me. It is surprising how liberating that realization can be!

In recent years, psychology has come to see an encounter with our mortality – even in our imaginations – as a dramatic and empowering method for working out what gives our lives meaning. Different methods can be used to achieve this. For example, one way would be to think about what you want written on your tombstone. Another is to imagine attending eulogies read at your funeral, whilst a third way would be to consider what you would do if you only had six months to live. Whichever method you use, the aim is the same – to conduct a mental spring-clean that allows you to shed false values, goals, and stories you have outgrown (remember Principle No. 1?) and wake up to what really matters.

The following exercise is a very powerful method for clearing away the clutter and discovering what you want your life to be about.

> **Warning**: this exercise is liberating but can also be unsettling. If you are in doubt, go through it with the support of a coach, therapist or a coaching partner.

Exercise 6. The tribute

Find a place where you will not be disturbed, make yourself comfortable and take a few slow breaths to clear your mind.

Imagine that your life is now over and you have recently died. A newspaper (or magazine or journal if you prefer) whose values you admire is compiling a special edition to honour you, your life and your contribution. The special edition includes interviews with family, friends, colleagues, and other people whose lives you touched and who wish to pay tribute to you. (Remember, the special edition represents what you would most *like* to be said about you, not what you imagine people might *actually* say). Write your answers to the following questions in your learning log.

- What would be written about you and why?
- Who contributes to the special edition and what do they say?
- What impact do people say that you have had?
- What achievements and talents does the edition celebrate and honour?
- For what strengths do people honour and celebrate you?
- What is your legacy (to those you love, your work, your community, and globally)?

The above exercise is about helping you discover what has meaning for you. So what did you learn? What do your answers tell you about what really matters to you? What contribution do you want to make? How do you want to live your life? Answer these questions in your learning log.

Make your map and live your meaning

Your answers to the questions in Exercise 6 reveal something very important about you – the legacy you wish to offer the world. When it comes to clarifying your sense of meaning, this is a good place to start. If you know what you want to leave behind, what impact you would most like to make, you can start to identify goals that will help you get there. Your actions become aligned with your larger sense of purpose.

Look back over your special edition. What would it mean to place your legacy – your sense of personal meaning – centre stage in every area of your life? Would it result in a life radically different from the one you are leading now? Or one that is very similar? What areas would need to change? If you put this framework of meaning at the centre of your life, what implications would it have for:

- your relationship with yourself (including your self-esteem, self-care, and lifestyle)?
- your intimate and family relationships (e.g. spouse, partner, children, and family)?
- your friendships and social life?
- your career and work (including relationship with colleagues and work–life balance)?
- your financial planning?
- your hobbies and interests?
- your spiritual life?
- your goals for the short-, medium, and long-term?
- your commitments?

Write the answers to these questions in your learning log.

Think about how you could start living more of your meaning every day. Even the smallest of steps can pay big dividends.

Take home message

Assuming that the meaning of life really isn't 42, then we are left with only one real conclusion: that discovering the meaning of our lives is not about locating a pre-determined formula but, rather, engaging with a personalized quest of self-discovery. Your meaning is something you create, not something that was assigned to you at birth, and deciding on your personal definition is probably the most creative act you will ever undertake.

Creating your meaning also involves beginning to broaden your visual field of possibilities. We have identified some of the many areas through which meaning might be found: family, work, personal development, spiritual worship, leisure interests, the arts, service to community – all provide potential routes into a person-ally crafted definition. Your task is to create a structure in which, like a rope, different strands are woven together to create a tough fabric that can sustain you through good times and bad.

Of course, while having a personal definition of meaning may be essential to happiness, it does not guarantee happiness. Indeed, having a sense of meaning may lead a person to make choices that are in direct contrast to happiness, such as fighting for a cause you believe in, being prepared to speak out against the crowd, or making an unpopular or controversial choice to leave behind a familiar way of life in favour of a new path. However, if your sense of meaning is personally defined, then your capacity for tolerating distress, difficulty, and setbacks will increase very considerably. After all, you will always have a compelling reason for carrying on, regardless of where the twists and turns of life might lead you.

Uncovering the Meaning of Your Life

One thing I will take away from this chapter is . . . (write the answer in your learning log).
One thing I will do differently as a result of this chapter is . . . (write the answer in your learning log).

Bibliography

Baumeister, R. F., & Vohs, K. D. (2005). The pursuit of meaningfulness in life. In: C. R. Snyder & S. J. Lopez (Eds.), *Handbook of Positive Psychology*. New York: Oxford University Press.
*Frankl, V. (1959). *Man's Search for Meaning*. New York: Pocket Books.
*Frankl, V. (1969). *The Will to Meaning*. New York: New American Library.
*Pavlina, S. (2005). *The Meaning of Life: From Purpose to Action*. Online. Available at www.StevePavlina.com. Accessed 22 June 2008.

CHAPTER SIX

Principle No. 3: Discovering Your Signature Strengths

'How can we expect a harvest of thought who have not had a seedtime of character?'

(Henry David Thoreau)

Welcome to Principle No. 3: discovering your signature strengths. In this chapter, you will:

- *discover your unique profile of signature strengths;*
- *find out how you can use your signature strengths to create a happy and meaningful life for yourself and those you care about.*

Over the years, I have discovered that there is one question guaranteed to strike fear into the hearts of virtually everyone I meet: 'What are your strengths?' It doesn't matter whom I ask – clients, colleagues, my students, family, or friends the response is always the same – an embarrassed silence, followed by a sudden fascination with their shoes and then a mumbled reply along the lines of 'I hate it when people ask me that question.' And yet, ask these same people about their limitations and they reel off a list of perceived weaknesses more quickly than I can write them down!

There is something very powerful about modesty in our culture. We feel resistance when people publicly declare pride in themselves or their accomplishments – no one likes a bighead, after all. But the danger is that this can turn into a false modesty, and when we start to impose this false modesty on ourselves we lose contact with one of the very qualities we need to harness to fulfil our potential and achieve the results we want: the strengths within our character that reflect the influence of the authentic self.

Your strengths are vital to everything you do and everything you want to become – they influence what you set your heart on and what you decide is meaningful in your life. They also influence the options you see as available to you, the type of future to which you believe you are entitled, and the choices you subsequently make. In short, if you are going to create a life that inspires you, you need to know what you are good at.

So my first question is this: do you know what your strengths are? If you put aside all modesty (and remember that no one else is going to see this list apart from you), what are some of the talents, accomplishments, or resources that are central to you and your life so far?

Exercise 7. Identifying your strengths

Take a moment to list your ten main strengths (talents/accomplishments/resources) in your learning log.

> **Helpful Hint**. If naming your strengths is a struggle for you, start with small successes or accomplishments that you might be inclined to dismiss as nothing out of the ordinary. If you cannot list at least ten, this area needs special attention and you should check out Chapter Twenty-three on how to improve self-esteem. This is definitely a growth area for you!

Take a look at your list. Chances are you will have identified a number of different areas. Maybe you included key skills acquired through formal training, knowledge of certain topics (such as career based expertise, how to raise children, or DIY), or some of your accomplishments (qualifications, certificates, and awards, etc). Maybe you identified certain successes in your life, such as events of which you are particularly proud.

But your list might also contain examples of another type of strength – those qualities that you appreciate in yourself, or that others value about you that seem quite separate from anything you have achieved. Examples of these kinds of strength include qualities such as kindness, concern for the well-being of others, a sense of justice, the courage to overcome obstacles, or zest for living. Unlike your accomplishments, these types of strengths are not a reflection of what you *can do*, but rather a reflection of what you *stand for* – the essence of your values, principles, and beliefs about what matters. These strengths are your 'signature strengths'.

Your signature, or character, strengths are those qualities that contribute to the unique brand of human being that is you. They highlight the best of who you are rather than the best of what you can do. The way you have organized your life will give you some important clues as to the nature of your special qualities in these areas, as will your answers to the following questions.

- What are some of the qualities and characteristics you appreciate in yourself?
- What are some of the qualities and characteristics that other people value in you?
- What qualities do you most want to give and share with others?
- On what occasions (when you have exercised certain choices, or behaved in certain ways) have you felt most true to yourself?
- Whom do you really admire? What choices has this person made that really impress you?
- What causes would you fight for?
- What would be the one thing, above all else, on which you would refuse to compromise?
- What type of person, with what sorts of qualities, would you not want to be?

What do your answers tell you about your main signature strengths? Jot down any key themes in your learning log (we'll come back to them later in the chapter).

What exactly are signature strengths? The science bit . . .

Signature strengths are part of that special formula that determines the essence and direction of your Mission. Unlike your talents and abilities, which to some extent you are born with (arguably not all of us have the potential to be Nobel Prize winning physicists or great composers), signature strengths refer to stable characteristics and core values which have high personal value.

Think of your signature strengths as being like your heart pumping away inside your body – that little muscle that supports and sustains you, oxygenating your entire system so that your brain can decide what you need to do and co-ordinate your muscles and limbs to carry out its wishes. Invisible to the outside world, your heart is at the very centre of your being, helping every other system in your body operate smoothly and effectively. Like your heart, your signature strengths provide a vital life force that can sustain you as you coach yourself towards the successes that matter most. And, just like your heart, if you look after them and attend to their needs, your signature strengths will serve you well.

Ground-breaking research by psychologists Chris Peterson and Martin Seligman has identified six core virtues, or strengths of character that, if systematically developed, enable us to live in a way that inspires us. These core virtues are:

1. Wisdom.
2. Courage.
3. Love.
4. Justice.
5. Temperance.
6. Transcendence.

What is interesting about these strengths of character is that they have been valued throughout history and seem to be shared by virtually all cultures. They were identified as highly prized qualities in the teachings of the Buddha, Christ, Socrates, Plato, and Aristotle, as well as psychologists and coaches of today. Almost every society, it seems, understands that these core virtues are a path to wise, harmonious, and fulfilled living.

Although the six core virtues are not new knowledge, Chris Peterson and Martin Seligman have gone one step further by attempting to define and measure them. Their research has identified 24 unique strengths, each one stemming from one of the six core virtues. Check out the list below. Which ones do you think are your signature strengths?

The 24 character strengths

1. Wisdom and knowledge. Cognitive strengths that entail the acquisition and use of knowledge:
   (a) Creativity (originality, ingenuity): thinking of novel and productive ways to conceptualize and do things; includes artistic achievement but is not limited to it.
   (b) Curiosity (interest, novelty-seeking, openness to experience): taking an interest in ongoing experience for its own sake; finding subjects and topics fascinating; exploring and discovering.
   (c) Open-mindedness (judgement, critical thinking): thinking things through and examining them from all sides; not jumping to conclusions; being able to change one's mind in light of evidence; weighing all evidence fairly.
   (d) Love of learning: mastering new skills, topics, and bodies of knowledge, whether on one's own or formally; obviously related to the strength of curiosity but goes beyond it to describe the tendency to add systematically to what one knows.
   (e) Perspective (wisdom): being able to provide wise counsel to others; having ways of looking at the world that make sense to oneself and to other people.

2. Courage. Emotional strengths that involve the exercise of will to accomplish goals in the face of opposition, external or internal:
   (a) Bravery (valour): not shrinking from threat, challenge, difficulty or pain; speaking up for what is right even if there is opposition; acting on convictions even if unpopular; includes physical bravery but is not limited to it. (We shall look at this more in Principle No. 4.)
   (b) Persistence (perseverance, industriousness): finishing what one starts; persisting in a course of action in spite of obstacles; 'getting it out the door'; taking pleasure in completing tasks.
   (c) Integrity (authenticity, honesty): speaking the truth but more broadly presenting oneself in a genuine way and acting in a sincere way; being without pretence; taking responsibility for one's feelings and actions.

(d) Vitality (zest, enthusiasm, vigour, energy): approaching life with excitement and energy; not doing things halfway or half-heartedly; living life as an adventure; feeling alive and activated

3. Humanity. Interpersonal strengths that involve tending and befriending others:
   (a) Love: valuing close relations with others, in particular those in which sharing and caring are reciprocated; being close to people.
   (b) Kindness (generosity, nurturance, care, compassion, altruistic love, 'niceness'): doing favours and good deeds for others; helping them; taking care of them.
   (c) Social intelligence (emotional intelligence, personal intelligence): being aware of the motives and feelings of other people and oneself; knowing what to do to fit into different social situations; knowing what makes other people tick.

4. Justice. Civic strengths that underlie healthy community life:
   (a) Citizenship (social responsibility, loyalty, teamwork): working well as a member of a group or team; being loyal to the group; doing one's share.
   (b) Fairness: treating all people the same according to notions of fairness and justice; not letting personal feelings bias decisions about others; giving everyone a fair chance.
   (c) Leadership: encouraging a group of which one is a member to get things done and at the same time maintaining good relations within the group; organizing group activities and seeing that they happen.

5. Temperance. Strengths that protect against excess:
   (a) Forgiveness and mercy: forgiving those who have done wrong; accepting the shortcomings of others; giving people a chance; not being vengeful.
   (b) Humility/modesty: letting one's accomplishments speak for themselves; not regarding oneself as more special than one is.
   (c) Prudence: being careful about one's choices; not taking undue risks; not saying or doing things that might later be regretted.
   (d) Self-regulation (self-control): regulating what one feels and does; being disciplined; controlling one's appetites and emotions.

6. Transcendence. Strengths that forge connections to the larger universe and provide meaning:

   (a) Appreciation of beauty and excellence (awe, wonder, elevation): noticing and appreciating beauty, excellence, and/or skilled performance in various domains of life, from nature to art to mathematics to science to everyday experience.

   (b) Gratitude: being aware of and thankful for the good things that happen; taking time to express thanks. [We look at this in Principle No. 7.]

   (c) Hope (optimism, future-mindedness, future orientation): expecting the best in the future and working to achieve it; believing that a good future is something that can be brought about. [We look at this in Principle No. 5.]

   (d) Humour (playfulness): liking to laugh and tease; bringing smiles to other people; seeing the light side; making (not necessarily telling) jokes.

   (e) Spirituality (religiousness, faith, purpose): having coherent beliefs about the higher purpose and meaning of the universe; knowing where one fits within the larger scheme; having beliefs about the meaning of life that shape conduct and provide comfort. [Peterson & Seligman, 2004, pp. 29–30, reproduced with permission]

Helpful hint. You can find out for sure which signature strengths you possess by completing the Values-in-Action Strengths Survey which can be found at www.authentichappiness.org. This free, on-line test developed by Martin Seligman and his colleagues will give you immediate feedback on all 24 signature strengths and your all important top five.

Know your signature strengths

What do your answers to the above tell you about your main signature strengths? If you were going to identify your all important top five, what would they be? Write these in your learning log.

Now revisit your answers to Exercise 7. Can you fit the strengths you identified with the system of classification Chris Peterson and

Martin Seligman have devised? Do the results you have obtained feel true for you?

Martin Seligman suggests that there are a number of key signs that we have identified the signature strengths that speak to our own truth. In particular, he suggests that they tend to recur. So, look for patterns across time and place: are they qualities that crop up time and time again? Are they qualities for which other people tend to appreciate you? Are they associated with good feelings for you, such as joy, zest for living, and enthusiasm? Does expressing them in your life lead to improved self-esteem, greater happiness, and a sense of fulfilment?

If you are unsure that you have captured the essence of your strengths, check through your list again and keep revising them until your top five really resonate.

How living out your signature strengths will change your life

If you commit yourself to using your signature strengths every day, then you are well on the way to creating a life that is rich in meaning and inspiration. What you actually do in terms of work and leisure may or may not change, but you will find that the core areas of your life start to become more aligned. Life becomes more harmonious and easier to manage. You will stop chasing after those things that don't speak to your soul and it will be easier to select meaningful goals, honour your responsibilities, and protect your time, because you are clear about what really matters.

When you are living life from your signature strengths, everything becomes more exciting, more alive, and more real. Learning becomes an adventure, obstacles that once overwhelmed you become challenges that arouse your curiosity, relationships become more rewarding and work becomes something that enriches your life. When you live from your strengths, you have a clear sense of direction.

Honour your signature strengths in everything you do

Your signature strengths come from a place of personal authenticity, and so every time you put them into practice you are giving life to an essential part of yourself and will feel positive and more fulfilled. The key is arranging your life so that your signature strengths can be expressed in each of the core domains we looked at in your Inspiration Inventory (Chapter One).

Imagine a life in which, from now on, all your major choices and life goals are based on your signature strengths. Imagine how you will spend your time, how you will be in your work, your relationships, and your free time. How will you take care of you, and what do you want to contribute to the world? Write down your responses in your learning log.

Now think about how you might arrange your life to give your signature strengths more prominence in your life. What, if any, changes are needed? Use the following exercise to guide your choices and actions.

Exercise 8. Making your signature strengths work for you

Take each of your top five signature strengths and think about how you can build more of it into your life, every day. How might you use each one in the following areas:

- your relationship with yourself (including self-esteem, self-care, health and lifestyle);
- your intimate relationships (partner, spouse, children, and family);
- your friendships and social life;
- your responsibilities to your community, country, and the wider world;
- your career and work (including work–life balance);
- your financial arrangements (including financial planning and spending);
- your hobbies and interests;
- your spiritual life?

Helpful Hint: You might find it useful to review your answers to the Inspiration Inventory in Part I.

Stretch your strengths

Although your signature strengths are a stable and enduring influence on your life, their development and expression will also have been influenced by those around you – your family, friends, community, and society. If early teachers and mentors encouraged the expression of a certain strength, for example, this may feature highly on your list of priorities now. Similarly, if particular strengths were discouraged, you may be less likely to have developed them yourself.

In order to allow your signature strengths to blossom, you will need to be mindful of external conditions, how they impact on you and the ways in which you can express your core virtues. Sources of influence will include your relationships, your professional context, and other organizations and communities in which you are embedded, as well as the values of your wider social and cultural communities. So, for example, if you work in an environment that is highly cut-throat and competitive, favouring gaining the market advantage over all else, and one of your top five signature strengths is the civic strength of fairness, you are likely to experience some inner conflict when your competitors lose out. Your environment is not supporting the expression of your particular strength in this area. Similarly, if you possess the strengths of bravery and live in a community where conformity to traditional values and roles is highly encouraged, you may find yourself with some difficult choices.

As you start to think of ways to implement your signature strengths, look around you. Cultivate relationships with those who have similar signature strengths, or those who have the strengths you are wishing to develop. Seek out work environments that appear to have similar values, or at least no obvious clash of values. If your environment seems to include people with very different values, see if you can identify what their signature strengths might be (understanding often aids respect). Obviously, you cannot change them, but there may be areas of common ground that you can start to work with, as well as areas where you can agree to differ.

One final thing to note about signature strengths is that, to an extent, they are consciously chosen. So you can actively acquire those strengths that are consistent with your authentic self to enrich your life and the lives of others. If you review the 24 strengths listed previously, can you identify any that you would particularly like to develop at this point in your life? How would they change your life for the better? And how might you go about incorporating them into the fabric of your life? Jot down your thoughts in your learning log.

Take home message

A large part of coaching yourself in the art of inspired living comes down to knowing what you bring to and can offer the world. Unlike achievements and accomplishments, your signature strengths reflect who you are, not what you want to achieve. But they are also a compass, pointing you in the direction of wise choices and informed actions. As a reflection of the authentic you, these core values can usefully influence not just the decisions you make, but also the goals you prioritize. So, get to know your signature strengths. Build them into your life wherever you can. But most of all, celebrate them: they are part of your unique contribution to this world.

Honouring and Building on Your Signature Strengths

One thing I will take away from this chapter is . . . (note this in your learning log).
One thing I will do differently as a result of this chapter is . . . (note this in your learning log).

Bibliography

Peterson, C., & Seligman, M. E. P. (2004). *Character Strengths and Virtues*. New York: Oxford University Press.
*Seligman, M. E. P. (2003). *Authentic Happiness*. London: Nicholas Brealey.

Resources

*Values in Action Institute. Online. Available at www.viastrengths. org.

CHAPTER SEVEN

Principle No. 4: Having the Courage to Live

'To have principles first have courage'

(Chinese Proverb)

Welcome to the fourth Principle of inspired living: finding the courage to live your Mission. In this chapter, you will learn:

- *why both fear and courage are essential to success;*
- *how to redefine your relationship to self-doubt so it doesn't hold you back;*
- *how to harness your courage to achieve what you want.*

Imagine I said to you that you could do, be, and have everything you want. But there is a catch. In order to achieve transformational results, you must be willing to tolerate a good deal of fear along the way – perhaps more fear than most people experience. If I offered you this deal would you take it? How much fear would you be willing to put up with before you decided the price was too high?

Now let me offer you another deal. Let's imagine for a moment that I could guarantee that you will achieve everything you want to achieve, and then some. You will be successful beyond your wildest dreams. But this time the catch is that in order to have this level of success, you must be prepared to have more than your average share of failures along the way. Would you accept this deal?

Take note of your answers – they tell you something very important about how far you are prepared to go to live the life you want.

Doing the deal

When I was writing my first book, I had absolutely no doubt in my mind that I wanted this opportunity more than anything. It was, for me, a dream come true. But once the contract came through and I began to get under way, I felt anything but joyful and inspired. Every morning as I sat down at my PC, I felt sick with anxiety. I was plagued with doubts and wondered who on earth I was kidding that someone like me could write a book. I couldn't get my head around how I was feeling. If I wanted it this badly, shouldn't it have been different – shouldn't I have been delighted instead of terrified?

After literally months of feeling lousy every morning, I had a realization that transformed the problem completely. I realized that, however bad I felt in the morning, once I started working, the fear would subside and my passion for the subject – a particular topic in academic psychology – returned. The anticipation made my insides do somersaults, but the reality was very rewarding: I was learning an enormous amount, developing my skills as a writer and doing something that genuinely felt like part of my Mission.

The second insight was that if I was going to fulfil my ambition of writing a book, then I would need to be willing to tolerate a lot of uncomfortable thoughts and feelings along the way. As long as I tried to get rid of them, the doubts and fears would double. But if I could change how I saw the fear – if I could recognize it as a feeling that automatically occurs in response to doing what matters most – it removed the sting. The penny had dropped. For the first time I understood – really understood – what Eleanor Roosevelt had meant when she said, 'You must do the thing you think you cannot do.' Pursuing those goals that inspired me didn't mean having a life that was fear-free; it meant pursuing my chosen path in spite of it.

Similarly, if you are going to get what you want from life, you need to know that you will experience fear, doubt, and uncertainty along the way. Any dream worth pursuing will *always* evoke some degree of discomfort. I can guarantee it because that's the deal.

Dreaming, daring, doing

In her inspiring book about her life with the actor John Thaw, Sheila Hancock recalls a piece of advice that John was given, early in his career, by the great actor Laurence Olivier. The advice was to 'amaze yourself at your own daring'.

Although I am not suggesting that you start doing bizarre things in the name of inspiration, a little more of the Laurence Olivier philosophy in your life might open up some interesting possibilities. For example, how often have you gone along with the crowd when deep down you wanted something very different? How many times have you wished you could be more like a favourite character in a novel or movie who is always prepared to stand up for what they believe in, even when there is a cost involved? How many times have you compromised your authenticity and left your signature strengths lying dormant all because you didn't quite feel up to dreaming, daring, and doing?

We may not all be able to strut our stuff with unlimited self-assurance, but if you could embrace even a microcosm of this motto, your life would probably blossom in some very rewarding ways. All meaningful change involves a little risk-taking and in the end, burying your head in the sand is no safer than grasping the nettle. Daring is what links the big picture you hold in your mind to the concrete action steps you need to take to get there.

Awaken your courage

If fear is the price you must pay to pursue what matters, then courage is the currency used to settle the debt. The word 'courage' comes from the Latin word 'cor' meaning 'heart'. This captures the essence of courage – the need to engage the heart over and above the emotions and thoughts that might be screaming at you to retreat.

As one of our basic human characteristics, courage is a strength that protects our mental health and emotional well-being, allowing us to stay motivated when challenged by setbacks and to heal ourselves when confronted by life's disappointments. It also fosters a genuine self-respect – one that mirrors our core values, respects the needs and drives of the authentic self, and supports us in following our Mission.

The ability to act with bravery might even be essential to our survival. As Chris Peterson and Martin Seligman observe, in the context of a future that is marked by so much uncertainty and unpredictability, the ability to exercise courage may be essential to everyday living. Certainly many of my clients would agree, choosing to put themselves through many difficult and challenging tasks to overcome difficulties and achieve their goals – sometimes even to reclaim their ability to do things that others would take for granted. What tremendous acts of courage – and for me, a never-ending source of inspiration!

The choice you need to make

Although you might be tempted to see courage as an emotion, it is perhaps more helpful to view it as a decision – the decision to pursue a desired direction despite experiencing fear, doubt, and other unpleasant feelings. Notice also that what is courageous for one person would not be courageous for another. For example, my colleague, Rachel, is frightened of public speaking. My friend, Matthew, loves the chance to perform. Both have jobs that involve giving presentations to groups of experienced professionals. Every time Rachel stands up to address her audience she is choosing to exercise her courage, because she is choosing to put herself in a situation which she knows will evoke fear. For Matthew, however, this part of his job is something he relishes – it involves no courage because the situation evokes no fear.

So, if we look at the essence of this remarkable human quality and how it operates in our lives, we can see that to be courageous means to

- take 100% responsibility for yourself and your life;
- make choices and own those choices;
- be willing to confront what is no longer working in your life;
- recognize and accept that there are potential costs involved in changing your life;
- take appropriate, life-enhancing risks in pursuit of your goals;

- persist with your efforts, even when the results don't pay off straight away;
- override uncomfortable feelings in the service of something greater (for example, honouring your authentic self and your signature strengths);
- be open to feedback and prepared to learn from your mistakes.

How comfortable are you with these elements of courageous behaviour? How often do you exercise them in your own life and in what areas? Where does your courage tend to fail you? Make a note of your answers in your learning log.

Making fear work for you

Fear sometimes gets a bad press – we don't like how it feels and so we try to get rid of it. But fear has a very important role to play in our lives. It is part of a survival instinct that we have inherited from our ancestors. When our ancestors were confronted with a threat to their survival in the form of say, a predator, essential changes in the functioning of the brain and body enabled them to be stronger and faster – either to fight the predator or to run away. This reaction is known as 'the fight or flight response'.

This reaction is so deeply embedded within us that I can guarantee if you suddenly found yourself confronted with a lion, tiger, or any other threat to your physical survival, you would react in the same way as your ancestors. You wouldn't have to think about it, it would happen automatically.

The problem, however, is that most of the challenges we face today do not involve wild animals but what I term 'head level' worries. Here are some examples of common 'head level' fears. See how many feel relevant for you:

- fear of failure;
- fear of success;
- fear of not belonging;
- fear of not being your own person;
- fear of making mistakes;

- fear of upsetting others or not living up to their expectations;
- fear of the future;
- fear of the past;
- fear of staying stuck;
- fear of moving forward.

Do any of these fears resonate with you? In your learning log, list some of the main fears that have got in the way of you fulfilling your ambitions and potential over the years.

Now think about how these fears have impacted on your life. In what ways have they kept you safe? In what ways have they led you to sell yourself short? How have they influenced your actions for good or ill? Write down your thoughts on this in your learning log.

Survival-based fear vs. paralysing fear

Of course, sometimes it really *is* better to be safe than sorry. Some of your fears have probably been quite valuable to you. Courage is not about rash or impulsive behaviour. In fact, it is the opposite: after all, anyone can do pretty much anything if they experience no fear, but that is not exercising courage. Without fear, you are not likely to live for very long.

The point is, there are those fears you need to attend to and those you need to push through. If you are honest, you probably know the difference. Look at your list of fears again. Which are the ones that have undermined you, that have prevented you from honouring your authenticity and that have got in the way of you using your signature strengths? If you are not sure, ask yourself the following question:

Would I want someone I really loved to have the same fear as me?

If the answer is no, then ask yourself why not. Is it because yours is a paralysing rather than a survival-based fear? Remember Mark Twain, who is famously quoted as saying, "My life has been full of disasters, most of which have never happened". Is it possible that most of the fears that hold you back are like this – problems that exist inside your mind rather than problems that have actually happened or are ever likely to happen?

Take heart! Building courage into your life

Courage involves mastering your fears – acknowledging their presence but refusing to see them as reliable indicators of danger. In order to do this, you need to increase your sense of mastery. Whenever you find that your fear is preventing you from living your Mission, use the following steps to help you:

Step 1. Name it

The great French Renaissance thinker and philosopher Michel de Montaigne said we have nothing to fear but fear itself. How true this is for most of us most of the time! Learning to accept your fear takes away its sting and, paradoxically, makes it easier to manage.

Close your eyes and think about a situation where you are currently holding yourself back due to fear. Imagine the situation in as much detail as you can. Now allow yourself to get in touch with the fear that goes with it. Can you:

- identify where it is in your body?
- name the sensations and feelings you experience (without telling yourself catastrophic stories about what they mean)?
- call it by its proper name: fear? (Don't confuse it with danger unless you know you are facing a threat.)
- remind yourself that there is nothing to fear beyond fear itself?

Step 2. Check it out

As a psychologist, I am all for taking our views seriously – until they start to contradict the facts! Given that so much of what holds us back is based on nothing more than fear itself, make sure you subject yours to some serious interrogation before you decide to base your life decisions upon it. Use the following questions to guide you.

- What are you really afraid of?
  - How likely is this to happen?
  - If it did happen would it really be as bad as you think?

- What is holding you back?
  - What old stories is your fear based on? (Remember the limiting story you uncovered in Principle No. 1?)
  - What new story would help you feel more courageous? (Remember the new version of 'My Story' you developed in Principle No. 1?)
- Is your fear totally accurate? Are there any distortions in your thinking that are disempowering you, such as extreme or exaggerated perceptions that another person wouldn't regard as accurate? (We will look again at this in Principle No. 10.)
- What would be a more accurate and helpful way of viewing things that could allow you to rise above the fear?
- Is there anyone else who has achieved what you want to achieve? If so, how did they succeed?
- What small step could you take right now that would empower you to do what you need to do, in spite of the fear?

Step 3. Tackle your fears head on

Now it is time to put these principles into practice – what a client of mine once referred to as the 'feel and deal' stage. Make a list of those things you avoid doing because they scare you. Put them in order, starting with the least anxiety provoking at the bottom of the page and working up to the most anxiety-provoking at the top, like progressively steep rungs on a ladder.

Work out a schedule for reclaiming these activities. Take each rung at a time, and bite the bullet. Keep practising it until it becomes easier, and before you know it you will find that what you once feared has become second nature.

Once you have reclaimed these activities, list the things you most fear will happen if you start to pursue your Mission. What resources do you need to fulfil your most cherished ambitions? What stories about you will you need to ignore to move forward? Revisit the stories you uncovered in Principle No. 1 on Authenticity. What actions will you now need to take? What behaviours will you now need to let go of? Be as specific as you can. Think of one thing you can do every day that pushes you gently beyond your comfort zone and towards the bigger vision you have for your life. If you introduce one new activity every week and stick with it, you will soon find that those things that used to cause you anxiety have become second nature.

Seek out success rather than trying to avoid failure

A successful business women I once met told me, 'It's not that I've failed. It's just that some things haven't worked out.' This was a woman who had maintained considerable drive and motivation to succeed, despite having more than her fair share of failures along the way. Her words sum up the essence of courage in action and the mentality with which you need to approach life: the need to be a success hunter rather than a failure fleer.

The difference between seeking success and avoiding failure might sound like little more than playing with semantics. However, there is a world of difference between the two in terms of the attitudes, actions, and motivations with which life is approached.

Success hunters and failure fleers experience the world in totally different ways. From the outside, they might look pretty similar – they might achieve equally good results, have similar lifestyles, and have achieved similar goals. But their experience of life will be radically different.

Failure fleers are driven by self-doubt. The prospect of 'failing' seems so catastrophic and overwhelming that their *raison d'etre* seems to be organized almost entirely around doing things that will prevent their worst fears from materialising. These are the people who invest enormous amounts of time and energy in their goals but are able to take little pride in their accomplishments – only a sense of relief that, on this occasion, they have managed to avoid failure. When you are a failure fleer it is only a matter of time before you burn out.

In contrast, success hunters are able to see apparent failures as an opportunity to accrue experience that they can use to their advantage. Failure is not some terrible monster lurking in the shadows and so there is freedom to pursue what really matters – and freedom to experiment with the best ways of achieving it. If you want to succeed in life and coach yourself effectively in the art of inspired living, you need to adopt the perspective of a success hunter.

Success is *never* about avoiding failures. In fact, I would argue that if you take any supremely successful person, regardless of their field, you will discover someone who has not only had more successes than others – but also more apparent 'failures' than others. Some things *won't* work out. This is just the way of life. But whether you see them as a sign of your failure, or simply an experience that moves you closer to getting what you really do want, is a choice you need to make. And this is where courage comes in.

The inventor Thomas Edison is probably one of the best examples of this mentality. When asked why he had continued in his efforts to invent a light bulb when he had accumulated over 2,000 failed attempts, Edison replied, 'I didn't fail, I found 2,000 ways how not to make a light bulb; I only need to find one way to make it work.' My point exactly. Each apparent failure brings you closer to what you are aiming for, if you know how to use it to your advantage and are prepared to exercise the courage that will bring you clear vision.

Exercise 9. Making apparent 'failures' work for you

Think of something in your life that didn't go as planned, something that you classify as a failure. See if you could apply the Thomas Edison strategy and discover how this could be interpreted as a stepping stone to success. Use the following questions to guide you.

- What didn't work out as planned?
- Can I identify the different reasons that led to things not working out in the way I had hoped?
- Without resorting to self-blame, what was my part in this?
- What did I overlook, under-estimate or fail to account for?
- What can I learn from this?
- How can I use this experience as the basis for success next time?

> **Helpful hint.** Don't worry if your answers don't feel entirely credible to you to begin with. Learning to recognize the opportunities in our apparent 'failures' involves altering our mindset which takes time and practice.

Write down your thoughts and ideas on these questions in your learning log.

Now think of an occasion when you succeeded. Give yourself a moment to really connect with that success and the thoughts and feelings that went with it. See if you can dissect this experience in the same way.

- What are the different elements that contributed to things working out so well?
- What was my part in creating this success?
- What uncomfortable feelings did I choose to override to pursue my ambition or goal?
- What self-doubting, undermining, or self-critical thoughts did I need to ignore in order to achieve this result?
- What can I learn from my success on this occasion?
- How can I use this experience as the basis for success next time?

Again, write down your thoughts and ideas in your learning log.

Take home message

Bravery is not something that we are born with. It is something we can develop, a way of being in the world that we can cultivate through observing other people and putting ourselves in situations that stretch us beyond our comfort zones. Like all four principles that make up the Mission section of MAP, the decision to act courageously is not one that you make once and for all, but rather one to which you need to commit over and over again.

You cannot eliminate fear – in fact, it would not be in your best interests to do so. But you can choose your response to it. You can take it as a sign that you are moving in the wrong direction, and stay in your comfort zone. Or you can choose to live your life to the full, in spite of it.

This is important, because exercising courage is not about fairy-tale endings. It's about putting yourself on the line, even though you do not know how things are going to work out. Choosing to exercise courage – the courage to express your authenticity, to live

65

by your personal definition of meaning and to implement your signature strengths – may well evoke the disapproval of others. After all, take a good look at what happened to pioneers such as Emmeline Pankhurst, Martin Luther King and Nelson Mandela.

For most of us, however, our Mission is not organized around challenging the status quo in politically volatile circumstances. For many of us, the most painful place to be is that place where we take no steps at all. There is an old saying that captures the essence of this beautifully:

> The best decision is the right one.
> The next best decision is the wrong one.
> The worst decision is no decision at all.

Taking risks means that you have to accept things may not work out – that, after all, is the nature of risk. But in the end this is better than creating a life that is so safe you feel stifled. At the end of your life, you are more likely to be haunted by those things you didn't do, rather than those things that didn't quite work out as you had hoped.

So, let me ask you again: how terrified are you prepared to be, in order to achieve your dreams? It all boils down to this. The more willing you are, the more likely you are to live your Mission to the full.

The Courage to Live

One thing I will take away from this chapter is: (write the answer in your learning log).
One thing I will do differently as a result of this chapter is: (write the answer in your learning log).

Bibliography

*Hayes, S. C., with Smith, S. (2005). *Get Out of Your Mind and Into Your Life*. Oakland, CA: New Harbinger.

Hayes, S. C., Strosahl, K. D., & Wilson, K. G. (1999). *Acceptance and Commitment Therapy: An Experiential Approach to Behavior Change*. New York: Guilford.

*Levine, S. (1997). *A Year to Live. How to Live this Year as if it were Your Last*. New York: Bell Tower.

Resources

Acceptance and Commitment Therapy. Online. Available at www.contextualpsychology.org.

CHAPTER EIGHT

Discovering Your Mission: Pulling It All Together

In Principles 1–4, we explored everything you need to discover your Mission. You learnt how to tap into the wisdom of your authentic self, how to establish a personal sense of meaning, ways of identifying your signature strengths, and how to harness your courage in the service of what matters to you most.

Each of these Principles contributes to a unique constellation of qualities that makes up the essence of you. Before you can decide what you want, you need to know what you are bringing to your journey. Living from the authentic self enables you to honour your truth. Without crafting a unique form of personal meaning, you run the danger of becoming stuck in a narrow vision of what you want rather than investing in something larger that offers service to others and to the world. Similarly, to work out where you are headed with any clarity, you need to know how to implement the character strengths that you have to offer. Finally, without courage, your Mission will eventually falter. It is mustering courage that enables you to accept what you find out about yourself and translate it into meaningful and effective choices.

The great artist Michelangelo is credited with the idea that inside every slab of marble and block of stone lies a beautiful statue. The job of the artist is not, therefore, to 'create' a statue, but rather to remove the outer layers of stone or marble so that the beautiful statue can emerge. So it is with your Mission. As we have seen, uncovering your Mission is not about creating something from scratch, but about uncovering what is already present and waiting to be revealed.

If you have done all the exercises relating to the first four principles and really thought about their implications for your life, you will now have a lot of rich material at your fingertips. Before moving on to the next section, spend time sifting through it. What recurring themes or patterns did you find? What emerges as your story? What is the constellation of strengths that you have to offer the world?

One of the most helpful ways to pull together all your new knowledge and insights is to transform them into a Mission Statement. Below are some examples of Mission Statements produced by people I know and have worked with.

- To inspire and empower others to fulfil their potential.
- To offer healing to people who are suffering.
- To give my children the best start in life.
- To serve God in all that I do and in everything I am.
- To do what I can to help eliminate poverty.
- To offer my services, in whatever way I can, to conserve our planet.
- To share my knowledge and skills for the good of everyone.
- To be there for my family.

Notice how all of these Mission statements could spiral off in any number of directions. Pursuing any of the above will open up opportunities personally and professionally as well as involving choices that relate to work, lifestyle, relationships, and so on. Your Mission, remember, is about determining the broad landscape of how you want your life to be rather than getting into the specifics of what you want to do, where and when (we'll come to the specifics later on).

Your Mission – should you choose to accept it

If you were going to sum up your Mission, how would you put it into words? How would you summarise it, based on all the work you have done in Principles 1–4? Write your own Mission Statement your learning log, under the heading of 'I believe my Mission is . . .'.

Once you have your Mission Statement, put it to one side for a few days and then re-read it. How do you feel when you look at it again? If it is a true representation of your Mission, then you can expect the following types of reactions:

- a sense that it resonates with your values at a fundamental level;
- excitement and optimism;
- curiosity;
- energy and enthusiasm;
- a sense of empowerment;
- a desire to bring this vision of your life into being.

If you find yourself experiencing any negative reactions to your Mission statement, pay attention to these. Notice any thoughts you are having. Are they cynical ("I've read all this before, stuff like this never really works"), or overly demanding ("Now you know what you stand for, you'd better do it properly"), or overwhelming ("How can I ever put this into practice? I'm bound to fail."). Also notice any feelings that your Mission Statement evokes. If you find yourself feeling anxious, fearful, overwhelmed, or daunted, rework your Mission until it feels just right for you (remember, there is no such thing as a right or wrong Mission and our sense of purpose can and often does evolve over time).

Helpful hint. You might also find it helpful to compare your Mission statement to the area you selected from the Inspiration Inventory in Chapter one. Is it the same? If not, in what ways has it changed? Does your Mission statement shed any light on why certain things are going well or less well in your life? Check your answers and make any necessary adjustments to your coaching destination.

When you are satisfied that you have the right wording, write your Mission Statement somewhere that you can see it every day. Write it in your journal. You may also find it helpful to keep a post-it note on your fridge, an index card in your wallet, or set up a screen saver. Whatever method you use, you need to find a way to keep your Mission at the forefront of your mind in every major choice you make from now on.

Martin Seligman, author of *Authentic Happiness*, explains that the more we live from a place of personal integrity, the more inspired we feel and this in turn helps us make choices that reflect what we really want. So a further task is to start putting your Mission into practice every day, to the best of your abilities, both in terms of the choices that you make and the ways in which you behave. Write in your learning log 'Ways that I could start to implement my Mission are . . .' Think small to start with, but try to list at least four things.

You have now completed the first stage in mastering the art of inspired living and will know, or are starting to get to know, what the big picture looks like for you. In the next section we will look at the second part of 'MAP' – your Attitude and how to make it work for you.

CHAPTER NINE

Introducing Principles 5–8:
Your Attitude

> 'Men are disturbed not by events but the views
> which they take of them'
>
> (Epictetus)

Get an attitude: acquiring perspectives
that inspire and empower you

How you view the world is central to how you experience it. The extent to which you implement your Mission is not just down to what happens, but also what you make of it.

When something bad happens, you have a choice: you can let it destroy you, or you can see it as something you can turn to your advantage. Let's be very clear what we mean here. I am not suggesting that you subscribe to the naïve view that problems are all in the mind and that everything in life is wonderful if only we change our view of things. But what I am suggesting is that if you consider the outlooks and perspectives you bring to your life, and commit yourself to incorporating more of those that empower you, you will have begun a process of self-mastery that will prove highly rewarding.

Personal development trainer and author Jack Canfield is well aware of the power of mindset. In his best-selling book, *The Success Principles*, he encourages us to greet each new experience with the question, 'What is the potential opportunity that this is?' Imagine that you saw everything as a genuine opportunity. How would your life be different? If you knew, if you really believed, that every challenge was something that you could use to your advantage or the advantage of others, how would you respond to life's obstacles and setbacks?

An athlete with attitude

One of the most inspiring illustrations of choosing an Attitude that enables us to achieve remarkable things is Jane Tomlinson. Diagnosed as having incurable cancer in 2000 and given only six months to live, Jane chose, through example, to show how people with a terminal prognosis can still lead an active and fulfilling life.

Jane's numerous courses of chemotherapy resulted in chronic heart disease. However, this did not prevent her from completing the London Marathon in 2003. In addition to being the first person in the world to have run a marathon on chemotherapy, she was the only person with incurable cancer to have completed a full Ironman (4 km swim, 180 km bike ride and full marathon, to be done inside 17 hours), two half Ironmans, and three London Marathons – as well as the New York Marathon and three London Triathlons. Jane's amazing drive and commitment enabled her to raise £1.75 million for charity. She died in 2007, but by then her inspirational work had been honoured through numerous accolades and awards.

Jane is a shining example of the potential of human beings to achieve truly great things even in life-threatening circumstances. But perhaps what makes her story particularly inspiring is that she draws attention to how we all, potentially, have the ability to respond to adversity in the same way. She chose not to interpret her prognosis as a statement about who she was and what she could and could not do. This capacity to choose how we respond to events is what I mean by Attitude. So let's look at your Attitude in more detail.

What are your fundamental beliefs, perspectives, and outlooks?

Whereas your Mission is concerned with the why of your life, your Attitude refers to what you bring to it – the perspectives, outlooks, and beliefs that lead you to act in certain ways and not in others. This, by the way, includes the beliefs you have about success, failure, and your ability to fulfil your potential.

Knowing the perspectives, outlooks, and beliefs you bring to your life allows you to clarify some of the resources that will inform your coaching journey – as well as some of your stumbling blocks. The main Attitudes you bring, including even the idea that coaching can be of benefit to you, have been shaped by the knowledge, skills, and life experience you have accumulated over the years. They will also reflect the values, ideals, and standards of the family, community, work environment, and society in which you are embedded.

The psychologist Jerome Bruner suggested that each of us has what he termed a 'library of scripts'. These scripts, inherited from our family, community, and society more generally, shape – even determine – how we think and act. There are many scripts currently operating in our Western library. Some of the more dominant and pressuring ones include the following. See how many apply to you, and how they have influenced your choices and actions (for good or ill).

- The 'Don't get ideas above your station' script.
- The 'Don't aim too high because you're sure to be disappointed' script.
- The 'You must make sure you fit in' script.
- The 'You're a failure if you're not successful' script.
- The 'It's important to keep moving up the career ladder' script.
- The 'A person's worth is determined by their material wealth' script.
- The 'It's important to be attractive to be loved' script.
- The 'It's important to be thin' script (why else would we have invented the 'size zero' dress size?).
- The 'You should beat the ageing process' script.
- The 'You should try to have it all' script.

If you're honest with yourself, you have probably felt the pressure of some these scripts at some point in your life. However much you might like to think you are immune to them, the truth is they influence us all in some form or other.

Of course, there is nothing wrong with aiming for career success, wealth, or making the most of your physical attributes, and if they are priorities for you, then that's fine. Similarly, there is nothing wrong with having realistic standards that accommodate the fact you are only human. The problem is, however, that these attitudes about what is important are often based on what we think we *should* want rather than what that genuinely inspires us. Worse still, these 'scripts' are often given priority over nourishing our potential, nurturing our love of life, appreciating the gift of our individuality, and honouring our personal and collective humanity.

So, if you are to honour your Mission and decide on a destination that is truly of your own choosing, you need to know exactly what your library of scripts contains. Only then can you start to disentangle yourself from the web of values in which you're immersed, to identify those that still matter to you and those you have outgrown.

Think about the Attitudes you have inherited – the ones that have helped shape you into the person you are today. See which ones have nurtured your talents and which ones have got in the way, using the following questions to guide you.

- What Attitudes (perspectives, beliefs, values or ideals) do you hold about:
  - ○ yourself (including what you like and don't like about the person that you are)?
  - ○ other people and relationships?
  - ○ life and how the world works?

Once your answers to these questions start to emerge, consider the following.

- Where did your attitudes come from?
- Who and what have been important in shaping these attitudes?
- Which attitudes are valuable to you at this point in your life? (Remember, perspectives can change: what may have been useful to you earlier in your life may not work for you now.)
- Which ones have you now outgrown?
- Which attitudes have caused you to play at being small?

●   If you could start life over, would you choose the same attitudes or devise new ones? If you were to devise new ones, what might they be?

Again, write down your responses in your learning log so you can revisit and revise them as you work through the next four chapters.

In 'MAP', Attitude is not just about what you bring to the journey. It is also about cultivating the outlooks, perspectives, and beliefs that will help you achieve your goals. In the next chapters, I am going to share some Attitudes that are worth cultivating, that will help you get more out of life and enable you to coach yourself to success. These Attitudes in 'MAP' are:

Principle No. 5: Optimism
Viewing experiences and events in an empowering way; maintaining a hopeful outlook on life; looking for the hidden gifts in challenging situations.

Principle No. 6: Curiosity
The capacity to be open to experience and have a genuine interest in new situations and experiences; valuing exploration, learning and discovery.

Principle No. 7: Gratitude
A genuine appreciation for life and the many gifts bestowed upon you; the capacity to be thankful for all that is yours to give and receive.

Principle No. 8: Compassion
The capacity to respect and empathize with ourselves and others; the willingness to let go of past resentments; an active acceptance of what is.

CHAPTER TEN

Principle No. 5: The Power of Optimism

'The mind is its own place, and in itself can make
a heaven of Hell, a hell of Heaven'

(John Milton)

*Welcome to Principle No. 5: the power of optimism. In this chapter
you will discover:*

- *whether your current attitude is holding you back from achieving
  what you want;*
- *how becoming more optimistic can improve your health, happiness, and levels of success;*
- *how to achieve a more empowering, optimistic perspective.*

When Anne Frank said, 'I don't think of all the misery but of the beauty that still remains', she was describing the one power we can always exercise, regardless of the situation in which we find ourselves: the power to choose how we see things. Amid the horrors of incarceration in a concentration camp, Anne Frank exercised her power of choice to see not just the despair, but the beauty that lay beyond.

At a time when the power of positive thinking seems to be all the rage, it is easy to become cynical about optimism. After all, bad things do happen to good people and we cannot always determine what happens to us. But we *can* choose how we respond. Whether we sink into the depths of despair or embrace what experience has to offer is, to some extent, a reflection of how we exercise our power of choice. In this sense, the art of inspired living has less to do with the circumstances in which we find ourselves than it does the perspectives we bring to those circumstances.

How do you respond to setbacks in life? After the initial disappointment has subsided do you look at them objectively and see what you can do differently next time? Or ruminate on them endlessly, blaming yourself or others for failing? And what about the future, including your beliefs about your ability to achieve your goals? Are you cynical about your prospects for change? Do you worry endlessly about what the future may have in store or trust yourself to handle whatever comes along? Write your thoughts about these questions in your learning log.

Karen's story

When Karen came to see me, she was depressed. Her partner of six years, with whom she had hoped to start a family, had recently left her. Her self-esteem was in tatters, she was struggling to cope, and had been signed off work with depression. 'I feel like such a failure,' she told me. 'It's all my fault Robert left, I always ruin my relationships. I'm obviously destined to be alone. I just don't see the point any more.'

Karen was describing a sense of hopelessness true of many people who are experiencing depression. The loss of her partner, and the loss of her dream of starting a family with him, had triggered a belief that life was pointless and that she would always feel as unhappy as she did right then. She felt negative about herself, the world, and her future.

When I talked to Karen a bit longer, I discovered that she had always tended to look on the bleak side of things. 'I have always been a "cup half empty" person,' she admitted. 'But it's better to be realistic than to have your hopes ruined. Besides, my life is a mess, so what's the point of positive thinking? I'd just be kidding myself.'

Karen was missing the point. She was confusing optimism with 'positive thinking' and was mistaking her current feelings of despair for an accurate appraisal of her circumstances. She is not alone in this. Many people believe that being pessimistic is a more realistic way to view the world. Perennial pessimists will even tell you that there are benefits to anticipating the worst. It is not unusual, for example, for people to choose a negative outlook in an attempt to prevent disappointment: 'If I expect the worst, I won't be disappointed' is the rule that guides their outlook. But there is a terrible price to be paid for this type of attitude.

The price you pay for your pessimism

If you see yourself as one of life's pessimists, prepare yourself for a shock. Studies in psychology have shown that a pessimistic mind-set has a powerful negative influence on our health and happiness. Not only has pessimism been linked to depression and, in extreme cases, suicidal behaviour, but when we live our lives under its shadow, we are likely to under-perform at work and fail to achieve our goals. Pessimism even seems to affect the immune system, making us susceptible to illness and disease.

Pessimism also saps our energy and love of life. Think of someone whom you would see as pessimistic. How do they respond to challenges and setbacks? Their attitude may be one of doom and gloom or they may exude an air of cynicism that veils a quiet desperation. Think about how you feel after you have spent time with them. Positive or negative? Energized or drained? Do you enjoy being around them? Probably not.

Optimism, in contrast, has a major role to play in increasing the amount of satisfaction we get from life. Studies show that optimism is essential to success in many careers, including sales and competitive sports where rejection and apparent 'failures' are commonplace.

Think of someone you know who is naturally optimistic. How does this person respond to challenges and setbacks? What kind of energy do they radiate into the world? How do you feel after you have spent time with them? Do you enjoy spending time with them? Probably.

But why should optimism and pessimism have such a powerful impact? Both these attitudes give out and attract back a certain type of energy that becomes self-fulfilling. The more optimistic you are, the more positive energy you radiate into the world, which in turn attracts positive reactions from others – the very kinds of reactions you need to open up new opportunities. Conversely, a pessimistic outlook sends out negative energy, which leads others to react in an equally negative way. To some extent, it seems, we get what we expect.

As life coach Fiona Harrold observes, our outlook informs, if not determines, our landscape of expectations and possibilities. And yet, rather than expand our range of choices, many of us prefer to adopt inflexible and restricting beliefs that we fight to hold on to. So, whatever Attitude you choose from now on, you need to be clear about its impact and whether it is helping you move in the direction of the life you want.

Optimism and pessimism: different mindsets for different ends

Being optimistic is not about seeing the positive in everything. Nor is it about adopting a blind faith in the goodness of humankind. Total optimism in all situations is naïve, even dangerous. For example, if you start to experience chest pains whenever you take physical exercise and you have a history of heart problems in your family, to tell yourself that it is just indigestion could be overlooking an important message that your body is giving you. A healthy level of pessimism leads you to take action when action is required – in this case, seeing a doctor. Making a will, taking out life assurance, and buckling your seat belt are similar examples of healthy pessimism: you hope you will not need them, but by anticipating the worst, can protect yourself from possible hazards.

The problem occurs when pessimism starts to permeate your life in a way that limits your choices. If you see most things through the mental filter of pessimism, life becomes a disaster waiting to happen. You spiral into a vortex of negativity that soon feels impossible to break out of, fuelling feelings of helplessness, hopelessness, and despair, much like Karen.

Many of these mental filters simply come down to habit. If you get into the habit of interpreting everything through a pessimistic lens, your outlook on life will be equally negative. Similarly, if you adopt the habit of interpreting events through an optimistic lens, your outlook will be more constructive.

Optimism, then, is the mental habit of perceiving and interpreting events in a particular way. You can learn to develop this habit in much the same way you might develop any other good habit such as eating healthily or taking regular exercise. If you are not used to it, it may feel strange to begin with, but the more you do it, the easier it will get – and the results will be well worth your while.

Here are some of the benefits you can expect from developing a more optimistic perspective:

- feeling more inspired by your life;
- making the most of your gifts and talents;
- being more appreciative of your relationships;
- honouring your priorities and values;
- turning challenges and setbacks to your advantage;
- solving problems more easily;
- being able to take advantage of new opportunities.

The true nature of optimism

Having described some of the benefits you can expect from adopting a more optimistic Attitude, let's look at the nature of optimism in more detail. If it is primarily a mental habit, what is the nature of that habit and how can you acquire it?

Ground-breaking research by the American psychologist Martin Seligman and his colleagues has revealed fundamental differences between optimists and pessimists, not just in terms of *what* they think, but more importantly *how* they think.

What Seligman and his colleagues have discovered is that optimists and pessimists explain events in fundamentally different ways. Pessimists explain setbacks in ways that are personal ('It's *my* fault'), pervasive ('My *whole life* is ruined'), and permanent ('It'll *always* be like this'). But optimists see negative events as impersonal ('It's one of those things'), impermanent ('It will pass'), and situation-specific ('This is a tough situation but other areas of my life are working really well and I still have a lot going for me'). For optimists, difficulties are problems to be solved, not an indication of their flaws as a human being. Pessimists, in contrast, 'own' their difficulties and see them as all-encompassing.

As you might expect, this pattern is reversed for successes: it is the optimists who interpret positive events in a personal, permanent and pervasive way and the pessimists who put them down to 'fluke' events. In short, the difference between the Optimistic and Pessimistic mindset can be seen in Table 1.

Table 1. The mindset of the optimist and the pessimist.

Type of situation	Optimistic style	Pessimistic style
You see bad events as:	Temporary	Permanent
You see good events as:	Permanent	Temporary
You see bad events as:	Specific to that situation	Pervasive (relating to all of your life)
You see good events as:	Pervasive	Specific to that situation
You see bad events as:	Not personal (you attribute them to an external cause)	Personal (you attribute them to an internal cause)
You see good events as:	Personal (down to you)	Not personal (down to luck or chance)

Which categories do you tend to fall into? Think about a time in your life when something went well for you. How did you explain it? To what did you attribute your success? Write any insights in your learning log.

Now remember a time when something didn't go well – an event that left you feeling disappointed, disillusioned, or fed up. How did you explain this? To what did you attribute the difficulty? What did you believe it was telling you about yourself or your life? Again, write your thoughts in your learning log.

On balance, are you a natural optimist or, someone who leans towards the pessimistic end of the spectrum?

Transform your pessimism into inspirational optimism

One of the best ways to start developing an optimistic outlook is, paradoxically, to get to know your pessimistic mindset. Although it may have exerted a powerful negative influence at certain times, you have been doing it for a reason. Try viewing your pessimistic perspective as a misguided friend: someone who has your best interests at heart but whose dire warnings are often wide of the mark.

The following exercise is designed to help you discover what motivates your pessimistic Attitude and how you can transform it into an outlook that is truly empowering.

Exercise 10. Interviewing the inner pessimist

Close your eyes and allow your mind to quieten.

When you are ready, I'd like you to imagine you have arranged an interview with a leading pessimist who has been your personal adviser and coach up until now. Your job is to interview them to find out all you can about the art of pessimism and how their coaching style has influenced your life. Notice what your pessimist looks like and the impression they create, then ask them the following questions, writing down their responses in your learning log.

1. What is your motto in life?
2. What experiences and relationships have shaped your philosophy of life?
3. From what are you trying to protect me?
4. In what ways do you hold me back, cause me to lose out or create problems in my life?
5. How would you advise me to view my successes? Why?
6. How would you advise me to view challenges, setbacks and disappointments? Why?
7. What do you fear will happen if I become more optimistic?
\. What message do you most want to give me?

What do your answers tell you about what motivates your pessimistic mindset? In what ways does your inner pessimist empower and disempower you? Do you feel energized and inspired? If yes, then great! If not, thank your pessimist for everything he or she tries to do for you, but gently point out that his or her coaching style is costing you too much.

Now that you understand the motives and costs of maintaining your pessimistic mindset, it's time to meet the inner optimist – the one who will be running your life from now on.

Exercise 11. Interviewing the inner optimist

Close your eyes and allow your mind to quieten.

I'd like you to imagine you have arranged an interview with a leading optimist who will be your personal adviser and coach from now on. Your job is to interview them to find out all you can about the art of optimism, what positive qualities they will bring to your life and how their coaching style will enable you to live your Mission more fully. Notice what your optimist looks like and the impression they create, then ask the following questions, writing down their responses in your learning log.

1. What is your motto in life?
2. What experiences and relationships have shaped your philosophy of life?
3. What can you offer me? What can you help me accomplish?
4. In what ways might you create problems in my life?
5. How would you advise me to view my successes? Why?
6. How would you advise me to view challenges, setbacks and disappointments? Why?
7. What message do you most want to give me?
8. What action would you recommend that I take in my life right now?

Spend some time looking through your answers. If your optimist were to take charge of your life, in what ways might your life improve? What possibilities might emerge? Would there be any costs? Consider how each mindset interprets your successes and setbacks. Can you see the patterns of personalization, permanence, and pervasiveness that Martin Seligman believes lie at the heart of the optimism-pessimism distinction?

Coaching tips for expanding your optimistic potential

One way of helping develop an attitude of optimism is to start with the realities of your day-to-day experience. If you are not facing any major challenges right now, focus on developing a more optimistic perspective for day-to-day tasks. Choose a day in advance and, instead of focusing on all the things you have to do, identify all the positive things. For example, you might focus on:

- how you will feel good for completing household chores, or clearing paper work;
- how the day will enable you to earn a day's wages;
- how your work, including daily chores, will benefit others;
- cherishing the chance to read a good book or listen to the radio.

If you are currently facing challenges, work on depersonalizing them. Avoid taking responsibility for what is not wholly or even partially your fault. Remind yourself that problems pass, that all setbacks contain discovery opportunities and that however bad the problem seems, other areas of your life are working well. Reframing problems as challenges enables you to grow. What can you learn for next time? Similarly, own your successes and remind yourself of all the good things that have sustained you in life. As we saw in Principle No. 1, there are always other ways of telling your story that present new choices.

As the optimistic mindset becomes more robust, you will find that it gradually becomes incorporated within your authentic self. To help you on your way, try using the ideas in the coaching tool kit below.

Your Coaching Tool Kit: Top Tips for Increasing Your Optimism

1. Watch your language! Next time something bad happens, change 'always' and 'never' words to 'sometimes' and 'lately'. When something good happens, insert 'always' and 'never' words and notice the difference.
2. Make a list of all the ways you will benefit from developing a more optimistic outlook and remind yourself of the benefits of developing this perspective in your life.
3. Every time you encounter an obstacle ask yourself: what can I learn from this? How can I turn this to my advantage?
4. Make a list of all the optimists and pessimists in your life. Whose pessimism do you benefit from (for example, your legal or financial adviser) and whose pessimism drains you? How can you limit your contact with the unhelpful pessimists in your life?
5. Find an optimistic role-model. If it is a celebrity, read their biography. Analyse their thinking and experiment with their Attitude. Imagine how they would explain their successes and setbacks. If it is someone you know personally, talk to them about how they see the world.
6. Start an Optimism File. Collect inspiring quotations and stories to bolster your own optimism potential.

Take home message

The difference between optimism and pessimism may be the difference between living a life that inspires you and one that leaves you feeling unfulfilled and unmotivated. Because of this, optimism is one of the most important outlooks you can acquire and an essential Attitude for your coaching journey. Even if you think you are one of life's more optimistic types, you can consciously choose to implement and enhance this strength – the results are likely to prove highly rewarding.

The good news, as we have seen, is that optimism is a habit rather than a personality type, and, like all habits, it is something you can learn. Whatever the circumstances, there are always opportunities for developing a more optimistic outlook that has the potential to benefit your health and happiness. So take advantage of everything that comes your way to strengthen your inner optimistic coach. By learning good mental habits you can develop an Attitude that will support you in achieving your dreams – wherever they may lead.

Cultivating The Right Mindset: The Power of Optimism

One idea I shall take away from this chapter is . . . (write the answer in your learning log).
One thing I will do differently to create more of an optimistic outlook in my life is . . . (write the answer in your learning log).

Bibliography

Carver, C. S., & Scheier, M. F. (2005). Optimism. In: C. R. Snyder & S. J. Lopez (Eds.), *Handbook of Positive Psychology* (pp. 231–243). New York: Oxford University Press.

*Harrold, F. (2002). *The 10-Minute Life Coach. Fast-Working Strategies for a Brand New You*. London: Hodder and Stoughton.

*Seligman, M. E. P. (1990). *Learned Optimism: How to Change your Mind and Your Life*. New York: Free Press.

CHAPTER ELEVEN

Principle No. 6 – Cultivating Curiosity: Develop Your Passion for Knowledge

'I have no special talent. I am only passionately curious'

(Albert Einstein)

Welcome to Principle No. 6: the power of curiosity. In this chapter you will:

- *discover why curiosity is essential to the art of inspired living;*
- *learn about your own curiosity and preferred learning style;*
- *discover how to develop curiosity so you can get more out of life.*

If you could learn about anything at all, what would it be? What fascinates you so much that you can lose track of time just by doing it?

Personal development guru Tony Robbins suggests that as long as you are genuinely curious, nothing is boring. But curiosity is more than the antidote to boredom; it is also a source of inspiration in its own right.

People who are curious have an added dimension to their lives. They have an insatiable appetite for information and knowledge and can appreciate new places, new people, and new experiences as the adventure that they are.

Curious people have a different perspective on learning, too. They tend not to take things at face value, or comply with the received view of things. Rather, they possess an ability to see things from different and novel angles and are open-minded enough to change perspectives when an existing one is not producing the right results. If they were holding the diamond that we talked about in Principle No. 1, they would never be happy with seeing just one colour, however beautiful, but would rotate it and hold it at different angles to see how many colours might emerge. That is the essence of curiosity.

Ralph's story

One of the most inspiring people I have ever met is Ralph, a former colleague and long-standing friend. Ralph, now retired, had held a senior position within a large television company. His work required not only a high level of technical skill but also an ability to co-ordinate team-working in situations involving high pressure and immovable deadlines.

I met Ralph when I was working as a secretary for the company, long before I began my training as a clinical psychologist. A kind and sociable man, he did not consider his abilities to be particularly outstanding. But even then, I recognized something remarkable about him.

Ralph was passionately interested in many subjects and his knowledge and skills were wide-ranging. Among pursuits that spanned broadcasting, travel, transport, and DIY, he was an accomplished photographer and possessed an impressive collection of his own work. Indeed, the standard of his work was so high that when the television company needed some scenic shots as background, Ralph's photographs were an obvious choice.

What was particularly extraordinary was that a large amount of his knowledge was self-taught. As I got to know Ralph, I realized that one of his defining features was an insatiable curiosity, coupled with a genuine enthusiasm for learning. Despite a lack of formal training in many of the areas in which he possessed high levels of skill, he had cultivated an attitude that enabled him to learn and grow. And his curiosity and enthusiasm were contagious. An evening spent in his company would leave me feeling inspired to learn about places and subjects that I would previously have dismissed as being of no interest to me. Quite literally, his curiosity and love of learning sparked my own.

Reconnect with your love of learning

Most of us start out with an insatiable passion for knowledge. Just look at babies. Their innate curiosity leads them to touch, taste, shake, push, pull, look, listen, and mimic most things with which they come into contact. Within the first two years of life their curiosity propels them to achieve the miracles of walking, talking, and building relationships.

A friend of mine once told me about her little girl, Annabel, who at the time was nine months old. Her mother left her for a moment to make a cup of tea and, realizing that things had gone rather quiet, went to check up on her. Annabel was transfixed by the sight of a large, black spider scuttling across the floor. Unhampered by any preconceptions of what spiders are (and how she should react to them), Annabel was totally enraptured by the unexpected appearance of this remarkable creature. Imagine if we could approach everything with this same sense of wonder and awe. Imagine how much more interesting and stimulating life would be if we greeted everything we encountered as if for the first time.

Making sense of the world is one of the first challenges with which life presents us. Our brains come hardwired with an ability to identify and classify objects, experiences, and events. We are cognitively primed to identify patterns in time and space and learn about cause and effect so that we can start to gain mastery over our world. Just like Annabel, we learn when our existing classification system needs refining (for example, to include a new 'spider' category) so we can discover more about what the world has in store for us.

As a young child you, too, would have been wide-eyed with curiosity about everything you saw, absorbing each new experience like a sponge. Life was an adventure, and as the explorer that you were, you set out to discover this strange new terrain, learning what the world had to offer. Through the little, yet monumental, expeditions of your young self, you discovered the world of objects and relationships, what you liked and disliked, what was right and wrong, and how to succeed. Over time, this became a more elaborate map of thoughts and feelings, actions and reactions, and preferences and choices. Behind it all, driving all of these expeditions, was your innate curiosity.

Unfortunately, by the time we are immersed within the education system, many of us have had our innate curiosity knocked out of us. We have learnt that there are right answers and wrong answers, good test results and bad test results, and that our expeditions, adventures, and constant questions can annoy the adults around us. We also learn that there are certain things we shouldn't ask about (because they seem to make people uncomfortable) and that we live in a world in which answers are often deemed more important than questions.

But the dampening of our curiosity comes at a terrible cost and in this chapter, I want to reawaken that innate ability within you – your passion to know, your thirst for knowledge, and your love of learning.

Why love learning? The curious facts . . .

Although scientists are not yet able to define the precise mechanisms through which curiosity enhances our abilities, they do know that the thirst for knowledge, the desire to learn, and the ability to remain open to what experience has to teach all have positive effects on our emotional well-being. Those of us who are highly curious can expect a greater abundance of positive emotions such as excitement and enjoyment of life, as well as healthy self-esteem. Curious people are more creative, enjoy challenges, and have better relationships. It has even been suggested that curiosity can enhance life expectancy!

Curiosity is also vital to fulfilling our potential. It helps us learn better and enhances our skills in problem-solving and complex decision-making. We remain flexible when events do not quite fit our current expectations and are likely to persist in the face of setbacks and obstacles. Like Ralph, people who experience high levels of curiosity do not see themselves as passive recipients of life events; they actively engage with them and are motivated to use setbacks to best advantage, seeing them as challenges rather than failings.

In this sense, being curious is a self-invited challenge to our existing Attitude that allows us to look beyond the confines of our own perceptual prism towards new possibilities and dreams. To be open in this way enables us to explore and integrate the novel ideas, strategies, skills, and approaches that we need to learn and grow. So, if you find yourself bored by life or stuck in the mundane, get ready to buck up and brush up! You need to re-engage with your passion for learning.

What is your learning orientation?

The extent to which you use your curiosity to its full potential will depend in part on your approach to learning. There are two distinct learning orientations you need to be aware of when building your curiosity. These are:

1. Learning that is active or passive.
2. Learning that is inwardly motivated or motivated by external reward.

Let's look at each of these learning styles in turn.

1. Are you an active or a passive learner?

We all differ in our desire for new experiences. Some of us need to face constant challenges just to feel alive, while others thrive on a more gentle and gradual approach.

If you are an active learner, the idea of novelty and challenge will excite you. You love learning and whatever you are doing, something will nearly always spark your desire to learn more. You tend to seek out opportunities to stretch yourself and feel good about the prospect of learning something new. Because you enjoy challenges, you are happy to work independently on problems, trusting yourself to come up with the solutions you need. You keep going when your efforts are thwarted because you have faith in yourself and your abilities.

If you are a passive learner, you tend to approach new tasks more warily, preferring to absorb information you are given rather than actively seeking to acquire it. You are more likely to be afraid of the unknown and anxious about making mistakes. Deep down, you are not sure you can trust your abilities and so may ask others for help because you lack the confidence to try things for yourself. While you may be relieved and pleased when you have mastered

---

Exercise 12. Are you an active or passive learner?

	Very true of me	Moderately true of me	Not really true of me
1. I thrive on the opportunity to learn something new.	☐	☐	☐
2. I find learning for the sake of it highly rewarding.	☐	☐	☐
3. There are many things that interest me.	☐	☐	☐
4. If I can't work something out straight away, I'll persevere until I can.	☐	☐	☐
5. I find challenges stimulating and exciting.	☐	☐	☐
6. Setbacks don't concern me too much.	☐	☐	☐
7. I feel confident about managing and supporting my own learning.	☐	☐	☐
8. I trust my abilities to learn new things, even if it's a stretch at first.	☐	☐	☐
9. Generally, I am able to come up with solutions to problems.	☐	☐	☐
10. I am confident that I will learn from my mistakes.	☐	☐	☐
11. I enjoy finding out more about the world.	☐	☐	☐
12. I think the world is full of interesting things, people and places.	☐	☐	☐

---

something, you would not describe yourself as passionate about learning. Acquiring knowledge is largely a means to an end.

To find out if you are an active or passive learner take the test below.

If you scored mainly 'Very true of me', then you are an active learner. If you scored mainly 'Moderately true of me' you certainly have the potential for active learning, but this could do with a little work. And if you scored mainly 'Not really true of me', then this is definitely a growth area for you, so read on . . .

2. Is your learning style intrinsically or extrinsically motivated?

An intrinsic love of learning refers to an inherent desire for knowledge and experience. The very act of engaging with your learning process sparks a sense of enjoyment and stimulation. You learn and absorb knowledge for its own sake and approach challenges with eagerness and interest.

Extrinsic learning is all about pursuing a means to an end. You may well be very motivated to learn but you acquire knowledge largely for strategic purposes, such as passing an exam or gaining a promotion that will lead to tangible rewards.

Intrinsic and extrinsic motivational styles are sometimes also known as the mastery *vs.* performance distinction. When we aim for mastery, we assess our progress in terms of self-improvement, personal development, and the outcome of our efforts to work towards something personally meaningful. We assess our progress in terms of questions like: What's changed? What have I discovered? How can I apply what I have learnt? A mastery orientation maps on to an intrinsic love of learning by increasing enjoyment and fostering a sense of effectiveness and control over our own learning. Mistakes are one more experience that you turn to your advantage, as you work out how you can do it differently next time.

The performance orientation, however, is based on measuring performance according to some externally imposed criteria – for example, the grade you get in an exam, whether or not you get the promotion, and how others judge you in the light of your performance.

95

Your learning orientation will influence the way you approach new tasks. If you are performance orientated you may well work hard, but your learning will be largely outcome-focused – for example, studying the curriculum for an exam, or putting in the hours to get a good performance appraisal at your next salary review. Your learning approach is likely to remain narrowly focused

---

Exercise 13. Is your learning style intrinsically or extrinsically motivated?

	Very true of me	Moderately true of me	Not really true of me
1. I enjoy learning for its own sake.	☐	☐	☐
2. External rewards are not my primary motivation for learning new things.	☐	☐	☐
3. I learn better when left to my own devices, rather than needing to study for a course, qualification or promotion.	☐	☐	☐
4. I rarely worry about how my efforts compare with those of others.	☐	☐	☐
5. I feel motivated to learn in the absence of external rewards (such as passing an exam or obtaining a qualification).	☐	☐	☐
6. I like looking for links between what I am learning now and what I already know.	☐	☐	☐
7. I feel good about myself when I have learnt something new.	☐	☐	☐
8. When it comes to learning something new, I prefer to work it out for myself.	☐	☐	☐

	Very true of me	Moderately true of me	Not really true of me
9. Where possible, I prefer to learn without the aid of formal training manuals or a pre-designed curriculum.	☐	☐	☐
10. Even if I know how to do something well, I enjoy exploring new ways of approaching the task.	☐	☐	☐
11. I regularly learn new things purely for the joy of discovering more about the world.	☐	☐	☐
12. I see myself as having a genuine love of learning.	☐	☐	☐

on what you have to learn, rather than enjoying learning for its own sake.

To find out if you are an inwardly-directed or outwardly-directed learner, take the test below.

If you scored mainly 'Very true of me', then you are an intrinsically motivated learner. If you scored mainly 'Moderately true of me' you are equally balanced between performance and mastery styles. And if you scored mainly 'Not really true of me', then your learning style is mainly performance-based or externally motivated.

In reality, we slip in and out of active and passive, intrinsic and extrinsic learning styles according to the task in hand. Each approach equips us with something valuable. As authors Christopher Peterson and Martin Seligman observe, in evolutionary terms, attraction to novelty is valuable because it increases our knowledge of the world. Conversely, the fear of novelty helps us approach potentially dangerous situations with caution. Intrinsic learning is inherently inspiring and extrinsic learning helps us maximize our potential through appropriate qualifications and experience. It's all about balance.

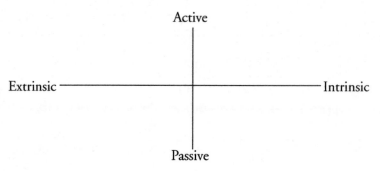

Figure 1. Your learning approach.

Copy the diagram (Figure 1) into your learning log and use it to plot different areas of your life. How many, and which areas of your life fit into each of the four sections? Do you have a balance or do you need a more active and intrinsically motivated approach?

Know the origins of your approach to learning

As we have seen, if you approach new challenges with a sense of competence, the experience of learning is likely to prove stimulating and rewarding. However, if your previous experiences of learning were based on being closely scrutinised or even being punished when you made mistakes, your passion to know may feel crushed beneath the need to do well. Engaging your curiosity could then feel like quite a challenge.

Think about your own experiences of learning. How was your learning helped or hindered by your parents, teachers, and peers when you were young? Were you encouraged to experiment or play it safe? Were mistakes seen as an inevitable part of learning or were they greeted with disappointment? What meanings did you attach to learning when you were young – a chance to engage with the world, or a sense of having tasks imposed on you that didn't really mean that much? Think about how you might now approach any previous obstacles from a more empowered perspective and jot down your thoughts in your learning log.

Whatever your prior experiences, know that you now have a choice. As an adult, you can stimulate your own interest and enjoyment through adopting a curiosity-orientated attitude. You can define tasks and activities in such a way to make them more interesting and further your learning journey. Even if the task is not intrinsically rewarding, you can still remind yourself of why it matters and how it fits in with your Mission.

Look for the miracles in the mundane

A teacher I once met gave me the following advice about nurturing a love of learning: start with what's right in front of you. 'Stop looking for the fantastic and start looking for the miraculous in the ordinary,' he said. 'If you open up to it, you'll see just how much there is, right in front of you.' He was right. When I opened my eyes, like Annabel and the spider, I saw miracles going on all around me.

Think about the kinds of things that might arouse your curiosity but that you may have overlooked – the small, daily events that make life more interesting. It might be the way you tend to get engrossed in a good book or movie; it might be the sense of awe and wonder that comes from watching the dramatic colours of a sunset; it might come from enjoying the challenge of a DIY problem, or coming up with a new way of approaching a work-related project. Next time you go shopping, take a moment to look at the people around you, how they move and what they do. Go to a café and observe who comes and goes. Look for the extraordinary right in front of you. It is there, I guarantee it.

Collect articles from newspapers, magazines, and the internet on any subjects that spark your interest. Spend a week keeping your learning log with you at all times, jotting down your observations, impressions, and ideas. Write down questions as they pop into your mind and keep them with you until the answers come to you. In the movie *Crossing Delancy*, the hero describes how he writes the questions to which he wants answers into a little book that he always carries with him. When he knows the answer, he writes it down. This is a great way of working creatively with your curiosity. Get into the habit of asking yourself what you would like to learn, even if it seems far-fetched. You never know what opportunities life has in store!

To get you started, jot down your answers to the following questions and see where they lead.

- What fascinates you?
- What sparks a sense of wonder or awe within you?
- What situations, events, objects, or people are most likely to arouse your desire to know more?
- If you could learn about anything at all, what would it be? (Identify anything that you have always wanted to know more about.)
- How could you extend the parameters of your curiosity to include new topics?
- Think of something you do regularly – something that you would judge as mundane or ordinary. How could you stretch yourself by seeing this in a new way?

Your Coaching Tool Kit: Ideas for Developing your Natural Curiosity

1. Put yourself in situations that are likely to arouse your curiosity. Do more of what truly interests you.
2. Try approaching a very mundane situation (e.g., going shopping, travelling to work) as though for the first time. How is it different when seen through fresh eyes?
3. If you are a passive learner, experiment with adopting a more active approach. How does this change how you feel about the task in hand?
4. If you are an extrinsic learner, experiment with adopting an intrinsic approach. How does this change how you feel about the task in hand?
5. Next time you have something new to learn, trust your abilities and see how enjoyable you can make the learning process.

Finally, remember to view your learning potential through an optimistic lens. Adopt the attitude that you can learn successfully and effectively and that the process will be enriching. Eventually, it will start to become so.

Take home message

Regardless of whether or not you see yourself as one of life's adventurous types, you can always enhance your love of learning and your passion for knowledge. The world is such an extraordinary place that, whatever your circumstances, there is always an abundance of things in which to be interested. But remember that in order to make your curiosity work for you, you need to have some faith in your own abilities to learn and grow; the drive to seek out new experiences requires a faith that you can handle what you encounter – whether it is a new creature, like Annabel's spider, or persisting in learning a skill that will help you achieve your goals and implement your life's Mission.

You are your own ultimate experiment. Your curiosity, love of learning, and a healthy desire to explore all provide an opportunity to create more of the life that you want. If you tap into your own unlimited supply, you will always find your efforts yield a rich harvest.

Cultivating Curiosity

One idea I shall take away from this chapter is . . . (write the answer in your learning log).
One thing I will do differently is . . . (write the answer in your learning log).

Bibliography

*Csikszentmihalyi, M. (1990). *Flow. The Psychology of Optimal Experience*. New York: Harper Row.

Csikszentmihalyi, M., & Csikszentmihalyi, I. (1988). *Optimal Experience. Psychological Studies of Flow in Consciousness*. Cambridge: Cambridge University Press.

*Fleming, N. D. (2002). *A Guide to Learning Styles*. Online. Available at www.vark-learn.com. Version 4.1.

Gibbs, G. (1992). *Improving the Quality of Student Learning*. Bristol: Technical & Educational Services. (Of interest to those wishing to follow up on the literature on different learning styles with a view to facilitating client learning.)

Ramsden, P. (1992). *Learning to Teach in Higher Education*. London: Routledge. (Of interest to those wishing to follow up on the literature on different learning styles with a view to facilitating client learning.)

*Robbins, A. (1991). *Awaken the Giant Within: How to Take Immediate Control of Your Mental, Emotional, Physical and Financial Destiny*. New York: Free Press.

CHAPTER TWELVE

Principle No. 7: The Gift of Gratitude

'If the only prayer you say in your whole life is "thank you" that would suffice'

(Meister Eckhart)

Welcome to the seventh principle of inspired living: infusing your life with the gift of gratitude. In this chapter you will learn:

- *why gratitude is essential for effective self-coaching;*
- *how enhancing your capacity for gratitude can enhance your well-being, health and happiness;*
- *essential strategies for nurturing the gift of gratitude in your own life.*

As Meg walked out of the hospital she could barely contain her joy. She had just been cleared of cancer: the symptoms that had been worrying the doctors had turned out to be nothing more than a scare. Meg had always tended to worry, but this time she had felt as though her life were in the balance.

At the main entrance to the hospital, Meg stopped and took a deep breath. As she drank in the hot, summer air she didn't notice the smell of traffic fumes or the fact that an argument had broken out between two drivers competing for the same parking space. The only thing she felt was a profound sense of gratitude – to whom or to what she had no idea. Somehow she had been given a second chance and in that moment, she promised never to take her life for granted again. And with this feeling of gratitude came, for the first time in her life, a profound sense of peace . . .

The transformational power of gratitude

Gratitude is a quality that expresses the highest of our potentials and is a core characteristic of people who are able to nurture and fulfil their potential to a high level.

Psychologist Abraham Maslow suggested that taking our blessings for granted is a primary cause of suffering and misery. But the pressures of modern life make it all too easy to fall into this trap. Life plods along, with all its irritations and frustrations, and much of the time we focus on all the things we have to get done, barely noticing how much we have going for us. Very often, it is not until we experience a serious threat to our lives that we realize how much we have to lose.

How many times do you make a conscious decision to feel grateful for everything that is in your life, both big and small? What kinds of experiences make you feel grateful and in which domains (for example, work, relationships, achievements, the thoughtfulness of others, beautiful scenery)? Before you go any further, jot down your answers to the following questions.

- What are you thankful for?
- What would you count as being among the most precious blessings of your life?
- What do you take for granted in your life that someone in a developing or war-torn country would see as a blessing?
- What would you badly miss if it were taken away?
- What experiences have you had, that have made you feel glad to be alive?

Meg's story

Following her health scare, Meg began to consider these questions very seriously. Like many of us she had grown up with the popular idea that she should 'count her blessings' but, although far from ungrateful by nature, she had spent most of her life worrying about everything that could go wrong. Having had a major health scare, however, counting her blessings took on a whole new meaning.

Meg decided to start a gratitude journal. Not a religious person, she didn't have a particular sense of to whom the journal entries might be dedicated, she just picked up a notebook and started writing. She began by recording the big things, such as her health, the love of her husband, having two healthy, happy children and a family who loved her. But as the weeks went by, she found herself thinking about other things she had taken for granted: the job that paid her a regular wage (a job she had formerly moaned about), food that was in plentiful supply, the roof over her head, and the fact that she could afford to live in a safe area.

But Meg didn't stop here. She realized the fact she had work, food, and a roof over her head was the result of many people's knowledge and efforts – the farmers who had grown and packaged the food, the builders who had the skills to build her house, the teachers who were trained to educate her children, and the healthcare professions who were able to carry out her recent medical investigations. After a few weeks, Meg told me that she had arrived at a surprising conclusion: that there was nothing and no one to whom she did not owe a debt of gratitude.

Had her life radically changed? No. She was still doing the same job and had to manage the same daily hassles that she had experienced before her health scare. But she now viewed her life through a completely different lens: being grateful had become part of Meg's Mission.

The secret ingredient of joyful living

The Roman philosopher and statesman, Marcus Cicero, said that gratitude is not only the greatest of virtues, but the parent of all the others. Whether or not this is true is a matter for debate. However, one thing is certain: gratitude is one of the richest sources of inspiration available to us.

Gratitude is a psychological state that enables you to connect deeply with others and the world around you. Originating from the Latin word 'gratia', or 'grātus', meaning grace, graciousness, or pleasing, gratitude is a felt sense of wonder, thankfulness, and appreciation for life that can be directed towards any dimension of your experience: the thoughtfulness of another person, the golden opportunity that comes out of the blue, the sheer joy of witnessing the sun rising, or a profound sense of spiritual connection. You may feel gratitude for the beauty that surrounds you, for others' excellence (for example, the life-saving skills of a surgeon who operates successfully on a loved one) or the small, mundane things, like changes in the seasons.

To experience gratitude requires an ability to appreciate the miracle of existence itself. Consequently, it is often closely associated with the meaning of our lives (remember Principle No. 2?). In this way, our appreciation prevents us from falling into the trap of disillusionment and cynicism and, as an essential part of 'MAP', enables us to live in accordance with our Mission.

The idea of including gratitude in a self-coaching programme may feel paradoxical. After all, coaching generally focuses on our needs as individual: how to enhance our *individual* potential, uncover our *individual* strengths or develop our specific, *individual* skills. Gratitude, in contrast, is about recognizing that we are not wholly responsible for our successes – that we are dependent on someone or something to whom we owe our appreciation. It reminds us that there are resources beyond our individual selves that sustain us and that we are part of an interconnected and interdependent universe. In short, gratitude teaches us humility.

Appreciation for yourself and your life also helps you stand back from the futile tendency of comparing yourself to others. When you do this, you focus on your limitations and can get sucked into a belief that you should have more, do more, and achieve more; you yearn for what you do not have and get seduced by a sense of entitlement to more. Comparing ourselves to others causes us to lose sight of the unique rhythm of our own lives and become fuelled by the limited, self-absorbed part of us that is always insisting that things should be different. Gratitude helps us live more consciously, more reflectively, more fully – and, therefore, more productively. It is one of the most potent reminders that our life is a gift that needs to be treated with respect and consideration.

There is good evidence that those who are highly appreciative tend to experience

- greater levels of happiness and joy;
- a well-developed sense of meaning and purpose in life;
- a greater sense of life as fulfilling, meaningful and productive;
- a greater abundance of positive emotions;
- more vitality;
- higher levels of optimism;
- greater peace of mind;
- more satisfying personal relationships.

There are important physical consequences of gratitude, too. As with optimism, higher levels of gratitude are related to improved health and general physical well-being, as well as lower levels of depression and stress. Even positive changes in our cardiovascular and immune systems have been observed.

As with optimism, it is easy to be cynical about gratitude, to perceive it as a Pollyanna-style naïvety that blinds us to the reality of how tough life can be. However, this is far from the truth. Those who experience relatively high levels of gratitude are not immune to suffering or naïvely optimistic. Rather, they have made a conscious decision to search out and honour the gifts inherent in even the toughest of situations. The capacity to do this equips us with a more balanced awareness of both our life and our choices – an ability that lies at the heart of effective self-coaching.

Exercise 14. Experiment in mood manipulation

I'd like you to participate in a short experiment, so you can test out the benefits of gratitude for yourself.

Make yourself comfortable, and when you are ready, I would like you to rate your mood from 0–10 (0 = the lowest you have ever felt; 10 = the best you have ever felt).

When you have chosen your rating, spend three minutes (no more than this) focusing on everything in the last week that has gone wrong in your life and anything that left you feeling cross, resentful, or bitter. Recall any disagreements you had, other people's inconsiderate behaviour or errors of judgement to which you were subjected, and anything else that comes to mind. After three minutes, re-rate your mood from 0–10.

What do you notice? If you could access the memories of the

last week, you probably found that focusing on all the negative events has lowered your mood. You might also find that there have been some changes in your physical state such as feeling more agitated, restless, or unable to think clearly.

Now I'd like you to spend another three minutes focusing on everything in the last week that has gone well in your life and anything that left you feeling positive, uplifted, or appreciative. Recall both major events such as work promotions, positive feedback, or expressions of gratitude from others, and minor events such as someone smiling at you, apparent lucky breaks, or the kindness of strangers.

After three minutes, re-rate your mood. What do you notice? If you could get into the memories of the last week, you probably found that focusing on all the positive things has enhanced your mood. You might also find that there have been some changes to your physical state and that you now feel more relaxed, energized, or inspired.

This experiment illustrates something vital to effective self-coaching: that what we focus on has a big impact on our mood and physical state – and that gratitude provides an empowering lens through which to view your world.

Increasing your capacity for gratitude

To some extent, appreciation of all that we have is a choice. We can choose to allow our minds to indulge in futile comparisons with others, to let it meander through our troubles and become preoccupied with our short-comings, or we can choose to guide it towards a more fruitful outlook in which gifts overlooked might be reclaimed. Just like optimism, gratitude is not solely an emotion, but a state of mind, a perspective we can cultivate. So how can we achieve this?

Professor Bernard Weiner has developed a formula for increasing the gratitude we experience in our lives. His three-stage approach is as described below.

1. Identify something in the last week that went well and which you felt was not entirely of your own doing.

2. Think about who or what came together in order for this positive event to occur.
3. Allow yourself to connect with the feeling of gratitude: where do you experience it in the body? What kinds of emotions do you experience? What happens to your level of hope, optimism and faith in your ability to fulfil your ambitions?

Here are Meg's responses when she first started using this approach.

1. Event: I got to see my daughter's school play. She had really wanted me to be there and would have been so disappointed if I hadn't been able to go.
2. Sandra (colleague) offered to swap shifts, so I could get to the school on time.
3. Felt great: relaxed and calm but also excited and able to enjoy the play. I felt really proud of Gemma (daughter) – she looked so grown up and confident! Sandra is a great pal – I must say thank you to her when I see her tomorrow.

Now do the same, taking an event from your own life:

1. Identify something in the last week that went well and which you felt was not entirely of your own doing and make a note of it in your learning log.
2. Think about who or what came together in order for this positive event to occur, and write this in your learning log.
3. Allow yourself to connect with the feeling of gratitude: where do you experience it in the body? What kinds of emotions do you experience? What happens to your level of hope, optimism and faith in your ability to fulfil your ambitions? Write down your answers in your learning log.

Once you have some practice at using this formula with positive events, see if you can build your ability for appreciation even further by selecting something that seemed to go wrong, or was difficult or upsetting in some way. Can you find something for which to be grateful – even in that?

Remember, this is not about naïve optimism, but about opening yourself up to elements of the situation that you might have overlooked. This will feel like a stretch to begin with, but will get easier with practice, so don't give up! (Re-read the optimism chapter if you need some help with this.)

Helpful hint. When doing this exercise watch out for any tendency to see yourself as a passive victim, any sense of entitlement, or beliefs that you are justified in feeling angry or upset. Your reactions may be justified, but continuing to focus on all the ways in which you were wronged can keep you stuck in a mental rut that limits your options rather than increases them.

The life review

An additional way of expanding your capacity for appreciation is to look back over your life so far, dividing it into specific sections: 0–5, 5–10, 10–15, 15–20, 25–30, etc. Write these sections in your learning log, leaving space to write things of significance for each period. Then, as you think about each chunk of your life, make a list of anyone whom you feel made a positive difference to your life, even if on a very subtle level. Remember to include any times that felt particularly difficult, and who was there to sustain or support you, whether family, friends, professionals, or even the kindness of strangers. Also notice any events or situations that seemed to conspire to create good outcomes for you. Record these, also.

You may have noticed how, as you got under way with this task, your list expanded to include more and more people, situations, and experiences. Notice what and whom you have included on your list. Is there anyone to whom you owe a debt of gratitude that you have never acknowledged? Could you find a way to say thank you now – in person, by letter, or even symbolically if you are no longer in contact?

Keep a gratitude journal

Another very powerful way of building an attitude of appreciation is to keep a gratitude journal. In a study designed to investigate the benefits of gratitude, researchers Robert Emmons and Cheryl

Crumpler found that those who kept gratitude diaries on a regular basis experienced a number of important positive effects, including greater optimism, enhanced satisfaction with life, and fewer physical symptoms. They also exercised more regularly than those participants who kept a diary of neutral or unpleasant events.

Start this in your learning log, or use a separate notebook if you prefer. You want to put aside some time each day to record those things for which you are grateful and which have added to your appreciation for life. This should include not just major events, but also everyday activities and tasks, such as the opportunity to eat, go to work, your health, being able to pay the bills, and so on. It is also important to include encounters with others and apparent 'coincidences' that result in positive outcomes.

Helpful hint. If this feels strange to begin with, try choosing something in the personal domain (e.g., chance to eat), the interpersonal domain (something someone did for me, something I did for someone else, which teaches you about the qualities of giving), a personal success/attribute, and something society/government did for me (having the opportunity to live in a democracy).

Commit yourself to doing these exercises and you will start to see the difference in a few days.

Just as you are sustained by others, so others are supported by you. You will be a source of gratitude for others and make an important contribution to their successes in many different ways. So, develop an appreciation of the myriad ways in which you have touched people's lives and the world around you. In the meantime, if you need some tools to get you started, try my coaching tool kit below.

Take home message

In cultivating appreciation, the aim is both to increase your awareness of the possibilities for your life and to allow more room for joy. Both are essential components of effective self-coaching. However, this doesn't mean that gratitude is easy to acquire. Indeed, to

Your Coaching Tool Kit: Top Tips for Enhancing Your Appreciation of Life

1.   Make the decision to be thankful for each and every day from now on, whatever it brings. Remember, this day will never come again.
2.   Identify at least 10 people who enrich and make your life easier (it doesn't necessarily have to be people whom you know personally). And then identify 10 more . . .
3.   Look for the miracle in the mundane. Get into the habit of identifying one thing to be thankful for at the beginning and end of every day.
4.   Think of everything you have accomplished so far – big and small. Identify people, situations, events that conspired to help you achieve these things. Can you allow yourself to feel gratitude for their role in your successes?
5.   Take one area of your life and see it through fresh eyes, with a sense of wonder. For example, think about everyone who has contributed to your being able to make something as mundane as a cup of tea. Imagine the sunshine warming the tea leaves, the tea-growers working in the baking sun, those who package the tea and send it abroad, etc. Notice how easy it is to take all this for granted.

experience gratitude repeatedly requires considerable, sustained effort. We might appreciate the principle, but when life takes over, it is easy to lose sight of everything we have to be grateful for.

You might be tempted to ask what would have happened if Meg had discovered that she was seriously ill. After all, it's easy to feel grateful when we've just had good news. But, as you've discovered, gratitude is not something to which we should confine ourselves when the news is good. It is what Christopher Peterson and Martin Seligman have described as 'an interior attitude of thankfulness' for whatever life throws your way.

I have always found it useful to see gratitude as being like a muscle in the body. With practice and training, my muscles will get stronger and better defined. But if I stop exercising, I will lose muscle tone and start to look flabby. Your gratitude muscle is always present and waiting to be used, but you must keep exercising it until eventually, you can experience gratitude even for those challenging events that would have once thrown you off course.

And you will always need a maintenance programme if you want this character strength to be in top condition.

So here's what I recommend. When you get out of bed tomorrow morning, before you start dwelling on what lies ahead, take a moment to say thank you. It doesn't matter if you know to whom you are saying thank you or not. As Meister Eckhart says, if the only prayer you say in your whole life is 'thank you', that will be enough.

The Gift of Gratitude

One idea I shall take away from this chapter is . . . (write your response in your learning log).
One thing I shall do differently/more gratefully is . . . (write your response in your learning log).

Bibliography

Emmons, R. A., & Crumpler, C. A. (2000). Gratitude as a human strength: appraising the evidence. *Journal of Social and Clinical Psychology, 19*: 56–69.

Maslow, A. (1987). *Motivation and Personality* (3rd edn). New York: Harper and Row.

Weiner, B. (1985). An attributional theory of achievement motivation and emotion. *Psychological Review, 92*: 548–573.

CHAPTER THIRTEEN

Principle No. 8 – The Power of Compassion: Anchoring Transformation in the Wisdom of the Heart

'The power of compassion has no bounds'

(Sogyal Rinpoche)

Welcome to Principle No. 8: how to cultivate the power of compassion. In this chapter you will discover:

- *how developing compassion can contribute to personal transformation;*
- *simple ways of nurturing your compassionate self;*
- *guided imagery exercises to expand your capacity for compassion, towards yourself as well as others.*

So far, we have explored the Attitude section of 'MAP' through optimism, curiosity, and gratitude. In this chapter, we will explore a different, but complementary and equally powerful approach to inspiration and growth – the gift of compassion.

Have you noticed how, in nature, everything occurs in opposites: masculine and feminine, winter and summer, night and day? Each one balances and completes the other – without one, the other cannot be whole.

In the same way, effective self-coaching involves balancing the need for change with the need for acceptance. In your journey of personal transformation, you need to know that there is a time to strive and a time to rest, a time to push forward and a time to accept what is, a time to work on refining yourself and a time to lose yourself in something bigger. All effective coaching involves a willingness to know when it is time to work on change and when it is time for graceful acceptance. Each complements the other and is vital to the timing and pacing of the methods you use.

Without this balance, there is a danger that your attempts to excel could amplify your dissatisfaction. When we cherish ourselves too much, when we pursue our goals with a fervour that borders on the unrelenting, we are at risk of becoming unhealthily self-absorbed. We lose sight of our Mission, our ambitions become rooted in pride, and our successes are hollow with materialism. We can even become lost in an endless search for self-improvement that turns personal development itself into an addictive pursuit.

Compassion helps us bridge the tension between acceptance and change. Unlike passive forms of acceptance, which breed resignation and cynicism, compassion embraces an active form of acceptance through which an expanded self can be awakened. Unlike optimism, compassion is not so much concerned with altering your mindset as it is opening yourself up to, and immersing yourself in, the ever-changing world around you. Compassion is an attitude that is anchored in the heart rather than the mind.

Awaken the power of the heart

Professor Eric Cassell, expert in Public Health, observed that compassion goes straight to the heart of what it means to be human. It speaks to that which is best in us, that part of ourselves which, for all the confusion and chaos in the world, never quite loses faith in humanity.

We all have the capacity for compassion; it is anchored in our hearts from very early on in life. Paul Gilbert, Professor of Clinical Psychology, even suggests that the ability to experience compassion is essential to our survival. As social animals, we live in and through our relationships, and at some point it is inevitable that we will experience disagreement and friction with those we love. The capacity to understand and forgive is essential for reconciliation, allowing us to rebuild and maintain the bonds that give our lives meaning.

As with all the other principles we have explored so far, there is good evidence that compassion will have a strong, positive effect on your life. Not only is it associated with high levels of emotional and psychological well-being but it also enables us to manage distress more easily. The practice of self-orientated compassion (that is, offering compassion towards ourselves) is excellent for our physical and mental health, with benefits including lowered blood pressure, reduced muscle tension, and improvements in sleep, anxiety, panic and depression.

Exercise 15. Experience the gift of compassion

We have all been touched by compassion at some point in our lives – whether it comes from someone who loved us deeply or the kindness of a stranger, somewhere, at some point, you will have been the recipient of a kind or thoughtful act. Think back to a time when someone showed compassion towards you. What did they do? How did they make you feel? Write down your memories of what happened in your learning log.

It is likely that in that moment you felt cared for, supported, nurtured, and empowered, even in the smallest of ways. Some part of life became that bit more bearable once again.

Now think of a time when you showed compassion to another. What did you do? For whom? How did you show that you cared? How did it feel to respond to them in this way? Again, write your recollections in your learning log.

Chances are, you not only made the other person feel better, you made yourself feel good, too – you found a way to reach out to another when they were experiencing doubt, fear, confusion, or pain. In that moment, the barriers between you and the other person began to dissolve as you found you could resonate with that person in a deeper way.

When we are compassionate, we step beyond the confines of our small, insular world to appreciate the world as seen and experienced through the eyes of another. For a moment, we set aside our own concerns to be moved by another's story. Temporarily, all criticism and judgement cease. Compassion requires a particular kind of open-heartedness – one that nudges you gently towards expanding the narrow lens through which you view the world.

Offering compassion to yourself

The quality of compassion is not just something we need to extend to others; it is one of the greatest gifts we can offer ourselves. Developing your capacity for self-orientated compassion enables you to access a powerful route to self-healing. It can also help you achieve deeper and greater appreciation for the feelings, attitudes, and beliefs that permeate your choices and actions.

In our modern and often frenetically-paced lives, our relationship with ourselves can become fractured. Rather than fully experiencing the gifts and contradictions of our humanity, we get caught up in judgement. Our experience is filtered through an internal running commentary on whether we are doing well enough and all the areas in which we are falling short. If you are like most people you'll be familiar with the 'inner secretary', whose commentary constantly reminds you of all the things you need to get done, the 'critical coach', whose commentary continually reports on your failings and all the ways you need to improve, and the 'anxious pupil', who is trying to respond to all the instructions and advice and typically feels pretty overwhelmed! Offering yourself the gift of compassion enables you to look beyond the different voices competing inside your head to reconnect with the wholeness that is you.

How often do you experience yourself just as you are, without criticism, judgement, or censorship? Do you show yourself compassion, or does the idea feel weak, woolly, or somehow as though you are letting yourself off the hook? In your learning log, make a note of any reactions you have in response to the idea of offering yourself compassion, including any objections or feelings of resistance.

Daniel's path to inspired living

When I first met Daniel, the concept of self-orientated compassion was totally unfamiliar to him. In fact, Daniel had spent the first 35 years of his life perfecting the art of self-criticism. Whatever he did, in his eyes, it was never good enough. However successful he was, he could always have done better or tried harder. He lived under the shadow of guilt and failure, which dominated every area of his life. For him, life was a series of tick boxes. As he put it, 'I either get the ticks in the boxes, or I've failed.' Not surprisingly, Daniel spent most of his life exhausted, depressed, and anxious. Even his successes brought little joy, as he would dismiss them as luck or attribute them to the expertise of others.

Although Daniel learnt how to develop a more optimistic perspective through challenging his thoughts (as you learned to do in Principle No. 5), he needed a change of attitude that engaged his emotions as well as his intellect. I suggested that instead of focusing on all the ways in which his personal standards were unhelpful and unreasonable, we should help him develop an approach to self-enhancement that was more nurturing, support-ive, and compassionate.

Not surprisingly, Daniel was sceptical. For him, the whole idea of compassion smacked of weakness – a benign but ineffectual attempt at introducing a religious dimension to his coaching that he believed had nothing to offer him. As he put it, 'How will patting myself on the back and saying "there, there" make a differ-ence?'

Like many self-orientated people, Daniel had no difficulty offer-ing compassion to others; indeed, he was regarded by his colleagues and friends as a warm, generous, and empowering person. But the idea of developing a more compassionate attitude towards *himself* felt indulgent, if not immoral.

In his mind, Daniel had confused compassion with pity. Pity is implicitly patronising – we might feel sorry for the person but are not truly touched by their experience. It took Daniel some time before he could understand that compassion is about strength rather than weakness, empowerment rather than helplessness, and resilience rather than resignation. So before you find out what happened to Daniel, here are some important points you need to know about what compassion is *not*.

- It is *not* about pity.
- It is *not* something you have to work hard to 'deserve'.
- It is *not* being a 'soft touch' (icons of compassion such as Gandhi and Mother Teresa display enormous strength, deter-mination, and courage).

- It is *not* about making excuses for what you did and didn't do.
- It is *not* letting yourself off the hook from taking responsibility for your actions.
- It is *not* letting others off the hook from taking responsibility for their actions.
- It is *not* about seeing the world through rose tinted spectacles.
- It is *not* about saying 'it's OK' to someone who treated you badly and letting them do it again (unfettered compassion is subservience stemming from a lack of self-respect).

Self-orientated compassion helps us understand our lives more clearly. Whereas harsh judgement impairs rational problem-solving, decision-making, and life planning, compassion allows us to examine our circumstances and choices in a way that accepts our human failings and encourages us to take responsibility for changing them. We can self-soothe when life's journey becomes tough without slipping into a swamp of self-pity. We can honour and validate our experiences without being blinded by them. When you look at things without harsh judgement, you can begin to decide what is skilful and helpful and what is unwise and unhelpful – a capacity that psychologist and Buddhist teacher Jack Kornfield refers to as 'discriminating wisdom'.

Compassionate qualities: lessons from the East

Although compassion has only recently come to the attention of Western science (including human sciences such as psychology), its power to heal and transform our lives has long been recognized in Eastern traditions, which provide fascinating insights into how to develop and use this quality to enrich our lives and achieve our potential.

In Eastern philosophies and religions such as Buddhism, compassion towards self as well as others is taught as a powerful means of liberating and healing ourselves. Compassion – or *metta* (which means loving kindness) – enables us to unhook from what we crave and fear, and from the attitudes and actions that prevent us from fulfilling our potential.

The concept of *metta,* or loving kindness, is often a difficult one to grasp. In Western culture, the concept of love has become somewhat problematic. We often use the term to refer to states of desire and use the word 'love' to depict a whole range of feelings about objects of people – 'I'm in love with you'; 'I love chocolate icecream', and 'I love Friday nights' are just three examples of how we use the idea of love to refer to a type of yearning that, when unsatisfied, leads to dissatisfaction or suffering.

But loving kindness is of a completely different order. The quality you are aiming for derives from two words meaning 'gentle' and 'friend'. It involves an openness to the experience of self and others in an accepting and non-judgemental way while also evoking a desire to relieve suffering.

Psychologist Paul Gilbert provides a helpful description of the elements of compassion. Do they fit with your experience of giving and receiving compassion? The different components are:

- sympathy;
- sensitivity to the distress of self/others;
- ability to tolerate the distress of self/others;
- empathy;
- care for the well-being of self/others;
- non-judgementalism.

When Daniel learned about the qualities that made up compassion, he began to realize the extent of his harsh treatment of himself, and the cost involved. Daniel was stuck in what I call 'the guilt trap': he would set personal standards that were sky high, focus on all the difficulties he encountered and fail to notice how well he was doing. He saw these difficulties as a sign of failure which led him to feel guilty and ashamed for being such a lousy employee, husband, father, friend . . . the list was endless. He was stuck in a judgemental cycle of blaming and shaming in which he offered himself neither sympathy nor empathy, was insensitive and intolerant of his own struggles and did not feel entitled to care for and support himself when feeling low. Learning to develop a compassionate mind was, I told him, a powerful way to break the cycle. For good. Once he understood this, Daniel was truly ready to start learning the compassionate abilities he would need to get the most out of coaching – and life.

How to build your compassionate self

Of course, you cannot 'force' yourself to be compassionate; you can only create conditions that invite its presence into your life. Although the hassles and strains of everyday life can cause you to become disconnected from your compassionate nature, you can reconnect with this part of yourself by creating the right conditions for its expression.

To help Daniel start developing his abilities for self-orientated compassion, we explored his reactions to the following questions. Use them to guide you in your own explorations:

- What events have particularly touched or moved you?
- By what kind of suffering or distress do you feel most moved?
- What 'good causes' lead you to put your hand in your pocket?
- What situations or circumstances are most likely to arouse your compassion?
- What moves you most: the plight of individuals, the needs of a group or community, the needs of a nation or of the planet?
- For whom and what have you been willing to sacrifice your precious time and resources? (Consider any generous and compassionate actions to individual people, communities, and organizations.)

Write your answers in your learning log.

Allow yourself to connect with these experiences as best you can. Notice how you feel as you imagine each of them. Where do you feel compassion in your body; what sensations are present? What feelings do you experience? What thoughts or images come to mind? What kinds of actions did your compassion lead you to take? Note all of these in your learning log.

Keep those memories, thoughts, feelings, and images at the forefront of your mind. You are going to need them for the next exercise.

Exercise 16. Inviting compassion into your life

The following exercise is a powerful tool for developing self-orientated compassion. It is relevant for you and your coaching journey, regardless of whether you have a religious faith or not.

Find yourself a quiet place where you will not be disturbed. To begin with, you need to allow 15 minutes of total privacy (as you become more experienced, you may want to extend this). If you can, create a pleasant surrounding for yourself; clear away any clutter and open a window if you would like some fresh air.

Make yourself comfortable. You can either sit on the floor or in a chair, but wherever you choose, make sure that your back is straight and that you can breathe easily. Your eyes can be open or closed; if they are open, allow your gaze to soften, rather than stare. Take a few slow even breaths and, as best you can, put aside any responsibilities, worries, or anything else tugging at your awareness.

Now I would like you to recall a time in your life when someone showed you loving kindness that touched your life in an important way. It may be a family member, a friend or colleague, a neighbour, or even a stranger. It can be an act of extraordinary generosity or an act of simple kindness that made a difference to your life at that moment. Elaborate this memory as best you can, including your recollection of where you were, what was going on around you, and the nature of your needs. Make the image clearer and clearer in your mind.

Notice how the kind act of the other generates a feeling within you – a feeling of gratitude perhaps, or humility, care, or concern. Allow yourself to reconnect with the feelings that their loving kindness generated within you. Let that feeling arise again now, stronger and stronger. Notice how, as these positive feelings arise, you can extend your own loving kindness towards that person in return. Immerse yourself fully in this feeling. Notice the qualities of sympathy, sensitivity, empathy, caring, and non-judgement arise within you and how the barriers between you and the other person momentarily melt as you too feel loving kindness for them.

Now, without forcing the feeling, see if you can turn that energy of loving kindness towards yourself. Allow the feeling to turn inwards. If it helps, think of a time when you were struggling in some way – big or small, a time when you needed compassion. Can you direct that feeling of loving kindness towards yourself as best you can? Where do you feel it in your body? What emotions do you notice? What quality of mind is present? Allow yourself to connect with the qualities of compassion: sympathy, sensitivity to your own distress without being overwhelmed by it, empathy for your self, kindly concern, and non-judgementalism.

When you have felt some degree of compassion for yourself – even if it is only in a small way to begin with, allow yourself to open your eyes and come back to the room.

Write down your observations from this exercise in your learning log. What was easy and difficult? Can you imagine how developing this ability for self-orientated compassion will empower you to achieve your goals?

When you have had some practice at this exercise and sense that your compassionate qualities are beginning to grow, let your heart open more as you allow an image of someone else you care about to come to mind. Visualise them as clearly as you can and then extend this feeling of compassion out to them. Then turn your attention to someone else you care about, each time evoking the same feeling of loving-kindness. Gradually, extend this feeling of compassion to encompass your family, your friends, your colleagues, your community – and ultimately, all living beings.

Generally, it's a good idea to start with those you find it easy to be compassionate towards and gradually build up to more challenging relationships – perhaps people with whom you are in conflict or who have upset you. Don't worry if directing compassion towards yourself feels strange to begin with; after all, you've probably never done it before! The more you practise, the easier it will become and the more liberated you will feel.

Daniel's progress on the road to inspired living

Early on, Daniel struggled with the idea that compassion could support him in transforming his life, as it didn't quite fit with his goal-driven and results-focused approach to success. When he did appreciate how it could be a powerful aid, he tried to 'acquire' compassion with the same driven mentality that he brought to everything; it was simply another goal at which he would succeed or fail. And he was very determined not to fail! Learning to soften his heart, to let go of some of his fierce judgements, involved the realization that he, too, was entitled to the full range of experiences that come with being human – joy and pain, hope and doubt, disappointment and joy.

As he began to develop his capacity for self-orientated compassion, Daniel's self-esteem and self-respect improved exponentially. This had an enormous impact on his life: he felt lighter in himself, more motivated and energized in all areas of his life, his relationships improved, and he was succeeding more than ever. But, even more importantly, he could enjoy his successes. By developing compassion he could both accept himself and develop those skills that would add value to his life. Compassion had enabled him to become a success hunter rather than a failure fleer.

When our work together ended, Daniel told me that he had learnt some important lessons. He now understood that without self-orientated compassion, he had been out of touch with this authentic self, unable to implement his signature strengths, and disconnected with what made his life meaningful. He understood that his Mission – which was bound up with the desire to inspire others to fulfil their potential – would always be blocked if he continued to see life as a series of tick boxes. He needed a new lens, one that allowed him to embrace all the talents and gifts, as well as limitations and failings, that go hand in hand with being human.

Daniel subsequently found a new job and now holds a senior position in a major banking establishment. He continues to inspire others around him. Gradually, he is learning that how he lives his life can be a source of inspiration to him as well.

Your Coaching Tool Kit: Expanding Your Compassionate Self

1. Find ways of practising compassion in action. What small things could you say or do to relieve another's burden?
2. Practise loving kindness every day. Smile at someone, offer to carry their shopping, or give up your seat. Small gestures go a long way.
3. Look for ways that you can become an instrument of care and kindness in your own family, work environment, community and society. Think about how your personal meaning and signature strengths could be used for the benefit of others.
4. If you find yourself caught up in judging someone, ask yourself what a compassionate perspective might add to your view of things. This not only sets the other person free, it sets you free also.
5. Be gentle with you. Practise awakening the feeling of loving kindness and, when you have that feeling, invite it gently towards you.

Take home message

Compassion is one of the most powerful resources available to us. When exercised through the filter of 'wise mind' it allows us to connect directly to the wisdom of our hearts and enables us to temper the logic of our rationally-driven, goal-focused selves with a profound sense of interconnectedness. Compassion enables us to begin a process of personal transformation, but it can also play a role in the transformation of our communities and our world.

Developing self-orientated compassion provides a solid foundation for seeking and honouring your own truth while respecting the rights and needs of others, and your responsibilities to them. As Jack Kornfield reminds us, compassion is not merely a helpful idea; it is a powerful, living force – one that nurtures, heals and inspires. To harness it is to enrich the world. To offer it to yourself is to enrich your life and the life of others, which will provide you with a limitless supply of inspiration every day.

The Power of Compassion: Anchoring Transformation in the Wisdom of the Heart

One idea I shall take away from this chapter is . . . (write the answer in your learning log).
One thing I will do differently is . . . (write the answer in your learning log).

Bibliography

Boorstein, S. (1995). *It's Easier than You Think: The Buddhist Way of Happiness.* New York: HarperCollins.

Cassell, E. (2005). Compassion. In: C.R. Snyder & S. J. Lopez (Eds.), *Handbook of Positive Psychology* (pp. 434–445). New York: Oxford University Press.

*Dalai Lama (2002). *It's Easier than You Think: The Buddhist Way of Happiness.* [[CITY]]: HarperCollins.

Gilbert, P. (Ed.) (2005). *Compassion. Conceptualisations, Research and Use in Psychotherapy.* Hove: Routledge. (Note: this book is also relevant for Chapter Twenty-three on self-esteem.)

*Kabat-Zinn, J. (1990). *Full Catastrophe Living.* New York: Dell.

*Kabat-Zinn, J. (1994). *Wherever You Go, There You Are. Mindfulness Meditation in Everyday Life*. New York: Hyperion.
*Kornfield, J. (1993). *A Path with Heart*. New York: Rider.
*Kornfield, J. (2000). *After the Ecstasy, the Laundry*. New York: Bantam.
(This reference is also relevant for Chapter Twenty-three on self-esteem.)

CHAPTER FOURTEEN

Cultivating the Right Attitude

In the last four chapters you have learned about four essential Attitudes that can help you work towards achieving what matters most. You (1) learnt how to view the world through a more optimistic 'lens' (and why this is so important); (2) discovered how to harness your curiosity so that you are never short of inspiring ideas; (3) found ways of nurturing gratitude so you can appreciate your life for the miracle that it is; and (4) learnt about the power of compassion as a gift you can offer to yourself as well as others.

Each of these Attitudes contributes something unique to your Mission. In order to translate your Mission into an action plan for your life, you need to have an outlook that is optimistic (positive yet realistic). Curiosity keeps your mind open to what you do not yet know and provides fertile ground for your creativity to flourish. Without gratitude, you can reach for the stars but will never feel satisfied – your goals will be an attempt to fill in the missing pieces, rather than reflecting a fuller and more balanced appreciation of how you can add to the richness that your life already is. Developing your compassionate abilities enables you to honour the person that you are, and all people everywhere. Through appreciating your interconnectedness your choices become more responsible and genuinely empowering for others as well as yourself.

Pulling it all together

If you completed the exercises in the previous four chapters, you will know a great deal about your own attitudes, and the attitudes you now need to cultivate to coach yourself in the art of inspired living. If you review your thoughts, ideas, and insights from the previous chapters, what themes did you find? How do you need to broaden your Attitude in order to move forward in the core areas you identified in Chapter one and in your Mission Statement?

Construct your council of advisers

One of the best ways to build an optimum Attitude is to create a council of advisers. This is a light-hearted exercise with a serious message. Equipped with your council of advisers, you are guaranteed to have a ready supply of new ideas, encouragement, and inspiration whenever you need them.

In order to construct your council, think of ten people whom you really admire and who might make up a group that exists solely to support you. Ideally, members will include men and women, people of different ages and backgrounds, those who have achieved a variety of things with their life and who have made a positive difference to the world in some way. You may want to include people who have displayed courage in overcoming the odds and whose Mission was similar to yours. You might also choose someone who has a character strength you would now like to develop.

They can be real people (living or dead) or fictional (such as a character in a movie or novel), famous people, or someone special to you. You do not need to know them personally, you just need to have a sense of the qualities that they embody – and those qualities need to be ones that inspire you. See if you can include in your council someone who captures each of the four Attitudes we have discussed in this section: optimism, curiosity, gratitude, and compassion.

Whenever you need help or inspiration, you can call an emergency meeting and the council will attend to offer you their support, suggestions, and advice. Before you admit any new member, however, make sure that their values are consistent with your own (that is, they do not conflict with your authentic self and what matters most to you).

To give you an example, my council currently includes the following members:

- Albert Einstein (for intellect and creativity);
- Queen Elizabeth I (for courage and political acuity);
- Gandhi (for courage, compassion and strength);
- Molly, one of my teachers on retreat (for compassion);
- Professor David Lane, my mentor in psychology (optimism, curiosity);
- Little Dorritt, a character from a Charles Dickens novel by the same name (for love, devotion, and gratitude).

. . . to name but a few!

Who would be your top ten members at this point in your life, and why have you chosen them? List your own preferred council members in your learning log.

Once your council is complete (remember, you can appoint and retire members whenever you choose), you have a ready-made supply of inspiration that you can draw upon whenever you need it. You can turn to your council when you want advice about a decision you have to make, when you need to make a choice, or are struggling with a problem. You can also request consolation and encouragement when you doubt yourself and when you feel like giving up.

You can also turn to your council when you want to approach something from a radically different perspective. The most helpful councils involve quite a bit of variety, with different members offering different 'lenses' through which to see the world. It is like the diamond we looked at in Principle No. 1; each character radiates a different colour, allowing you to consider a situation in new ways. So the council is a great way of extending your library of scripts. Because of this, it can often be helpful to include someone who challenges your existing views a little. Remember what Einstein said: 'The significant problems we face cannot be solved by the same level of thinking that created them.' There will be times when, in order to get the most out of your life, you will need to step out of your existing ways of viewing the world and adopt a novel perspective.

Whenever you need the advice of your council all you need to do is find a place where you will be undisturbed for a few moments. Close your eyes and allow the mind to quieten. Then imagine yourself sitting with your council in a place that feels safe and nurturing (it can be a formal setting such as a board room, or much less formal, such as sitting on a picnic blanket!). Visualise each member of your council in turn, then share your dilemma, problem, or question, and ask for their help. You may wish to direct your question to a particular member of the group, or the council as a whole. Stay as long as you need, until you have some new ways of seeing things and new ideas to try out.

At the end of the meeting, thank your council members for their advice and then say goodbye. Before you do anything else, write down any suggestions your council made. What ideas struck you as useful? How could you implement these ideas? How will you monitor their effects?

The more you work with your council the more effective it will be. Experiment with it now. Think of something that you would like to be different in your life – it might be a problem you want to solve, a decision you have to make, or an ambition that you are unsure how to take forward. Imagine yourself in the presence of the council and then ask your question . . .

Write down any useful, interesting or provocative ideas that emerged in your learning log.

You have now completed the second part of 'MAP' and know how to build Attitudes that will help you achieve your ambitions, enhance your well-being, and enable you to feel more fulfilled. You have also learnt a powerful way of expanding your outlook through the method of council. If you have completed the exercises in the previous chapters and are incorporating the ideas into your life on a regular basis, you will be well on the way to mastering the art of inspired living. In the next section, we will complete the journey by exploring the Process component of 'MAP': those tools that are essential for translating your Mission into action.

CHAPTER FIFTEEN

Introducing Principles 9–12: Your Process

'Action may not always bring happiness, but there is
no happiness without action'

(Benjamin Disraeli)

Designing your process: essential tools for creating your action plan

If your Mission is concerned with the 'why' of your life, and your Attitude examines what you bring to your journey, the Process is how you get there: the steps you need to take to get from where you are now to where you want to be.

Of all the stages of MAP, the Process stage is the most practical. It involves establishing a clear and achievable action plan, setting specific and realistic goals, and making sure you stay on task. It is about the nuts and bolts of rolling up your sleeves and getting on with it because, without a clear Process, your Mission will always remain a day-dream. More than any other aspect of MAP, Process involves doing rather than being and requires a commitment to putting your plans into action time and time again until you get the results you seek.

For example, if the core area you selected in your Inspiration Inventory (Chapter one) was to change your career to a field more in tune with your Mission, you will need to design a concrete plan of action for achieving this. Your Process, like most good action plans, will probably involve several steps, such as conducting an audit of your current skills and experiences so you know what you have to offer, constructing a new CV that highlights your areas of expertise, researching new career areas, networking with people who know about your chosen area, and so on. Each small step builds on the last until, through consistent, committed action, you are where you want to be.

How successful are you in designing your own Process?

The art of inspired living means knowing how to devise an action plan that will take you in the direction of your choice. How successful are you at devising concrete action plans for achieving your goals? What are your strengths and limitations when it comes to designing an effective strategy?

Think about a time when you succeeded at something that really mattered to you, and which required sustained effort and commitment on your part. How did you achieve the results you wanted? Be as specific as you can and record your thoughts in your learning log, under the heading 'I achieved success because . . .'.

Now remember a time when, despite your good intentions, your action plan fell apart. What went wrong? And more importantly, what would you want to do differently from now on? Write your thoughts in your learning log, using the heading 'My action plan did not give me the results I wanted because . . .'.

With all the self-coaching you have done so far, you are in a stronger position to design an effective plan of action than you have ever been. So, based on your Mission and your new Attitude, give some thought to what, practically, you want to achieve at this point in your life. Imagine a time in the future where you are consistently implementing your Mission. Identify the specifics of what you did, how it makes you feel, and how your life has changed as a result. How did you get there? What did you do? What steps did you take? Be as specific as you can in writing the answers to these questions in your learning log.

The ability to design a good Process involves a number of key skills. These are: (1) knowing how to set appropriate goals; (2) essential thinking skills that open up new possibilities; (3) drawing on and developing your creative skills; and (4) harnessing (and regularly topping up!) your motivation to succeed.

In Principles 9–12, I am going to introduce you to the essential tools and resources you need to design your own Process. These are:

Principle No. 9
Goals: knowing the difference between aims and goals, and how to set goals that help you implement your Mission and fulfil your potential.

Principle No. 10
Thinking style: how to empower your mind by asking the right kinds of questions that help you invent new ways of approaching your life and your choices.

Principle No. 11
Creativity: harnessing your creativity as a source of inspiration in its own right and as well as a means of achieving success.

Principle No. 12
Motivation: understanding what motivation is and how to work with it to get the results you want, even in the face of setbacks.

CHAPTER SIXTEEN

Principle No. 9: Transforming your Mission into Goals

'Enthusiasm needs to be nourished with new actions,
efforts, aspirations and visions'

(Anon)

Welcome to Principle No. 9: how to transform your Mission into specific goals that enable you to move, step by step, towards a life of your own choosing. Together, we will explore:

- *why goal-setting is an essential skill for the inspired life;*
- *how to transform your vision of life into a workable action plan;*
- *easy steps for creating goals that will inspire you.*

It is a curious fact that people who set themselves clear, concrete, and practical goals tend to be more successful than those who do not. Take anyone who is highly successful, in any sphere of life, and I will show you a very practical person.

Goals are a vital tool for implementing, monitoring, and evaluating your progress towards the vision you have for your life. It doesn't matter how often you refine your Mission or how much effort you put into cultivating helpful Attitudes, living a life that inspires you is ultimately an action-orientated business.

Setting tangible and achievable goals is the point at which you commit yourself to a specific, focused course of action. It is also a means through which you can monitor the implications of living your Mission; if the results are not producing what you had expected, a more fundamental review might be required.

Having clear and achievable goals helps you:

- decide if what you thought you wanted is something you really do want;
- plan the practicalities of achieving what really matters;
- anticipate obstacles;
- develop new knowledge and skills;
- monitor your progress;
- identify missing life skills that might increase your chances of success;
- observe the effects on you and those around you;
- keep motivated. (As you see yourself turn your dreams into outcomes, your motivation and confidence increase.)

Let's look at how these principles apply to you.

Exercise 17. Creating inspirational goals

What are your goals for the next five years? What do you want to have accomplished? What do you want to be able to look back on with pride?

Take a few moments to think about this now. Be as bold as you wish, doing your best to put aside that part of your mind that insists on censoring your great ideas and heartfelt hopes for the future. Write down in your learning log what you would like to be, own, have experienced and accomplished in the next five years, in all of the different areas of your life (Hint: you may find it helpful to look back over the core domains you rated in the Inspiration Inventory in Chapter one).

Have a look at your goals. If you have allowed your imagination free rein you will probably find that your list includes a wide range of goals. Some might be concerned with experiences you would like to have for the sheer fun of it (for example, going for a ride in a hot-air balloon), while others seem related to enriching your life (for example, visiting a foreign country that has always intrigued you). Other goals might be concerned with sense of achievement: for example, completing a course, gaining a degree, writing a book, or setting up your own business, while others still may relate to material possessions, such as owning property or having a particular level of income.

You will also have noticed that some of your goals will require more effort to achieve than others. A fun-related goal such as going for a ride in a hot-air balloon will require relatively little in the way of planning – you find out who provides such opportunities, book the event, and turn up on the day. Others, however, will involve sustained effort. Completing a course is a good example of this type of goal: there is an end point in sight but there will be multiple stages involved in achieving the goal, each of which will involve time and effort in its own right. Other goals will require sustained effort over a more prolonged period of time, such as establishing and maintaining a successful business.

Do your goals fit with your Mission?

In order that our lives continue to inspire us, it is helpful to have a wide variety of goals that stretch our imaginative and creative potential, as well as our knowledge and skills. But when it comes to the larger goals of life – those that require a sustained commitment on your part – it is vital to keep asking yourself whether your goals are consistent with your Mission.

Goals only have meaning within the broader context of your Mission: your authenticity, personally defined sense of meaning, signature strengths, and the courage to exercise your power of choice. So, if you find that one of your goals doesn't fit your sense of the bigger picture, then eliminate it; it's not the one for you.

The river bank analogy

Before we look at how to set goals, let's look at their role in your life. A helpful way to think about goals is using the river bank analogy.

Imagine that you are on one side of a river and you want to get across to the other side. On your side of the river, it's cold and raining and you don't like being there. On the other side of the river, the sun is shining, the birds are singing, and the landscape is full of beautiful flowers, shrubs, and trees. The river bank opposite you is exactly where you want to be, but the river is too wide for you to jump across it.

However, when you look closer, you notice that embedded in the river is a series of stepping stones. The stepping stones may not seem that appealing at first. You'll have to scramble down the river bank to get to the water and will need to be prepared to get your feet wet. The stones are uneven and wet so you might even lose your footing temporarily. But, despite these unappealing possibilities, the stepping stones get you to where you want to be. And it's the only way to get there.

In this analogy, the stepping stones are our goals – not important in themselves. For example, you would not stand on a stepping stone and throw a party because you had mistaken it for the other side of the river! At best, they can only ever take you one step closer to where you want to be. But that, in itself, is a triumph. Every time you get your feet wet, every time you falter, you are none the less moving closer to your chosen destination.

The three steps to inspirational goals

Goal-setting is, in many respects, the most exciting stage of creating an inspired life because it is the point at which you see all your previous learning come together. But it is also a skill in its own right. So, before you devise a strategy, it's important to be aware of some of the fundamentals of effective goal-setting.

Step 1. Make them 'SMART'

One of the most powerful goal-setting approaches for self-coaching is the 'SMART' formula. According to the SMART model, goals need to be:

- Specific (clear and concrete);
- Measurable (so you know when you've got there);
- Attractive (they have to be appealing, or why bother!)'
- Realistic (so you have every chance of succeeding);

- Time-framed (organized around a deadline by which you expect to have achieved a result).

This formula strips goal-setting down to the nuts and bolts for a good reason: it aids effective, action-orientated planning and it works. The mistake that many people make is having goals that are too broad or vague rather than organizing their efforts around strategic success planning.

I come across this a great deal in my work with clients. For example, when we start to look at goals, people often tell me that their main goal is 'to be happy' or 'feel better about themselves'. Admirable though they may be, these broad aims don't specify what my clients intend to do, how they intend to do it, and when. Aims like this also don't give you any indication of how you will know when you have achieved the results you were looking for. Another problem with broad aims is that they often harbour unrealistic expectations and fantasies about change: for example, that increased self-esteem will lead to supreme confidence in all situations, or losing weight will lead to a totally new sense of self inside and out. Making your goals SMART is a reality check whereby you define and refine your strategy until you are clear you know exactly what you are aiming for.

Think back to a time when you achieved success and a time when you didn't. Could the SMART model help explain this?

Exercise 18. Make your goals SMART

Take one or two of your goals from the previous exercise (Exercise 17) and see if you can make them SMART. Write the heading 'My overall aim or general goal is . . .' in your learning log, and then identify the goal or aim.

Then write 'To make this goal SMART', and list and answer the following questions.

1. What Specific (clear and concrete) step will I take?
2. How will I Measure my progress towards the goal (so I will know when I have achieved it)?
3. Is this goal Attractive to me? Is it worth pursuing?
4. Is this goal Realistic? How confident am I that I can achieve it? Have I given myself the best chance of success?

5.   What Time-frame do I have around this goal? By what date and time will I expect to have achieved this?

Finally, summarise your results by defining in your learning log what your SMART goal is (e.g., 'By next spring I will have set up an internet business', or 'In six months' time I will have gone down one dress size').

Step 2. Turning your goals into action steps

As part of being 'SMART', it is helpful to turn your goals into specific action steps that you can evaluate for their potential effects on your life. Breaking big goals into manageable, bite-sized pieces will also help you build on your success by allowing you to plot a route through the process of change. Below, I describe how I used this process with Rebecca.

Rebecca's story

When Rebecca asked me for help in losing 70 pounds in weight, I encouraged her to think about the Mission that lay behind this goal. She told me, 'I want to have a positive relationship with my body, in which I like what I see in the mirror. I want to take care of my body, treat myself with respect, and nurture myself with healthy eating.'

Once she was clear about why losing weight mattered to her and, with the aid of her doctor, we had established that 70 pounds was an appropriate target, we began to look at different ways of achieving this. I asked Rebecca to list all the different ways she could think of to lose weight. Having come up with many different ideas, she settled on four main possibilities.

'Potential ways of achieving my goal of losing 70 pounds are:

- crash dieting;
- starting a weight loss programme, in discussion with my doctor;
- going for a 30-minute walk four times a week;
- not drinking alcohol until I have lost at least 14 pounds.'

We then looked at each potential course of action more thoroughly to see which ones might be most helpful and which, if any, might undermine her Mission of having a positive relationship with her body. Rebecca used a goals analysis sheet to help her consider the different options. This, together with her responses, is set out in Table 2 (p. 144).

The aim of the goals analysis sheet was to help Rebecca break a large goal down into more manageable chunks. Trying to lose 70 pounds is a daunting task for most people, but identifying a range of steps, some of them small, some of them slightly bigger, Rebecca was better able to see which areas she was prepared to tackle first. This enabled her to start creating a plan of action that would lead to experiences of success, that would inspire her to keep going, and that would help her avoid the setbacks that in the past had led her to feel like a failure (such as binge-eating in response to crash-dieting).

Simon's story

Simon's goals were quite different from Rebecca's. Through working on his Mission, Simon clarified his life purpose as one of needing to make a contribution to the well-being of others. He wanted to start a new career that would enable him to fulfil his Mission, but had no idea what form this might take.

Because Simon was thinking about taking a U-turn in his life, it was important that he didn't rush into big decisions until he was really sure of his course of action. Instead, he decided to create some interim goals to clarify his options. Here is the list he came up with.

- Contact an occupational psychologist for careers advice.
- Carry out an inventory of skills acquired in my career to date, to clarify the resources I already have.
- Find out about options for voluntary work overseas.
- Contact my favourite charities to ask about career openings in their organizations.

Simon's Goals Analysis Sheet is shown in Table 3 (p. 145).

Table 2. Rebecca's goals analysis sheet.

Potential goal	How will I feel when I achieve this?	How does this goal fit with my Mission?	On balance, does this still seem like a worthwhile goal?	Is this a goal for right now? If yes, when will I take action?
Crash dieting	I'll feel high for the first couple of days but I know from experience that I'll soon get hungry and eat more than ever.	It doesn't. It's a way of punishing myself for being overweight, which makes me feel terrible about myself.	No (although it's tempting to believe it's the answer).	No. Ideally, I would never do this again, as I know it doesn't work.
Start a weight loss programme in discussion with my doctor.	Good but scared. I know I'll be under regular reviews from then on. What if I don't succeed?	It won't feel comfortable, because I won't be able to hide my weight any more. But it fits with my Mission to build a positive relationship with my body. Doing it this way means I know I'll be losing weight safely.	Yes (if scary!).	Yes. Will phone doctor tomorrow to make an appoint-ment.
Go for a 30-minute walk four times a week	More energised, less stressed.	Exercise always makes me calmer and less stressed. I sleep better,too. I'll start to become more toned, which will motivate me to keep going with the weight loss programme.	Yes!	Yes. I could start this tomorrow, when I get home from work.
Not drinking alcohol until I have lost two stone.	This would be good but feels rather challenging.	This feels like a huge stretch for me right now. I might need to get some help with cutting down.	Yes	Not sure. I need to think about this before committing myself further.

Table 3.   Simon's goals analysis sheet.

Potential goal	How will I feel when I achieve this?	How does this goal fit with my Mission?	On balance, does this still seem like a worthwhile goal?	Is this a goal for right now? If yes, when will I take action?
Contact an occupational psychologist for careers advice	I'll have a clearer knowledge of my talents and weaknesses. Should boost my confidence.	Will give me an impartial overview of my strengths and weaknesses. Have never done this before and it will inform my decisions about how to move forward	Yes.	Yes. I'll get a list of occupational psychologists from the internet.
Carry out inventory of all skills and responsibilities over the years	I'll have a clearer picture of what I have achieved and what I have to offer. Will boost my confidence at a time when I feel unsure about my future.	It fits well. Hopefully, I will be able to think more creatively about my options.	Yes.	Yes. I'll start this at the weekend.
Find out about options for voluntary work overseas.	This will help clarify if this is something for me, or whether it's just a pipedream.	I have always been interested in the idea of doing voluntary work abroad and it seems to fit well with my Mission.	Yes. Nothing to lose.	Yes. Will start researching options on the internet this weekend.
Contact my favourite charities to ask about career openings in their organizations.	This could leave me feeling a little pressured if there is something definite available and I'm unsure if I want it.	Potentially a good fit, but not entirely convinced. Don't know why – just a feeling.	Yes, but maybe not a priority.	I'll wait six weeks and revisit this option when the other goals have been achieved.

You have probably noticed that the content of Simon's goals analysis sheet was very different from Rebecca's. While Rebecca knew exactly where she wished to be headed and why, Simon was at an earlier stage in the process. His goals were guided by his Mission, but he needed to have the freedom to explore a range of options before committing himself to a life-changing strategy. However, Simon's goals were still very achievable. By making them SMART, Simon could keep track of his progress and the results of his early goals would put him in a stronger position to decide what he needed to do next.

For both Simon and Rebecca, knowing that they were moving in the right direction kept them on target, enhanced their motivation by enabling them to see tangible results, and helped them organize their actions around those goals that really mattered.

When you start to see results, you too will feel good about yourself and your efforts to succeed. You can see more and more evidence of your Mission operating in your life and your motivation increases as you start to see new ways of enhancing your potential.

Use Exercise 19 to devise your own blueprint, based on your results on the Inspiration Inventory, and everything you now know about yourself having completed Principles 1–8.

Exercise 19. Your personal blueprint for inspirational goals

Write in your learning log, 'In relation to this area of my life, my Mission is . . .', and state what this is.

Then write 'What specific action steps can I now take?', and brainstorm as many ideas as you can think of.

Now draw up your own goals analysis sheet, using the same headings as shown in Rebecca's and Simon's sheets.

Finally, go ahead and implement your action plan. Be sure to record any observations in your learning log and think carefully about how you will evaluate the outcome of your efforts. Also see if you can anticipate any obstacles to implementing this goal. What steps could you take to get around them?

Step 3. Do your goals inspire you?

This question is often one that many people forget to ask themselves before committing to a particular strategy. It does not matter how carefully you have planned your goal, if it doesn't really matter to you, you will not achieve it. In my work, I see many people waste time and energy on goals that they think they should want, or should achieve, but which do not really inspire them. Exercise 20 contains some key questions that you need to ask yourself every time you set a new goal, just to make sure it's really worth the effort. Copy the exercise into your learning log, and tick either the 'Yes' or the 'No' column in respect of each question.

Exercise 20. Do you really want to achieve this goal?

	Yes	No
1. Is this really 'my' goal (or is it something someone else thinks I should achieve)?	☐	☐
2. Is this goal important to me?	☐	☐
3. Does this goal excite, energise, or inspire me?	☐	☐
4. Will I feel as if I have gained something when I have achieved it?	☐	☐
5. Is this goal specific enough for me to know what action I need to take and when?	☐	☐
6. Am I more than 80% confident that I have the ability to achieve it, even if it's a stretch?	☐	☐
7. Am I more than 80% confident that I have the motivation to see this through?	☐	☐
8. Is this goal moving me in the direction of the bigger picture I have for my life?	☐	☐
9. Is this goal consistent with my responsibilities in life?	☐	☐

If your answer to any of these questions is no, then think again. It may be that you are trying to pursue a goal that is really some-body's else's priority. Or it may be that it is too much of a stretch and you to need to break it down a bit further. Whatever the objection, take note of it and keep refining your goal until you have one in which you are willing and able to invest.

Don't forget to celebrate your gains

Do you remember Nina, whom we met in Principle No. 1? During our work together, Nina kept a log of her learning journey using what she called a 'Proud Book'. Into her Proud Book went all her accomplishments and successes, her mini-triumphs as well as her major ones. Over a period of time, she began to appreciate just how many triumphs had occurred, which helped her revise her former opinion of herself as unable to achieve much.

Nina had hit on a key formula for success: keep a record of your gains (you'll find a Gains Log at the end of the book). Keeping a Gains Log is a fantastic way of reminding yourself just how well you are doing. As we journey through life, most of us forget how much we have achieved. Even the most exciting of achievements starts to tarnish in our memories after a while. Things that were once very challenging become second nature, so we forget every-thing we had to do to attain them.

Reflecting on your gains also helps you learn from past successes. If a gain has occurred, then you have played a role in creating this outcome. You have a winning formula on your hands, so wouldn't it be worth knowing exactly what that formula is so you can use it again when you need to? Once you know how you have mastered challenges, you are in a strong position to bring those skills to future challenges.

Do remember, though, that gains are not permanent. In the same way that your goals are merely stepping stones that you leave behind once they have served their purpose, so your gains are achievements from which you are always moving forward. What matters is not that you cling to what you once achieved, but rather that you notice the fact that you are capable of achieving and think about how you got there. The gains may not last forever, but the work you undertake to achieve them does.

Get some guts in your goals

Now here's the bit that hurts. Remember how in Principle No. 4 we looked at the need for courage in relation to pursuing mean-ingful life choices? Well, here is where you need it!

If your goals are worth something, if they really matter to you, then pursuing them is not going to be a piece of cake. You select your destination, choose the strategy to help you get there, and learn to accept any discomfort that arises from your choice. In fact, implementing goals that are in keeping with your higher vision often involves feeling things you don't want to feel.

Jonathan was a good example of someone who had to manage this type of internal struggle. As a long-standing church member, he felt a strong calling to become ordained as a priest. He had experienced this calling for several years and felt that the urgency to respond to it was becoming greater. There was only one problem; Jonathan had a fear of speaking in public. His throat would go dry, his deep voice would become a mere squeak, and his legs turned to jelly. There was nothing that Jonathan hated more than public speaking. And yet, his Mission was calling him towards a path that would put him into direct contact with the thing he feared most.

I knew I could help Jonathan manage his fear of public speaking more effectively, but I also knew that this would not turn public speaking into a joyful experience! If Jonathan decided to follow his Mission, he would also have to choose experiencing something he did not want to feel. This is true of all of us and is, in fact, a key to success. When you select your goals, don't sell yourself short by settling for those that you think are within easy reach. Choose those goals that are true to who you are and your vision of what you want to achieve. The best goals are not those that eliminate uncomfortable thoughts and feelings, but those that are sufficiently meaningful for you to embrace the discomfort involved in their pursuit.

Take home message

Goals are so central to implementing any life plan that I have devoted a whole chapter to them. But, as we have seen, they are only a means to an end. Their value comes from their relationship to your Mission and the Attitudes that guide your vision of your life. While you want to be committed to action, it is also important to treat your goals lightly. I work with many clients who, in the process of doggedly pursuing their goals, somehow forget to live!

Goal-setting can become addictive, particularly if you are someone who thrives on self-imposed pressure. If coming from a conflicted place inside you, goal-setting can turn into a relentless striving that creates dissatisfaction rather than empowerment. When we get caught in this trap we are like children who have been let loose in a sweet shop and run from one delicious treat to another, grabbing as many as possible, without ever stopping to question which sweets we might enjoy the most. Sooner or later, all this indiscriminate consumption leads to nausea. So it is with our goals. Unless they are supported by a clear vision, we become seduced by one possibility after another and eventually burn out.

For some further tips on how to create goals that will really make a difference to your life, see the Coaching Tool Kit below.

Your Coaching Tool Kit: Top Tips on Getting your Goals to Work for You

1. Make your goals SMART.
2. Word them according to what you *do* want (e.g., to get fit by going to the gym twice each week) not what you don't want (to stop lazing in front of the TV every night).
3. Check that your goals inspire you.
4. Make sure they are consistent with your Mission.
5. Go for goals that stretch you beyond your comfort zone: the sense of achievement will be much greater.
6. Write them down and read them every day to help keep you focused.
7. Keep a Gains Log to remind you of all the efforts you are making.
8. Keep your goals in perspective: they are only stepping stones to something bigger.

So, go for your goals, make them SMART, and commit yourself to action 100%. But in the midst of all this, don't become a slave to them: they are merely a means to an end. The point of having goals is to keep you focused on what really matters. And when you are, you'll start to see some amazing results.

Setting Inspirational Goals

One idea I will take away from this chapter is . . . (write your answer in your learning log).
One thing I will do differently from now on is . . . (write your answer in your learning log).

CHAPTER SEVENTEEN

Principle No. 10: Essential Thinking Skills

'Our sickness is that we continually take our relative
perceptions as absolutely real'

(LeLoup, 2002, *The Gospel of Mary Magdalene*)

Welcome to Principle No. 10: how to increase your options and inspire your mind with the right type of thinking. In this chapter you will:

- *discover how to recognize and defuse toxic thinking;*
- *learn how to modify the distorted thinking styles that prevent you from transforming your life;*
- *learn how to look beyond what you believe you know about yourself, in order to create new possibilities.*

In this chapter I want to appeal directly to the most powerful tool that you possess: your mind. The power of your mind is truly awesome. Not only does it possess a highly evolved capacity for judgement, evaluation, analysis, and problem-solving, it also possesses a magnificent and seemingly unlimited ability for story-telling, creativity, imagination, and fantasy, unparalleled in other species.

You have the capacity to think of things that have never been thought before. You have the capacity to dream wonderful dreams and to envision different and better futures for yourself. Thanks to your mind, you inhabit a world of possibility. There is virtually nothing that the mind cannot do – and to top it all, studies estimate that at best, we use only a fraction of our mental abilities. What an extraordinary gift!

But with this gift comes responsibility and if you are to use it to best advantage you need to take responsibility for exercising, training, and guiding it in the right direction. In order to do this effectively, there are one or two things you need to know about how your mind operates.

Wielding the power of the mind

Have you ever noticed how your mind tends to leap from one subject to the next? Without any effort on your part, it pulls you into thinking about one thing and leads you to forget another. It makes up stories about everything you experience. It also seems to have an agenda all of its own that makes it virtually impossible to control – and if you doubt me on this just ask yourself whether you can predict what you will be thinking five minutes from now. The answer, I would imagine, is no. Left to its own devices the mind can – and frequently does – meander through all sorts of possibilities, some of which are more helpful to us than others.

Exercise 21. Noticing the activity of the mind

Spend a few minutes now observing how your mind wanders. Find yourself a comfortable place and then close your eyes. Allow yourself to bring your attention to your breathing and, without trying to force or control your attention, see how long you remain focused on your breathing before your mind begins to start chattering. As you become aware that your attention has wandered, make a note of where it has wandered to: what thoughts, beliefs or stories is it telling you in that moment? Then gently bring your awareness back to the breath. Allow your attention to remain gently focused on your breathing until you become aware that your mind has wandered again. Each time, bring your mind back gently to your breathing.

Spend five minutes or so staying with the breath, and noticing how the mind will start to wander even though your intention is to stay focused on your breathing. Then record any observations or reactions in your learning log.

If you are like most people, you probably found it difficult to keep your mind focused on your breathing. It was as though your mind had an agenda all of its own. Notice, too, the thoughts you were having. Your mind might have tried to convince you that the exercise was a waste of time, or reminded you of all the important things that you should be doing instead. Or it might have produced critical thoughts about how badly you were doing for being unable to keep focused on something as simple as the breath.

Whatever happened for you, the point of the exercise was to notice how the mind is constantly caught up in a stream of thinking, judging, evaluating, and story-telling. And this is entirely normal. The mind wanders because this is its nature. To try to stop it from wandering, to try to force it into a state of stillness is like trying to stop a lion from hunting prey. It cannot: it is just what it does.

Perhaps it is a good thing we cannot control our thoughts. After all, our minds can wander to some very interesting places. If we had total control over our minds, we would never be able to come up with any original ideas. A good friend of mine once told me that he has his best ideas when he is running; when he lets go of *trying* to come up with solutions and novel ideas, the mind serves them up for him.

However, the mind doesn't always produce pleasant or productive ideas. Sometimes it wanders on to difficult terrain, conjuring up painful memories, hurtful experiences, or telling us destructive stories about who we are and how we should live.

So, your most powerful tool can be either your greatest ally, or your deadliest enemy. If you are to turn your mind into your greatest ally, you need to know how to provide it with direction. Try seeing it as your young prodigy – your prodigy may have an unlimited supply of creative potential, but a responsible adult needs to set some limits to make sure that things don't get out of hand.

Similarly, you cannot control your mind (there is good evidence that trying to control our thoughts can actually create a lot of suffering – if you have ever tried *not* to think about something painful you'll notice how impossible this becomes, and how the very act of trying not to think about something can get your mind tied up in knots). But you can cultivate the mind in ways that are likely to increase your chances of inspired living: you can be the

155

responsible adult guiding your prodigy in ways that are likely to be beneficial to you and others.

The purpose of this chapter is to help you take responsibility for your mind and offer it a direction so that it becomes your greatest ally.

Craig's story

Craig is a great example of someone who learnt how to harness the power of his mind. When we first met, he had lost all sense of direction. He had tried different careers, undergone different courses and trainings, but had never stuck at anything. By the time he met me, he had no idea what he wanted to do with his life, he just knew he wasn't happy.

Not surprisingly, his confidence was at an all-time low. Having always doubted whether he was 'good enough', Craig was now more convinced than ever that he was not up to much and his lack of confidence was preventing him from thinking creatively about the kind of life he might want to lead.

But, over the course of our work together, Craig turned his life around – for the first time he knew exactly what he wanted. He was embarking on a new career as a personal trainer, which involved having the discipline to study, changing his diet and lifestyle, and putting himself through repeated physical and mental assessments. And he loved it.

At our last meeting, I asked him what had made the difference. If he was going to identify one thing in our work together that had had a transformational impact, what would it be? He grinned. 'It was when you suggested I eliminated the words "What if?" from my vocabulary,' he said.

The power of toxic thinking

When I first met Craig, he had been seduced by the power of what I call 'toxic thinking'. Toxic thinking is the psychological equivalent of taking slow-acting poison: you may not notice its effects at first, but it undermines your body's defences and eventually you start to notice obvious signs of illness.

Toxic thinking works on our psychological well-being in the same way. It weakens us through whispering messages about our inadequacies that undermine our ability to perform effectively. Over time, it attacks our efforts to change so that we feel paralysed about taking action and our cherished hopes for the future seem as ridiculous as they are impossible.

This is what had happened to Craig. Before he turned his life around, Craig's mind had been producing thoughts derived from a story that he 'wasn't good enough'. His mind would tell him:

- you're not as good as other people;
- things always go wrong for you;
- don't even try: if you do, you'll discover that your worst fears about yourself are true;
- play it safe – that way your inadequacies won't be exposed.

Craig could see how these thoughts led him to put barriers in the way of his own success in an attempt to protect himself from the shame and humiliation of failure. And because the story seemed so real to him, he never stopped to check whether these thoughts were as accurate as his mind insisted. So he allowed his life choices to be dictated by them. The tragic irony of this was that Craig was a remarkably resilient and gifted person. But he couldn't see any of this until he began to change his relationship to his toxic thinking.

Ditch the 'What ifs . . .'

For Craig, a particularly paralysing kind of toxic question was the 'What if?' question. Craig could spend hours ruminating on all the things that might go wrong. Listed below are some of his mind's favourites.

- What if I can't do it?
- What if I am just not capable of making changes?
- What if I make a fool of myself?
- What if this is it for me, and my life is like this for ever?

Because Craig could never find any answers to these questions (we'll take a look at why in just a moment), they haunted him.

Feeling overwhelmed and hopeless, he would try to silence them by watching TV and drinking alcohol. Unfortunately, however, these were the very behaviours that led his mind to criticize him for not being 'good enough' in the first place. It was a vicious circle.

'What if' questions are problematic because they usually focus on the worst case scenario. Because they seem so plausible, they seduce the mind into zoning in on the apparent imminent catastrophe, rather than encouraging you to think about things in a balanced way. Asking yourself a 'what if' question may seem like an attempt to anticipate and prevent problems, but if you think about productive approaches to problem-solving, you'll soon see that they are a poisoned chalice. Think about a time when you asked yourself a 'what if' question. What was the effect?

Why, why, why?

Another common type of toxic thinking is the 'why' question. 'Why' questions essentially demand explanations and asking them can be very useful when applied in neutral situations. For example, a mechanic asking why a car has broken down will lead to a series of investigations that will help identify and fix the problem. But when we apply the 'why' question to ourselves – whether it is our thoughts, feelings or actions, it is bad news. This is because when we ask ourselves 'why' we do or don't do something, we're often introducing a judgement. Let's look at some common examples of why questions that don't work.

- Why can't I give up smoking?
- Why don't I follow through on my goals?
- Why do I have so little will-power?
- Why do I always get things wrong?
- Why am I so stupid?
- Why does this always happen to me?

Read these statements out loud and notice their tone. Would you like someone to say these things to you? Probably not. You can see that these questions aren't really questions at all – they are judgements and criticisms wrapped up as questions that put you under pressure to come up with an answer when there isn't one.

Below are some more examples of toxic thinking. Copy them into your learning log, tick any that apply to you, and make a note of the situations in which you tend to get trapped by them.

Exercise 22. Examples of toxic questions and statements

Toxic question/statement	True of me?	Situation in which it occurs
Why has this happened to me?		
Why can't I . . .?		
What if I fail?		
If only . . .		
I can't . . .		
I'll try . . .		
I really should/shouldn't . . .		
I can't help it if . . .		

Notice how, on the surface, these questions and statements may seem perfectly innocent. You probably say them to yourself at least some of the time. You may even believe that they serve a purpose, such as protecting you against disappointment or helping prepare you for the worst. But don't fall into the trap! Like a drip-feed of slow-acting poison, they eventually start to wear you down and you pay a high price in terms of your happiness and well-being.

The tell-tale signs of toxic thinking

From what we've seen so far, you can see that toxic thinking tends to have the following qualities.

- It often involves questions that you cannot answer.
- You can spend hours thinking, without getting anywhere.
- It seems convincing but is not based on the facts.
- It increases your distress levels.
- It leaves you feeling disempowered and demotivated.
- It leaves you feeling inadequate.
- It undermines your confidence and self-esteem.
- It closes down options, rather than opening them up.

Exercise 23. Get to know your toxic thoughts

Think about times when you have felt unable to live in a way that is consistent with your Mission. What kinds of things do you tend to say to yourself that keep you stuck? Look out for dire warnings in the form of 'what if . . .' questions, judgements about your 'inadequacies' in the form of 'why' questions, or phrases that weaken your resolve and confidence (such as 'If only . . .' or 'I'll try . . .'). Include any other phrases that you can think of, that tend to entrap you. List your top five favourites in your learning log.

Take a moment to look at the thoughts you have written down. Can you spot the signs of toxic thinking and see how they have a detrimental effect on your life? And can you also see how they don't quite reflect the reality of all aspects of the situation – even if they feel completely true at an emotional level? If you were free of the influence of these toxic thoughts, what would you like to think instead?

Mind the gap between your mindset and reality

When it came to making changes, one of the big lessons Craig had to learn was that, when it came to judging himself and his potential, he couldn't always take his assumptions at face value.

We all like to believe that our thinking is pretty accurate, and some of the time this might be true. But when it comes to judging ourselves, our relationships, our competencies and needs, strange things can happen. Decades of research in psychology has found that when we experience strong emotions or encounter challenging situations, our style of thinking changes in predictable ways.

Specifically, our perspective becomes much more narrow. Our mind presents us with abbreviated versions of reality that fail to take account of the whole picture. It is like zooming in with a telephoto lens – you can see the detail but not the context.

Have you ever been in a challenging situation involving strong emotions where you were convinced that one interpretation of a situation was accurate – only to find later on, when you were calmer, that you had misread things? This is what I mean by seeing the world through a telephoto lens. The detail looms so large that, in the moment, we forget to look at the whole picture.

What the mind is doing at these moments is taking short-cuts in its style of information processing. In survival situations, there are very good reasons for doing this. If you are facing a threat to your life, you need to be able to zoom in on the threat to the exclusion of everything else. This ability enables us to stay alert to danger and sharpens our decision-making skills so that we can make swift judgements about whether a situation is safe or harmful.

If you are out in the African bush, for example, and you see the grass shimmering in the distance, you will stop gazing up at the birds or the trees and the beautiful landscape and will focus on the detail of the shimmering grass to the exclusion of all else. That particular aspect of your landscape will capture your whole attention while you try to work out whether the shimmering is just the breeze or a lion preparing to attack. In this situation, the ability to anticipate danger will enable you to zoom in on that danger. And doing so could well save your life.

Survival thinking is part of the fight or flight response that we looked at in Principle No. 4, and it works very well when you are faced with an immediate life or death decision. But because it diminishes your curiosity, depletes your creativity, and closes down your options, it cannot help you identify ways of fulfilling your Mission. This is important, because most of the choices we experience in our lives today are not true survival situations. We have choices to make about how we want to live our lives, the kind of work we want to do, and how we want to nurture our own gift of individuality so that we can offer it to the world. For these situations, we need to take a broad perspective that will arouse our curiosity, interest, and creativity: a style of thinking I call 'inspired thinking'. Table 4 highlights the different qualities of each approach.

Table 4.   Survival and inspired thinking styles.

Survival thinking	Inspired thinking
Closes down options (to aid quick decision-making)	Opens up options
Aims to minimize risk-taking	Aims to enhance (appropriate) risk-taking
Danger orientated	Development orientated
Judgement orientated	Choice orientated
Contractive: can see things from one angle only	Expansive: can see things from many different angles
Associated with uncomfortable emotions (such as fear, anxiety, anger)	Associated with pleasurable emotions (such as joy, humour, pleasure)
Occurs when we feel threatened	Occurs when we feel safe
Facilitates swift, incisive thinking (even if incorrect)	Facilitates day-dreaming and creative thinking
Concerned with right and wrong	Concerned with a world of possibilities
Keeps you alive in survival situations	Keeps you growing and learning

Both styles of thinking are important and have their place. But you need to know which style of thinking to use when. When it comes to fulfilling your potential, deciding on your goals, working out how you want to live your life, and implementing your Mission, you need inspired, not survival, thinking.

Avoid the thinking traps

Survival and inspired thinking are all about the way you process information, not just the content of your thoughts. Because survival thinking is all about taking short cuts, it tends to lead to biased thinking. Study Table 5, and see which types of biases apply to you, particularly when you feel disheartened, vulnerable or uninspired.

Table 5. Common thinking traps: which ones do you use?

Type of thinking trap	Description and example
All-or-nothing thinking (also known as dichotomous thinking)	Viewing situations and events from extreme perspectives, with no middle ground: e.g., 'If I don't get a distinction on every piece of work, it means I'm a total failure.'
Over-generalizing	Making sweeping, generalised conclusions based on a single event: e.g., a person has a minor setback and tells themselves, 'Things *never* work out for me. Sooner or later, it *always* goes wrong. I might as well not bother.'
Catastrophizing	Exaggerating the significance of an event: e.g., 'If I make a mistake on this project, others will realize that I'm a failure, my partner will leave me, I'll lose my job, won't be able to pay the mortgage and will end up homeless . . .'
Mind-reading	Assuming you know what people are thinking and that they are judging you negatively (even in the absence of evidence to support your view): e.g., when you are talking to someone at a party, you see them glance at their watch and you think 'They obviously find me really boring and can't wait to get away.'
Fortune telling	Predicting future events, usually in a catastrophic way, in the absence of any evidence (see catastrophizing, above).
Discounting positives	Discounting positive information about yourself or the situation and playing down your strengths and accomplishments. 'I know I've achieved my goals, but they weren't actually that difficult when you appreciate what other people achieve . . .'
Exaggerating negatives	You focus almost entirely on the negative aspects of a situation and fail to appreciate other, more positive aspects.
Labelling	You sum yourself up in a single, usually critical or judgemental word: e.g., 'I am stupid'; 'I am a failure.' This is often an extreme form of all-or-nothing thinking.

(continued)

163

Table 5. (continued)

Type of thinking trap	Description and example
Personalizing and blame	Blaming yourself for outcomes for which you are not totally responsible: e.g., 'It's my fault my son failed his maths test, because I'd been too busy to help him revise. If I'd been a better parent this would never have happened.'
Shoulds	Focusing on how you think things ought to be, rather than how they actually are. This often involves imposing arbitrary rules or standards on yourself or others that become difficult to live up to. For example: 'I should always make sure everyone is happy and well looked after before I even think about my needs.'
Unfair comparisons	You impose unrealistic standards on yourself by focusing on others who seem more successful than you and then judging yourself inferior in comparison.
Inability to disconfirm	This often appears in our thoughts or speech in the form of a 'Yes, but . . .'. You reject any evidence that contradicts your negative thoughts.
Emotional reasoning	You assume something is true because it *feels* true: e.g., believing that you are being taken advantage of by someone because you feel angry with them.
Preconceived notions or expectancies	Your implicit ideas about a situation or event act like a filter and prevent you from perceiving new information accurately.
Selective attention to confirmatory evidence	You attend only to information that confirms your existing beliefs. You edit out information that challenges your ideas, preventing a more impartial view of the situation.

Go back to your answers on the Inspiration Inventory at the start of this book. Are any of these thinking traps involved in those areas that aren't working so well? If so, how have they held you back? What thinking traps might get in the way of you fulfilling your Mission? Write down your reflections in your learning log.

Ask the questions that can facilitate your journey

As your own coach, I want you to get into the habit of asking yourself the kinds of questions that will consistently point you in the right direction. The best types of question, the thinking style you need for inspired living, allow you to frame a problem, life dilemma, or choice in a way that prompts you to come up with helpful solutions. They engage your imaginative and creative potential, as well as your problem-solving capabilities, and equip you with a framework for relating to your mind that you can apply to any situation you encounter in your life.

The kinds of questions you want to aim for are those that help you explore your thoughts, emotions and actions in a particular context and which source new ideas and possible courses of action. These tend to be questions that

- have no right or wrong answer;
- generate many possibilities, options, and choices;
- are simple to answer (you don't need a PhD to answer them!);
- evoke curiosity and interest;
- motivate and empower you;
- help you transform problems into opportunities;
- promote positive self-belief;
- lead to greater clarity about what you want;
- give you a focus for implementing your Mission and goals.

Inspired thinking also uses open questions that tend to start with the following types of words:

- how?
- what?
- where?
- who?
- when?

(Notice that 'why' questions are not included!)

Think about how you could use these kinds of questions in relation to your own coaching journey. Below are some examples that you may find helpful to explore.

- How many ways can I think of to turn my Mission into an action plan?
- How does this (idea/goal) relate to the core area in which I am coaching myself?
- How will my goals serve others as well as myself?
- Who will benefit when I achieve my ambitions?
- What's the first step I can take towards getting where I want to be?
- What other possibilities are there?
- What small steps do I need to take over the next six months?
- How will I know when I've got there? What do I expect to feel? Notice? Experience? Which bit of my new life will I like the most?

And, in relation to apparent obstacles or setbacks, how about the following questions?

- How have I played a role in bringing about this result?
- What Attitude could I adopt right now that would give me more choices?
- How many ways can I think of to solve this problem?
- What's the opportunity in this? What can I take from this, to create a different outcome next time?
- If I knew my success was guaranteed, how would I approach this situation differently?
- Who can help me think about this dilemma creatively?
- What advice would my council give me? (Remember the personal council of advisers you appointed at the end of the Attitude section? Here's one place where you can start to put your members to work.)

Notice that these questions are not just about replacing negative statements with positive ones, but are about learning a way of examining, evaluating, and relating to your thoughts and reactions so that you can increase your range of choices. Notice also how all the questions are likely to employ your mind in a helpful way – it will chatter on regardless, so you might as well make it work for you by giving it a job to do!

Your worksheet

Whenever you find yourself getting caught up in the stories that your mind is telling you, or when your current thinking style is not getting you the results you want, use the work sheet below. (Copy it into your learning log.)

Toxic thought	Thinking trap	Inspired thinking	Action
(write it below)	(name it here)	(your reframe)	(what is one thing you can do right now that would help you?)

Take home message

Creating the life that inspires you involves learning how to nurture your heartfelt ambitions and honour your potential. In order to do this consistently and effectively, you need to harness your most powerful tool: the mind. Cultivating the mind involves learning to guide it away from those forms of mental processing that generate distress and towards those kinds of processing that are empowering and nurturing and that trigger curiosity and effective problem-solving. The essential thinking skills for inspired living involve more than just altering the content of your thoughts. They also involve working with your thought *process* or thinking *style*. And, like all skills, working with your thinking style takes practice – the more you do it, the easier it will get and the more powerful and effective it will become.

From now on, tune into your thoughts on a regular basis. Search out disempowering phrases, learn to understand the thinking style that underpins them, and gently reframe them by changing your thinking style from one of survival thinking to one of inspired thinking. Do this every day for a week and the results will probably surprise you. Do this every day for a month and your life will start to change in profoundly positive ways. Make this the habit of a lifetime and you will always inspire others with your interest and creativity – as well as yourself.

Your Coaching Tool Kit: Top Tips for Thinking Right

1. Pay attention to your thoughts: if they undermine you, root them out.
2. Do not take your assumptions at face value. Just because they feel true doesn't make them true (after all, thousands of children believe in Father Christmas . . .).
3. Whenever you find yourself asking a toxic question, reframe it within an inspired thinking style, using a how, what, when, who, or where question.
4. Use your optimism skills to undermine any toxic pessimism.
5. Practise cultivating these qualities of mind every day.

Empower Your Mind with the Right Questions

One thing I will take away from this chapter is . . . (write the answer in your learning log).
One thing I will do differently as a result of this chapter is . . . (write the answer in your learning log).

Bibliography

Brown, J., & Isaacs, D. (2005). *The World Café: Shaping Our Futures Through Conversations that Matter*. San Francisco, CA: Berrett-Koehler.

*De Bono, E. (1994). *Parallel Thinking: From Socratic to de Bono Thinking*. London: Penguin.

*De Bono, E. (2003). *De Bono's Thinking Course*. London: BBC.

Gambrill, E. (2005). *Critical Thinking in Clinical Practice* (2nd edn). Hoboken, NJ: Wiley.

*Greenberger, D., & Padesky, C. A. (1995). *Mind Over Mood. Change How You Feel by Changing the Way You Think*. New York: Guilford.

*Leahy, R. L. (2005). *The Worry Cure. Stop Worrying and Start Living*. New York: Harmony.

Wheatley, M. J. (1999). *Leadership and the New Science: Discovering Order in a Chaotic World*. San Francisco, CA: Berrett-Koehler.

CHAPTER EIGHTEEN

Principle No. 11: Developing Your Creativity

'Creativity is the making of a life and a world'

(Zander & Zander, 2000)

Welcome to Principle No. 11: how to develop your creativity. This chapter dispels some of the myths surrounding this remarkable human gift and allows you to expand your creative potential in the service of your wider sense of purpose. Together we will explore:

- *the nature of creativity;*
- *the creative skills and talents you already possess (but may have overlooked);*
- *how you can become more creative across all domains of your life.*

How do you come up with ideas that have the potential to transform your life? What are the skills you need to turn great ideas into a new and exciting reality? If you want to bring your Mission to fruition, you will need to look beyond your analytical and problem solving skills to engage with a deeper quest: one of excavating and nurturing your capacity to imagine, design, and invent.

In the previous chapter, we looked at the importance of asking the right kind of questions. In this chapter, we will look at how to take this one step further by combining your skills in inspired thinking with your ability to create – an ability which speaks directly to the heart of inspired living.

If you are like most people, you probably radically underestimate your natural creative ability. So, before continuing with this chapter, complete Exercise 24.

Exercise 24. Are you a creative person?

Take a moment to think about your own creativity and then use the following questions to guide you.

- How does your creativity express itself in your life?
- In what areas are you most and least creative?
- Do you see yourself as a creative person?
  - If so, why? What is it that you observe yourself thinking, feeling or doing, that leads you to label yourself as creative?
  - If not, why not? What do you notice yourself thinking, feeling or doing that leads you to judge yourself as non-creative?

Write the answers in your learning log.

The gift of creativity

Creativity is prized throughout the world, and for good reason. When allowed to flourish, it has profound implications for our work, our lives, our relationships, and our communities. On a personal level, the ability to think and act in creative ways adds dimension, richness, and vitality to our lives. Author Julia Cameron has even suggested that the opportunity to express our creativity is vital to sustaining a sense of personal meaning.

Industries and organizations are increasingly aware of the power that creativity has, both in terms of how opportunities for its expression can enhance job satisfaction and as a means of gaining a competitive edge in the marketplace. In the commercial world, where organizations must continually reinvent themselves, their image, and their products in order to survive, considerable amounts of money are spent on enhancing the creative potential of the workforce. Creativity pays dividends and, as one of the highest of all human functions, is central to artistic expression, scientific discovery, political leadership, entrepreneurial endeavours, and successful businesses.

But what exactly is creativity? Think of someone whom you would judge to be truly creative. Try not to analyse your response too much – simply take the name of the first person who comes to mind.

Whom did you choose? Someone who is famous for their creative gifts or someone little known by the world at large? Now think about why you chose them. How do you know they are creative? What qualities do they possess? How is their creativity expressed? Your choice tells you something important about how you view creativity and, therefore, your ability to nurture this gift in your own life.

Creative genius and mundane moments: the Big C, small c distinction

If, in the previous exercise, you chose someone who is famous for their creative genius, then you are not alone. Many of us associate 'true' creativity with something bordering on genius. Ask one hundred people to identify someone whom they would judge as genuinely creative, and they will produce names such as Leonardo da Vinci, Michelangelo, Mozart, Beethoven, Newton, Einstein, Galileo, Edison, or Shakespeare: in other words, people whose creative abilities enabled them to achieve extraordinary results and, in some cases, results that changed the world.

Great artists, composers, scientists, inventors, and writers are undoubtedly examples of creative talent at work. But this is only one type of creativity, and when we associate it with such greatness we are in danger of seeing it as something bestowed on the gifted few – a mysterious quality that exists 'out there' and that is a million miles away from the everyday realities of earning a living, developing a career, running a home, or raising children.

The notion that creativity only 'counts' if it yields great outcomes is a myth. Abraham Maslow, a pioneer of the human potential movement, identified two distinct types of creativity: primary and secondary. Primary creativity refers to peak moments in our thinking and behaviour that leave us feeling inspired at some deep or transformational level. Secondary creativity, in contrast, refers to those more mundane moments we take for granted because they are so much a part of how we live.

More recently, these different types of creativity have been branded 'Big C' and 'small c'. Big C creativity is that which makes a lasting contribution to our society, culture, or history in some distinct way. It refers to the ability to make a truly original and exceptional contribution within the context of a particular field. This is where our creative geniuses shine; within their domains, they leave a lasting and transformational legacy. Picasso changed the way in which art was viewed. Wagner introduced a new type of musical form that changed the way in which music was understood. Their fields were never the same after they had been touched by these giants in Big C talent.

In contrast, 'small c' creativity refers to the art of applying our abilities, talents, and imagination to increase our options and enhance our quality of life. More mundane than Big C creativity, small c moments can none the less be equally profound. If you have ever noticed the look of delight on a child's face as you present them with an aeroplane you have just made out of old newspaper, or sent a thoughtfully worded card to someone whom you know is going through a tough time, you'll know what I mean. Small c creativity makes history too – just on a more modest scale.

Big C: the creative facts

There are several important facts to note about your own Big C potential. The first is that Big C is not something that you are born with or without. True, some people may be more naturally gifted in certain areas than others, but the differences between Big C and small c types are quantitative rather than qualitative. In other words, your creative potential exists along a sliding scale, and you can move towards greater expression of Big C in your life by heightening your awareness of your creative abilities and finding ways to implement them.

The second fact is that Big C creativity typically involves years of study, hard work, and persistence in order to manifest in some extraordinary way. Talent undoubtedly helps, but persistence is even more essential. For example, if you want to be a Nobel Prize winning physicist, having a natural inclination for the subject (however exceptional) will not be enough. You will need to spend many years refining your knowledge of the discipline, studying the efforts of others gone before you, and expanding your repertoire of technical skill before you can even begin to think about making an original contribution – let alone one that is of the Nobel Prize winning standard.

Sometime ago, I was listening to a radio programme about the great composer Ludwig van Beethoven. As a young student, Beethoven was mentored by another distinguished musician, Joseph Haydn. The programme quoted a letter that Haydn had written to one of his contemporaries, extolling the talent of the young Beethoven and predicting his brilliant future. However, in his letter, he described how he was going to help his prodigy to rewrite his Octet in E Flat, so that the young Beethoven could reshape it into a better and more elegant composition. This letter sums up something important about Big C creativity; the genius was present, but it existed as raw material. Beethoven needed to work hard to hone his ability and perfect his craft. And he needed experienced teachers to guide him. Without commitment, hard work, and discipline Beethoven's talent would have remained latent potential.

How much 'raw material' do you have that is currently lying dormant? What hidden talents are you currently ignoring, or have assumed you don't possess, simply because they have not been given sufficient time and opportunity to manifest? Is it possible that you have Big C potential that you have overlooked? If you approached your creative potential using the thinking skills you learnt in Principle No. 10, would you view your creativity any differently? Write any reactions to these ideas in your learning log.

Are there any ways in which you could now start to express your Big C potential?

A final, but equally important, fact is that many people with Big C gifts have to struggle with major setbacks and live with tremendous uncertainty about whether they will succeed in their chosen field. And even when it does come, success is often the outcome of a long and arduous journey. Thomas Edison 'failed' hundreds of times in his attempts to make a light bulb and Albert Einstein was a poor student who failed his maths exams.

Moreover, many innovations that we would now regard as truly creative were rejected at the time because they proved too challenging for the status quo. For example, the ballet *The Rite of Spring*, choreographed by the legendary dancer Vaslav Nijinsky, was a crashing failure at the time of its first performances. It departed so radically from the received wisdom of how ballet 'should' look that neither the dancers nor the public could understand Nijinsky's vision. As a choreographer, Nijinsky failed. Today, however, we would view his contribution as truly original.

Small c: the creative facts

Although you may have found the idea of connecting with your Big C potential quite a stretch, you will probably be more familiar with expressions of small c creativity in your life.

Small c creativity is central to a wide range of daily tasks, including solving problems at home and work, getting the most out of your relationships, and optimising your leisure time. Small c is all around you, and if you broaden your awareness of its influence you'll discover that it represents a wonderful source of inspiration in its own right.

My good friend Lorraine is a prime example of the power of small c creativity. Her busy life involves holding down a job, running a home, supporting a husband, and raising her young son. She weaves all these different strands of her life together with an ease that is remarkable.

All of these are ongoing creative projects in their own right, but what really inspires me about Lorraine is her immense talent for interior design. She looks at colours and fabrics and immediately sees their potential for creating a certain type of ambience in her home. Over the years, she has created – and recreated – a series of beautiful rooms, each with its own distinct décor. There is little doubt that Lorraine is an artist. However, she would not consider herself to be creative in the Big C sense; her way of arranging things is something that she takes for granted. However, whenever I spend time with her, when I talk with her about her choice of textures, fabrics, and colours, I come away feeling inspired. Her creativity encourages me to explore my own.

Exercise 25. Identify your small c potential

What creative skills and abilities do you use every day? Which ones are now so familiar to you that you have forgotten to recognize them as the talents that they are? If you approach your creative abilities using the thinking skills you learned in Principle No. 10, what might you now understand to be an expression of your creative self? Write any reactions to these ideas in your learning log.

Are there any ways in which you could now start to acknowledge the influence of your small c creativity – and even build on it?

Exploring the essence of creativity

The word 'creativity' comes from the Latin word 'creare', meaning 'to bring into being'. Although there are many different theories about creativity, there is fairly unanimous agreement that in order to be awarded the status of 'creative', an idea or invention must meet two key criteria, listed below.

new

1. Originality: the idea or invention must be new and perhaps even radically different from current thinking or practice.

applicable

2. Value: the idea or invention must be productive, having the potential to enhance some aspect of our lives, or the lives of others.

These qualities apply to virtually all of the major accomplishments of the human race. Transport, cinema, the internet, air travel, or the latest advancements in medicine can all be assessed according to the degree to which they are original and the extent to which they have helped us progress. True, some ideas may be controversial (for example, the internet has dramatically increased access to information and has also enabled higher incidences of web-based scams), but few would argue that they have been neither original nor valuable.

If you think about your own creativity, you will notice that you, too, mix the ingredients of originality and value all the time, and have done since you were a child. If you are not sure, think back to when you were little. Did you ever play 'make believe', conjuring up stories that kept you entertained for hours? Or have an

175

imaginary friend in whom you confided when you needed comfort or support? Or pretend that towels or rugs were magic carpets that could transport you to faraway places? As an adult, have you ever day-dreamed? Made something? Come up with a solution to get you out of a tight spot? If you answered yes to any of the above, then you are a creative person.

Use the questions in Exercise 26 to start developing a profile of your unique brand of creativity, taking account of your Big C and small c abilities. Write down your answers in your learning log so that you can review and add to them as you continue with your coaching journey.

Exercise 26. Developing a profile of your creativity

Think of a time in your life when you were creative in some way. This could be a major project, such as setting up your own business or completing a thesis. Or it could be something simple such as a time when you planned a special meal or invented a bedtime story to soothe a young child to sleep. Be as specific as you can. Write down a brief description of what you did. Then answer the following questions.

- What were the qualities (of thinking and action) you drew upon in order to be creative?
- What skills were you using?
- How did you feel? What sorts of emotions and sensations were you experiencing?
- What sort of mind-set did you have (inspired or survival thinking)? What were the thoughts and ideas relevant to how you approached that task?

Now think about a time when your creativity felt blocked or stifled in some way. Perhaps the great idea eluded you, or things weren't working out in the way you had hoped. Be as specific as you can. Again, write down a brief description of what you did and then answer the following questions.

- What were the qualities (of thinking and action) you drew upon in an attempt to be creative?

- What skills were you using?
- How did you feel? What sorts of emotions and sensations were you experiencing?
- What sort of mind-set did you have (inspired or survival thinking)? What were the thoughts and ideas relevant to how you approached that task?

Your answers to Exercise 26 reveal something unique about your own brand of creativity, so study them carefully. What themes or patterns do you notice? You might, for example, have discovered that your creativity tends to flow easily in certain areas, but gets blocked in others. You might find that your creativity tends to emerge when you are by yourself, with plenty of time for your imagination to wander. Or it may need the more active energy of a team of people around you in order to thrive.

Use your imagination

Whatever form your creativity tends to take, I suspect that during your most creative moments you are able to

- be playful with ideas without censoring or judging them;
- be willing to experiment;
- remain open to different possibilities;
- feel curious;
- feel involved and immersed in the moment;
- focus on solutions rather than problems.

Conversely, for those times when you feel less creative, I suspect that you are more likely to

- feel pressured into coming up with a good answer;
- view things from one particular angle (remember the thinking biases we looked at in Principle No. 10);
- feel your imagination was constrained in some way;
- be critical of your ideas;
- feel daunted by the challenge;
- focus on problems rather than solutions.

If this is true for you, then you have discovered something important about the quality of thinking that is needed for creative self-expression. We are far more likely to achieve our creative potential if we free ourselves from the constraints of logic and sensible thinking and are willing to look beyond the familiar, even if it is just for a moment. Perhaps one of the best examples of this was Einstein, whose creativity enabled him to undertake an imaginary ride on a sunbeam – a journey that led him to conclude that the universe was finite and curved. Einstein felt comfortable looking beyond the established and rational wisdom of his discipline to access a part of himself that was essentially non-scientific: the power of his imagination.

day-dreaming

One of the major obstacles against fulfilling our creative potential is, as author and psychologist Tony Buzan observes, that we are largely taught to think in only one way – we prize our analytical, rational, problem-solving skills over our ability for imagination. However, this doesn't seem entirely consistent with the advice of those well-versed in Big C creativity. Everything, so the poet William Blake tells us, starts in the imagination – a sentiment shared by Einstein himself, who claimed that imagination is always more important than knowledge.

When pregnant with her second child, a colleague of mine told me how she had taken her young son along to her three-month ultrasound scan. During the scan, the well-meaning doctor had asked the little boy, "What's inside your Mummy's tummy?" Totally unfazed, the little boy replied "A horse!"

Now, technically, we could argue this response is neither accurate nor rational. But to dismiss it as such is to miss the point entirely. It was no more accurate or rational for Einstein to contemplate going for a ride on a sunbeam. But it was only by liberating himself from the rational that life-changing solutions could be found. Just think what you could accomplish if your imagination was as free to roam as that little boy's!

Creative people, creative contexts: the interaction of the personal, social, and cultural domains

So far we have looked at how creativity is a combination of your own unique cocktail of personal qualities, willingness to think beyond the ordinary, and persistence (especially when it comes to Big C creativity). However, individual factors are only one component of your creativity. Working out which ideas are useful and which are not, and how to translate ideas into action, requires knowledge of the context in which you are living and working.

Creativity, then, is the outcome of an interaction between four different domains, identified below.

1. The personal.
2. The interpersonal.
3. The wider networks and systems in which we are embedded.
4. Global and historical influences.

All these factors will influence when, and how, your creativity manifests. At the personal level, think about how your creativity has been enhanced and inhibited by:

- your Mission (including your authenticity, what has meaning for you, your signature strengths, and the extent to which you are prepared to exercise your courage);
- your Attitude (the extent to which you are optimistic *vs.* pessimistic, how you harness your curiosity, experience gratitude, and offer compassion to yourself and others);
- your Process (the nature of the goals you set yourself, the way you think about your life, your abilities, and your creativity and the extent to which you persist and nurture your motivation to persist when confronted with obstacles);

At the interpersonal level, think about how your creativity has been enhanced and inhibited by:

- your relationships with family members and intimate others: their values, priorities, and perspectives;
- your relationships with friends – their values, priorities, and perspectives;
- your relationships with colleagues – their values, priorities, and perspectives.

At the level of wider networks, how has your creativity been enhanced and constrained by:

- the different communities to which you belong: professional, social, spiritual, and cultural?
- the organizations and industries in which you work?
- the Mission, Attitudes and Processes of those communities?
- the ideology of your society at this point in human history, as shaped by local politics and national political and economic interests?

Finally, at the level of global influences, how might your creativity have been shaped (for good or ill) by:

- trends in thinking about what it means to have a good life?
- trends in thinking about what it means to be successful?
- concerns and priorities for the future of humankind (including ideas about power, warfare, and economic security).
- concerns about the future of our planet?

How to harness your creativity

However creative you judge yourself to be, there is no doubt that you can increase your creative potential still further, and that doing so will increase your range of choices, your sense of resourcefulness, and your love of life. The art of inspiration is learnt and refined through experimenting in the context of our everyday lives.

A good way to begin this search is to pay attention to what inspires you, which will provide an invaluable trail of clues about your unique brand of creativity and how you can recognize opportunities for growth and inspiration from all four dimensions. You can also use Exercise 27 to work out ways of stretching your creative potential.

Exercise 27. Harnessing the power of your creativity

Think of an area in your life where you would like to be more creative. Make it as clear as you can and sum it up in single statement or question (such as 'How can I . . .?' or 'What I really want to achieve now is . . .').

Allow your mind to enjoy playing with this as a possibility for your life. What would need to happen for you to allow your creativity expression in this area? What steps could you now take to invent this for yourself? Consider what resources might be required, the type of thinking skills that will support your efforts and who, within your family and social circle, might help you give expression to this part of yourself.

For a further source of ideas for developing and expressing your creative potential, use the Coaching Tool Kit below.

Your Coaching Tool Kit: Suggestions for Enhancing your Creativity, Big and Small

1.   Build some unstructured time into your week and do something completely unconnected with your daily life and all its responsibilities. Unstructured time creates a space for your imagination to express itself.
2.   Get curious about your creativity and keep a diary of 'creative moments' in your life. Make a note of what form your creativity took, where it happened, how it happened, when and with whom.
3.   Build up your tolerance for appropriate risk-taking, uncertainty and ambiguity, even if it doesn't come naturally (remember Principle No. 4: Courage).
4.   Try something new every day – or if not every day, at least once each week!
5.   Build up your network of creative contacts – for ideas, feedback and support. See if you can identify the Mission, Attitudes and Process that guides them. In what ways do they conform to and disregard conventional thinking and behaving?
6.   Draw on the lessons learned by others. Creative geniuses often have a mentor to whom they can turn for inspiration. Remember the Council you created at the end of the Attitude section? Here is your chance to use it, or to invite some new members on board.
7.   Mix your media. Creativity is stimulated by drawing on skills and interests from multiple areas of our lives. Search out contact with the natural world, literature, the arts, science or spirituality to access your sense of adventure.
8.   Try approaching a situation or task from a radically new perspective. If you were an inventor, scientist, politician or human rights activist how would you approach that situation or task differently?

---

play

chaos

Take home message

Creativity involves a subtle blending of knowledge, skills, talents, curiosity, spontaneity, and a willingness to experiment that allows for nuances of the self to be explored.

Your brand of creativity is unique to you and needs to be expressed through every channel of your life. So, make yourself available to its call – in whatever shape or form it occurs.

Seeing yourself as creative may feel totally natural to you, or feel like a real stretch. Either way, learn to nurture this gift within you. See it as a young seedling – depending on the type of plant, it may need to germinate for a while before it bears fruit, but that does-n't mean it isn't growing. And, like so many of the other principles that make up the art of inspired living, creativity breeds more creativity: the more you work with your abilities in this area, the more robust and powerful they will become.

In this chapter, we have looked at ways of heightening your awareness of your creativity, both at the Big C and small c levels. We have also looked at how your natural creative talent already manifests in your life and considered how you might like to find new outlets for its expression.

In order to allow your creative potential to shine through, you may need to engage with a part of yourself that doesn't want to play by the rules of sensible, logical thinking. In fact, in order to thrive, creativity needs a degree of chaos and a willingness on our part to relinquish the desire to have our rational selves run the show. To live creatively means to sacrifice some of the control, certainty, and predictability that our education and environment insists is so vital to effective living.

In the end, harnessing your creativity is not about having extra-ordinary thoughts or achieving remarkable things. It is about knowing that you shape your world in small and incremental ways through your innate imaginative potential and your desire to invent. If you commit yourself to a life of creativity – both Big C and small c – you will always find life to be full of inspiring moments.

Developing Your Creativity

One idea I will take away from this chapter is . . . (write the answer in your learning log).

One thing I will do differently from now on is . . . (write the answer in your learning log).

Bibliography

*Buzan, T. (2001). *The Power of Creative Intelligence. Ten Ways to Tap Into Your Creative Genius.* London: Thorsons.

*Cameron, J. (1995). *The Artist's Way: A Course in Discovering and Recovering Your Creative Self.* London: Pan.

Csikszentmihalyi, M. (1996). *Creativity: Flow and the Psychology of Discovery and Invention.* New York: HarperCollins.

Maslow, A. (1968). *Towards a Psychology of Being.* New York: Van Nostrand.

Maslow, A. (1971). *The Farther Reaches of Human Nature.* New York: Viking.

Sternberg, R. (Ed.) (1999). *Handbook of Creativity.* Cambridge: Cambridge University Press.

CHAPTER NINETEEN

Principle No. 12: Managing Your Motivation

> 'Success is going from failure to failure
> without loss of enthusiasm'
>
> (Winston Churchill)

The last of the 12 Principles of inspired living looks at how to manage your motivation so you can be sure to achieve the results you are aiming for. In this chapter you will:

- dispel some of the common myths about what it means to be motivated;
- find out your own stage of motivation;
- discover the secret of keeping motivated;
- learn some great ideas for helping you get back on track when your motivation flags.

There is always a certain adrenaline rush that comes from deciding to make changes in your life. If you've ever been on a diet, promised yourself to give up a long-standing habit, or made a New Year's Resolution, you'll know what I mean. Nothing energizes us more than committing ourselves to a goal that really matters. For a short while, you find yourself full of enthusiasm and vitality as you go about making meaningful changes to your life. But be honest; how long do the good intentions last? A month or two if you're lucky?

For many people, loss of motivation is the fly in the ointment that prevents them from transforming their Mission into goals and from following their goals through to completion. Maybe the amount of effort required makes you question whether it's really worth it. Maybe you encounter setbacks and obstacles that leave you feeling as though you are failing. Perhaps other demands on your time take over, or maybe even success itself starts to feel scary as you see yourself edging closer to what you thought it was that you wanted.

Times like this are a real test and if you don't know how to manage them, it's difficult to keep going. But giving up on your dreams is the ultimate betrayal of your authenticity, personal meaning, signature strengths, and courage. So, if you want to sustain your motivation through good times and bad, there are one or two things you need to know.

The true nature of motivation

Motivation is big business. Businesses spend thousands of pounds each year on motivating their staff in the belief that motivated people are more productive people.

Motivation is also essential to exercising your creativity. Break-throughs and insights often occur as a result of our willingness to persist – even when confronted with obstacles or apparent failures. People who work in sales are very aware of this. For every sale they make, many will have fallen through. It is the determination to continue in the face of defeat that separates the highly successful from the less successful. This is where motivation is essential.

Motivation is a misunderstood concept. If you look at some self-help books, it's easy to come away with the impression that motivation is little more than a choice: you either choose to change things or you don't; the key to success is simply deciding what you want and going for it.

We all buy into this myth to some extent. Imagine, for example, someone who is highly motivated to start a new business. The market conditions are favourable, the person really knows their core area, and has capital behind them. Their Mission is clear, they have the right Attitude and they have SMART goals to help them get there. What do you think will happen next? If you are like many people, you probably imagine this person making changes relatively easily and quickly. You have a vision of them staying consistently motivated until they have a successful business, shrugging off any obstacles with determination until their dreams have come true. After all, will-power and determination are everything, right?

Wrong! According to change experts James Prochaska, John Norcross, and Carlo DiClemente, this is one of the most common and destructive myths about how we change. They highlight how we are often seduced into believing that change is (or should be) easy once we've made up our minds about what we really want. The truth is that most of us try repeatedly before finally getting the results we want – particularly when it comes to making major changes in our lives.

The stories of highly successful people in the media tend to reinforce this myth, focusing largely on the outcome of success. Pick up a magazine article on anyone famed for their accomplishments and, regardless of their field, you'll see what I mean. The story is all about *what* they have achieved, not the details of *how* they achieved it. In this sense, success is viewed as a 'product'. But behind this product is a more messy, meandering process of experimenting, stumbling, learning, and growing that is the foundation of true success.

When working with my clients, I often describe motivation as being like a sea voyage. You set out to sea on a small boat. Before you go, you plan your route and set a course. You hope your route will allow you to arrive safely, but the prevailing conditions will determine how the journey actually unfolds. Sometimes the conditions seem to smile on you. The sun shines and the water is calm, allowing you to enjoy the ride and take in the scenery. But at other times the weather gets stormy and the water becomes choppy. When this happens, you have to devote all your energy and skill to keeping yourself afloat. You cannot control the conditions; all you can do is respond to them as best you can. It may not be pleasant at those moments, but to abandon your journey because the prevailing conditions are not ideal is to miss the point. Choppy weather is part of the reality of sailing. Just like the weather, motivation fluctuates. Motivation is a direction not a fixed state of mind.

Before you read on, use Exercise 28 to help you clarify any myths you may be holding about the nature of motivation and how it relates to success.

Exercise 28. What does motivation mean for you?

Motivation is a word that evokes strong reactions in most of us, including resistance! Think about your own beliefs and assumptions about motivation, then answer the following questions.

- How would you define motivation?
- To what (if any) myths have you subscribed (such as the idea that change should be easy if you want it enough, or that will-power is simply about making a choice)?
- What implications have these myths had for your life?
- Think of a time when you have achieved something that required persistence and motivation. How did you do it? Break it down until you have a clear picture of the different components. How can you draw upon these components to help you now?
- Think of a time when motivation seemed to elude you. What got in the way? Can you identify the specific components? What do you want to do differently next time?
- What are your hopes and fears about making changes at this point in your life?

Based on your analysis, what do you need to remember about the nature of motivation generally, and your motivation specifically, to help you achieve your goals? Write any thoughts in your learning log.

Jasmine's story

When Jasmine began pursuing her dream of writing a novel, she found herself confronted with a major motivational block.

Although she had no formal training in creative writing, Jasmine had harboured a lifelong ambition to write a novel. She also believed she had a story that was burning to be told. After several months of hard work during which Jasmine refined her plot, developed her characters, and produced some drafts of the initial chapters, she decided it was time to get some feedback. She joined a writer's group where she read out part of her first chapter.

The reactions of the group were mixed. She received some positive feedback and useful suggestions. However, one member of the group was extremely critical, accusing her of spouting clichés. Jasmine felt humiliated and, despite her intentions, could not summon up the courage to return to the group. Two years later, the pages of her novel were gathering dust in a plastic bag under her bed. As her coach, Jasmine asked me if I could help her get back on track.

As we talked, I discovered that Jasmine's expectations of being a writer were quite realistic. She was not aiming to win the Booker Prize, but loved to write and believed that this was central to her Mission, which was concerned with reaching out to people through stories.

Given that she was not putting herself under pressure to come up with a literary masterpiece, I asked her what was getting in the way of her writing now. She told me that she could not get the critical group member's voice out of her head. 'When he told me that my writing was full of clichés, something inside of me curled up and died. I realized I was stupid to think I could write anything,' she sighed. 'Who was I kidding?'

Jasmine's motivation took a nose-dive because of a setback triggered by someone giving her unconstructive criticism. But her Mission – her desire to communicate with others through writing – was still a burning one. So we began to look at the situation in greater detail.

Jasmine had got caught up in the thinking trap of exaggerating negatives, in that she was focusing entirely on the negative aspects of the group's feedback and had failed to remember the broader picture. All she could remember was how critical this one person had been. I asked her what the other members of the group had said. Jasmine then remembered some positive feedback – people had come over to her after the group and told her that they had enjoyed her story. Others offered practical suggestions that she had thought would be helpful.

As we began to explore her experience at the group more objectively, Jasmine recognized that there had been some truth in what the critical member of the group had said – it was the tone of his delivery that felt hurtful. Moreover, he hadn't accused her of spouting clichés throughout – only in one section. We looked at how she might depersonalize the feedback through using a worksheet so that she could take on board the suggestions that were useful. I also reminded her that she had never written a novel before and so was learning a new skill; receiving feedback was part of her learning journey.

The next stage was to break the larger and quite overwhelming task of completing a novel into manageable chunks. First, we looked at how she could exercise inspired thinking (see Principle No. 10). We then looked at the SMART goals she needed to set herself. Jasmine decided it would be helpful to think about other resources she might need, including accessing novel writing guidelines on the internet and finding a tutor who could guide her through the creative writing process. Her plan also included basic organizational tasks like filing the pages of her novel properly and re-reading the story again for the first time in two years.

A week later, Jasmine had re-read the chapters she had written so far and was planning to start writing the following week. She knew it was far from perfect and that she would need to get more feedback, some of which might be difficult to hear. However, she was back on track and doing what she loved most.

Know thyself (and thy stage of change)

Is it worth it? For Jasmine the answer was a definite yes. She was ready to make changes but just needed some help depersonalizing the unhelpful feedback she had received and establishing a realistic plan of action. But what if you're not so sure?

The psychology of motivation shows that when we try to achieve our goals, we typically dance our way backwards and forwards through a series of stages. The best way of managing your motivation effectively is to make sure that your action plan accurately fits your stage of change.

Think about your own Mission, Attitudes, and Process at this time in your life and then read through the stages described in Table 6. See if you can identify where you are on the journey of change.

The key to managing your motivation is knowing your stage of change and planning your Process accordingly. If you aim for something for which you are not truly ready, the goal will not come to fruition and you'll lose self-belief. This is why so many New Year's

Table 6. Prochaska, Norcross, and DiClemente's stages of change.

Stage of change	Example
Precontemplation	You find it difficult to accept that you have responsibility for making things change and may be more interested in changing others than grasping the nettle yourself! This stage is characterized by denial, reluctance and often, feelings of despondency or hopelessness.
Contemplation	You recognize that something needs to change but are ambivalent about making it happen. In contemplation, you are beginning to reflect on your needs, but are still at the thinking stage and not ready to commit yourself to definite action.
Preparation	You are now starting to focus on the solution rather than the problem and are directing your energies more to the future than the past. You are preparing yourself to take action in the next few weeks and may have started experimenting with small changes. You still have mixed feelings, but are preparing to 'walk your talk'.
Action	You are now actively making changes and are probably aware of the commitment of time and energy involved in achieving your goals. You know that taking action is not the same thing as change and probably feel the need for some extra support. You may feel good about taking action but are also aware how far you have to go.
Maintenance	You have made important changes and your efforts are now directed towards consolidating your achievements. By now, you understand that achieving the goal is not enough; it is how you keep going that matters. You realize that the effort to sustain your gains is an on-going project.
Termination	This is the ultimate goal that most of us never quite reach! In the termination phase, you are completely confident that you will never go back to your old ways. This category isn't appropriate to all goals as there are some areas of our life that we can never be fully confident we've truly 'cracked' (such as keeping fit, giving up habits, running a successful business and so on).

Resolutions fall at the first hurdle; they are often based on a form of wishful thinking that fails to recognize how change involves more than good intentions. Effective self-coaching requires pairing your motivation stage with action steps consistent with that stage.

For example, if you are at the contemplation stage, you might simply need to gather information about how to achieve a goal for future reference. If you are in the action stage, however, you will probably want to develop a very clear and detailed plan of what you will do and when, and establish a support network that will sustain you through good times and bad. An analysis of your level of motivation might lead you to realize that, in order to bring your dream to fruition, you need to acquire new skills, as in Jasmine's case. It could even involve making more fundamental changes to how you live your life and who is, and isn't, a part of it.

What the psychology of motivation also tells us is that it is not only natural to experience setbacks, it is also normal to have mixed feelings. Ambivalence often gets a bad press, but in fact it is present in every major decision we ever make. We all want to feel comfortable with ourselves, and the most important changes we undertake involve making ourselves uncomfortable! Feelings of self-doubt, insecurity, even fear, are simply par for the course. Even letting go of problems can be scary – true, you may not want the problem, but sometimes the prospect of a life without it can feel unsettling. As a result, it's perfectly possible to want something and not want it at the same time.

Knowing that ambivalence is normal can help you manage your motivation more effectively. If you can recognize that pursuing your goals *will* involve mixed feelings, you are free to choose the response that best serves your Mission. In other words, your feelings are not always a reliable compass for determining how you should act and where necessary you can acknowledge but override them in favour of a course of action that will help you succeed.

How to steer your motivation through those tricky moments

If you can expect ambivalent feelings as part of making valuable life changes, how do you navigate your way through them?

Psychologist Robert Leahy suggests that when it comes to making changes we often have hidden agendas that handicap us from achieving our intentions. If you find yourself faltering, a useful place to start is to examine what seems to be getting in the way (note: to do this successfully, you need to be curious and non-judgemental about your struggles – you're not making things difficult for yourself intentionally).

Think about what you have invested in your goals and if there are any reasons you might be holding yourself back. Are you afraid, deep down, that if you try, you will fail? Are you making excuses in an attempt to protect yourself from the terrible failure you imagine will occur if you implement your dream? Or is your lack of motivation coming from a fear of success? Do you imagine that you or your life would change beyond all recognition if you were to achieve your ambitions, or that success would create new pressures you are simply not ready to handle? Do you see yourself becoming so caught up in your new success that others in your family or community start to suffer? Think about how you imagine your life will change as a result of your successes. Your responses may surprise you!

In your learning log, make a note of any fears you might have about pursuing your goals and any motivational blocks that could prevent you from seeing them through to completion. Remember also to keep a look out for any thinking biases and take steps to correct them, using the work sheet in Principle 10.

Once you know you are clear about potential blocks, try using the solutions chart (Table 7) to help yourself move forward.

Did you notice any motivational traps that you tend to fall into? What action do you now need to take so that you are free to pursue what really matters?

Exercise 29. Develop a personal motivation guide

You alone can know what will make the difference between persisting with your Mission and giving up on it. So, before we end this chapter, I would encourage you to develop your own personal motivation guide, which you can turn to whenever your enthusiasm needs a boost.

Table 7.   Solutions to motivational setbacks.

Motivational setback	Solution
Every time I think about trying to achieve my ambitions I see myself failing.	1. Look out for unrealistic fears and challenge them. 2. Cultivate optimistic thinking and images of you succeeding. 3. Make sure you have a realistic and achievable action plan, aiming for small steps that will build your confidence.
I keep trying but it all keeps going wrong.	1. See if you are missing any essential skills and learn them. 2. Success comes from knowing not just what to do but how to do it. Are you using the coaching methods for long enough, consistently enough, and rigorously enough to be successful? 3. Ask for support from a coach or therapist to help work out where you are going wrong.
If I achieve this goal, I will become selfish and self-absorbed.	1. Review your previous successes. Did you become selfish or self-absorbed then? If not, why would this happen now? 2. Make sure your action plan includes sufficient time for family and other responsibilities. 3. Keep your goals in perspective. No one is asking you to sign your soul to it!
I won't be able to handle the pressure of success.	1. Check what you imagine will happen if you are successful. Would someone impartial agree that your fears are realistic? 2. Challenge your unrealistic expectations of success. 3. Review your action plan. See if it reflects your Mission and is worthwhile and achievable.
I can't take action until I have found the perfect solution.	1. There is no such thing as a perfect solution. It doesn't have to be perfect, just effective. 2. Remind yourself that action is central to motivation. The main thing is to get going. 3. Remind yourself that setbacks are part of every every significant change: you will experience them no matter how 'perfect' your strategy.
I'm not sure I really want this.	1. Remind yourself that it is fine to change your mind. 2. Review where you are on the stages of change: are you pitching your action steps at the appropriate level? 3. Adjust your goals so they reflect your priorities right now.

A personal motivation guide can take many forms. It might be several pages of key ideas based on what you have learnt about yourself in this and previous chapters, which you can summarise in your learning log. Or it might take the form of a letter that you write to yourself. It can also be a series of bullet points on an index card that you carry in your purse or wallet for those challenging or 'high-risk' situations. Whatever form it takes, make sure that your personal motivation guide complies with the guidelines set out below.

1. It is written in language that is compassionate, supportive, and concerned (avoid self-criticism or judgement at all costs).
2. It draws on skills in optimistic thinking.
3. It reminds you of all the times you have succeeded and over-come obstacles.
4. It reminds you to view setbacks as part of your progress rather than as a sign of personal failure.
5. It reminds you why it is worth keeping going (how your goals relate to your Mission).
6. It contains specific, simple, achievable, and practical actions you can take in the next few minutes, hours, or days to help you get back on track.

Jasmine's motivational letter

Jasmine chose a personal motivational guide that took the form of a letter. This capitalized on her natural inclination to express herself through writing. Here is what she wrote:

Dear Jasmine

If you are reading this letter, then I know that you are having a tough time right now. Perhaps you are struggling with a particularly difficult chapter. Or perhaps someone has given you some critical feedback that was difficult to hear. Whatever the setback, you are probably having all those doubts about yourself and your book. You may even be wondering whether it's worth carrying on with it.

Please remember that these kinds of feelings and thoughts are natural: anything worth pursuing will throw up obstacles and challenges – it's not a sign that you can't do it, it's a sign that you are getting on with it! You started writing this book for a good reason – because you believe in the story and you believe in writing as a powerful way of connecting with people. So don't give up now: it would be such a waste of your talents and your dreams.

This project is very important to you and is incredibly worthwhile. Deep down, however bad you are feeling, you know this to be true. Not only that, but people have also given you positive feedback, telling you that they like the story and your writing style. Since starting it, you have been full of energy and enthusiasm and have never felt more inspired. So you can't tell yourself that it's not worth it.

If you're feeling hopeless, here are some things you need to do after reading this letter:

- Go back to your writer's notebook and read through all the positive things people have said about your book so far (remember, you have had a lot of positive feedback and people really seem to like your ideas).
- Look for any toxic thinking and complete a thinking worksheet so you can make sure your thinking style isn't making things worse.
- Make a date in your diary for the next time you will sit down and work on the novel and then do it (you always feel better when you are doing it rather than worrying about it!).

I believe in the project, so keep going.

Jasmine.

Jasmine's letter worked well for her because it reminded her of why the project mattered (how it related to her Mission), how she viewed things differently and more positively when she was not facing a motivational challenge, and gave her specific advice about what she needed to do next in order to get going again.

Motivational letters can be incredibly powerful, so you may choose to write one for yourself. You can write it from you, to you, in the way that Jasmine did. Or you can write from a member of your council of advisers if you prefer. Another method you may want to try is to enlist the support of a family member or friend who is non-judgemental, who knows what you want to achieve and who reminds you of your goals from time to time. Making yourself 'accountable' to another person can often be a powerful way of managing your motivation.

You might also like to include some of the tips outlined in your Coaching Tool Kit.

Your Coaching Tool Kit: Meaningful Motivators for when You Need a Little Extra Help

1. Remind yourself of the bigger picture. Why is your goal important? How does it relate to your Mission?
2. Celebrate your successes and triumphs, especially the small ones.
3. Identify times you have achieved your goals in the past. How did you do this? How did you keep your motivation going during challenging moments?
4. If change feels overwhelming, start by creating some mini goals that you can achieve easily. This will encourage you to keep going.
5. Depersonalize apparent 'failures': learn to see them as the result of you applying insufficient time, practice, or the wrong strategy, rather than due to a lack of ability.
6. Find someone who believes in you and your goals. Draw on them for support when you find yourself faltering.
7. Watch our for the twin enemies of self-criticism and pessimism. Work on developing your optimistic mind-set (see Principles 5 and 10).
8. Acknowledge yourself for your efforts to keep going. Write down validating messages in your logbook.

Take home message

In this chapter, we have looked at some of the myths that surround motivation. Motivation is not a mysterious quality that we are born with or without, but a mindset (an Attitude) and a set of actions (a Process) that we can acquire. High levels of motivation also involve a willingness to take the rough with the smooth.

Managing your motivation is all about understanding that mixed feelings are a natural and inevitable part of change.

However, as we have seen in previous chapters, feelings are not always a good basis for deciding how to act. What matters is your Mission – the bigger vision of who you are and what you want your life to be about – that is capable of sustaining you through all your motivational highs and lows. Tap into this, and you have found yourself a winning formula.

Getting Motivated, Staying Motivated

One idea I will take away from this chapter is . . . (write your answer in your learning log).
One way I will work differently with my motivation from now on is . . . (write your answer in your learning log).

Bibliography

Leahy, R. L. (2001). *Overcoming Resistance in Cognitive Therapy*. New York: Guilford.

*Prochaska, J. O., Norcross, J. C., & DiClemente, C. C. (1995). *Changing for Good. A Revolutionary Six-Stage Program for Overcoming Bad Habits and Moving Your Life Positively Forward.* New York: Quill.

CHAPTER TWENTY

Designing Your Process: Pulling It All Together

In Principles 9–12, you learned everything you need to start translating your Mission, and new Attitude into a Process – an action plan that will help you get from where you are now to where you want to be.

Each of these Principles contributes something unique – a tool, method, or approach that will increase your chances of following through to completion and success. Without knowing the power of goal setting, for example, your ambitions will lack focus. You will have a sense of the general direction in which you want to be headed, but will struggle to get there. Learning how to draw on thinking styles that enable you to approach challenges from new perspectives will increase your imaginative potential; working with your creativity will help you design a route to get to where you want to be and your motivation will need to be regularly topped up so that you don't lose heart at the first hurdle.

At this point, let's return to the exercise you completed at the start of the Process section. Think of a time now where you are living what, for you, is a life that inspires you. It doesn't have to be perfect and it certainly won't be problem-free. But it's a life in which you are living with a sense of purpose, experiencing greater levels of fulfilment and experiencing success more frequently. What's changed? How did you get there? What exactly did you do and when? What small steps paid the biggest dividends? Be as specific as you can and record your thoughts in your learning log.

Now come back to the present and think about the goals you could implement to help you get there. List five SMART goals in your learning log (think small – remember the popular saying about giant oak trees growing from tiny acorns).

Look carefully at the goal list you have devised. If you have the balance right, it should evoke a feeling of 'I can'. You want to feel a sense of positive anticipation and maybe even a slight tinge of anxiety if your goals are stretching you a little bit. If you achieve them, will you feel as though you have accomplished something worthwhile? Will they contribute to a big win for you? If not, keep refining your goal statements until they do.

Finally, make sure your action plan includes attention to the following questions.

- What's your deadline for achieving each goal?
- How will you know when you've achieved it? What will be different?
- Is this action plan realistic and achievable?
- What might get in the way of implementing your action plan and how could you prevent this? (You may find it helpful to think back to your previous successes and setbacks here.)
- What Attitudes and thinking style will help you achieve this action plan?
- What Attitudes and thinking traps will you need to watch out for?
- How can you bring your creativity to this action plan?
- How are you going to manage your motivation? How will you boost your morale so you keep going through any setbacks?

Once you have answers to all of the above questions, write your action plan in your learning log – including specifying deadlines of what you will do and by when, under the heading 'My action plan is . . .'.

On reaching the end of this section, you have completed the 12 Principles in the Art of Inspired Living. By working through the different chapters, you have developed a rich collection of insights, self-knowledge, perspectives, tools, and techniques that will help you capitalize on your talents, enhance your motivation, and fulfil your potential.

In Part III , we will look at some specific ways in which you can apply these principles to different areas of your life. Although there are a limitless number of areas with which coaching can help, I have chosen those areas for which my clients most commonly request help. These are listed below.

1. How to be inspired at work.
2. How to achieve a healthy work-life balance.
3. How to create healthy self-esteem.
4. How to have a happy and healthy relationship with your body.
5. How to develop and sustain rewarding relationships.

Just before we conclude Part II, however, let's have one last look at 'MAP'. In Figure 2 (p. 202), you'll see the full version of MAP, in diagrammatic form, which gives you an instant overview of how to master the art of inspired living and how to go about planning each self-coaching journey now and in the future.

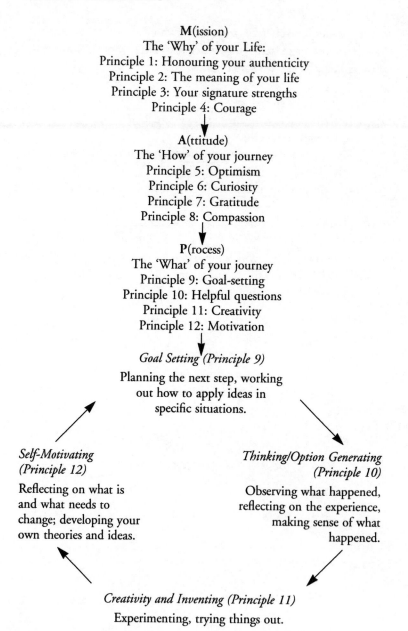

M(ission)
The 'Why' of your Life:
Principle 1: Honouring your authenticity
Principle 2: The meaning of your life
Principle 3: Your signature strengths
Principle 4: Courage

A(ttitude)
The 'How' of your journey
Principle 5: Optimism
Principle 6: Curiosity
Principle 7: Gratitude
Principle 8: Compassion

P(rocess)
The 'What' of your journey
Principle 9: Goal-setting
Principle 10: Helpful questions
Principle 11: Creativity
Principle 12: Motivation

Goal Setting (Principle 9)

Planning the next step, working
out how to apply ideas in
specific situations.

Self-Motivating
(Principle 12)

Reflecting on what is
and what needs to
change; developing your
own theories and ideas.

Thinking/Option Generating
(Principle 10)

Observing what happened,
reflecting on the experience,
making sense of what
happened.

Creativity and Inventing (Principle 11)
Experimenting, trying things out.

Figure 2.   Your coaching 'MAP'.

PART III

CHAPTER TWENTY-ONE

Being Inspired at Work: How To Choose Your Vocation and Love what You Do

> 'Work is love made visible'
>
> (Freud)

Work is one of the main channels through which we can enrich our lives. The aim of this chapter is to help you think about the place of work in your own life, whether career is central to your Mission or primarily a means of supporting another core area. By the end of this chapter, you will:

- *know your career orientation;*
- *be able to identify the kind of work that will prove most rewarding for you;*
- *have a new, creative way of approaching career planning.*

Preparatory reading: To get the most out of this chapter, you will need to have worked through the chapters on Principles 1–4. You will also need to be familiar with the MAP coaching model described in Part I.

Does your work inspire you? Does it stimulate your intellect, nourish your potential, and provide a rewarding outlet for your creativity? Or do you feel as though you have never quite found your niche, that you are misplaced in your line of work – or even that the working day is just one more thing to get through?

Neil, a good friend of mine, recently took the plunge and underwent a radical change of career. Having spent almost 25 years in the finance industry, he left to set up his own travel company – a decision that involved sacrificing a regular salary, pension, and company share scheme. It was a step into the unknown that required every ounce of his passion, courage, and self-belief. When he returned home after a five-month sabbatical, and by now with the anxiety biting at his heels, he contacted his former colleagues to alert them to his new venture. A response from one was particularly telling. "Great to hear from you," she e-mailed back. "It's amazing to think that you have gone off and actually *done* all this. Here we are, having yet another tedious day in the office." If ever Neil needed confirmation that he had done the right thing, this was it. For his former colleague, work life had continued in the same uneventful way it always had. But he was on an adventure of an altogether different kind.

The sad reality for many people is that work is a drain on their resources rather than a crucible for their potential. Of course, even great jobs have their downsides; if you are a natural entrepreneur or creative thinker, for example, you probably won't relish the admin generated by your great ideas. But when the tedious elements become too frequent or time-consuming, it's time to think again.

Think about your own working life. Consider all the different things that you do including both the work for which you get paid and any work that is salary-free (such as running a home, raising children, caring for family members, or doing voluntary work). List the different components in your learning log.

If you take all of these areas as a whole, how satisfying do you find your working life? If you were going to rate your satisfaction on a scale of 0 (totally unsatisfying) to 10 (totally satisfying), where would you place yourself?

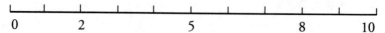

| 0 | 2 | 5 | 8 | 10 |

If you rated yourself anywhere between 8–10, then you should feel well pleased! You have a working life that is adding to your quality of life quite substantially. If you scored between 6–7, your working life may benefit from a review and a little tweaking. If you scored below six, however, your vocation definitely needs some clarification. Perhaps it's time to set your sights a little higher . . .

What is the 'perfect job'?

Knowing what you want from the workplace is vital to inspired working. But knowledge of your abilities, interests, and values is not in itself sufficient to ensure that your work remains a source of inspiration. Our working lives are embedded in a range of contexts that influence the ways in which our career choices manifest. These contexts present us with a range of potential opportunities and constraints that we must negotiate in order to arrive at a specific career plan.

In the past few decades, one of the biggest changes in Western career culture has been the shift away from employment towards employability. With the end of a 'jobs-for-life' culture and all the trappings that come with this, there is a strong argument for seeing ourselves as essentially self-employed. Even if you are in paid employment, more than ever before we are increasingly expected to take responsibility for our working lives.

This change in culture presents us with significant challenges, but it also creates unlimited opportunities. Taking control of our careers, professional learning, and development means that we need to be clear about what we want, what we have to offer, and the type of environment in which our talents and skills are most likely to be well received.

I believe that you are entitled to work in an environment where you feel respected, valued, and rewarded, where your talents, creativity, and motivation are able to flourish, and where you have the opportunity to use your potential in ways that benefit yourself and others. Whatever you do – whether you are on your way to the top of the career ladder, or have a working life organized around creating a comfortable home for your family, it makes no matter. This is your fundamental right.

In an ideal world, I believe your work should

- be interesting;
- allow you to express your skills and talents;
- provide a vehicle for expressing your creativity;
- challenge you to learn and grow;
- offer an appropriate level of independence;
- provide appropriate levels of support;

- give you feedback on your performance;
- reward your best efforts.

Let's look at these criteria in more detail. First, the work you do has to stimulate your interest. This doesn't mean that your intellect needs to be stimulated every minute of the working day, but that overall you find the nature of your work engaging. Second, it should give you opportunities to implement your knowledge, talents, skills, and creativity. Third, you need to feel challenged at a level that encourages you to learn and grow; too much challenge and you feel as though you are failing; too little and you soon become bored.

The opportunity for feedback is vital. When we've done well we need to know that others have noticed and appreciated our efforts. When there are areas of our performance that need improvement, we need to know this, too. We also need an optimum balance between autonomy (being micro-managed is frustrating for most of us) and appropriate dependence (being thrown in at the deep end without sufficient training or support is disempowering). Finally, meaningful work should bring tangible rewards – not just in the external sense (although this is often highly rewarding!) but also internally through the satisfaction that comes from seeing ourselves develop and achieve.

But the perfect type of work for an individual is not just about following objective criteria. It is also about the mindset we bring to it and the extent to which we are willing to contribute our own resources to our working lives.

Develop your career 'MAP'

In his book *The Work We Were Born to Do*, Nick Williams describes how we need a vision that enables us to share the best of ourselves in the workplace. From my perspective, this comes from knowing and having defined your Mission, cultivating the right type of Attitude so that you can appreciate opportunities that are available to you, and being able to design a Process to help you implement your intention. In other words, to design a working lifestyle that is optimally fulfilling, you need a career-focused 'MAP'.

Below is what our coaching framework – 'MAP' – looks like in relation to career decisions.

Mission: *General.* Your sense of purpose, the vision you have for your life, what you are aiming for and why it matters to you.
              Career specific. What is your Mission in relation to your professional or working life? What purpose does your career serve? What is your overall vision for your working life? What results do you hope to achieve in the long-term?

Attitude: *General.* The outlooks, perspectives and beliefs that you bring to your life, as well as the attitudes and perspectives you need to succeed.
              Career specific. What are your beliefs about and attitudes towards working life? What Perspectives underpin your Mission? What values, beliefs, models, prior learning and knowledge do you bring to your career at this time in your life? How might you need to expand them, based on the ideas we looked at in Principles 5–8?

Process: *General.* The methods, tools, procedures and techniques you need to get from where you are now to where you want to be.
              Career specific. Based on your Mission and Attitude, what is the Process you need to use to get to where you want to be? What specific steps do you need to take? How could you design a way of getting there, drawing on the tools and skills you learned in Principles 9–12?

One of the advantages of using MAP is that thinking about the why, what, and how of your career can help you identify features of yourself, your circumstances, and your context that you might have overlooked. By revisiting your Mission, you can become clear about the 'why' of your work and where it fits into your overall list of priorities.

Reviewing your Mission: where does career fit in your list of priorities?

Before you can make informed decisions about what you want from your career, you need to ask yourself some fundamental questions that relate to the Mission you uncovered in Principles 1–4. How much of yourself do you have invested in your career? To what extent do you see your work as a source of meaning in your life? How much of your identity is based on what you do for a living? Is career essential to your Mission, or simply a means to support another kind of purpose, such as raising a family or pursuing an extra-curricular passion?

There are no right or wrong answers here, but there will be answers that are more or less true for you at this point in your life. There might also be more or less helpful influences that are guiding your choices. For example, in his book *Lifeshift*, occupational psychologist Andrew Ferguson points out that many of us rely on our careers to bolster our sense of self-worth. If this is true for you, this might leave you vulnerable to burnout or, if you are made redundant, stress or depression.

Moreover, if your desire for a career comes from a false self (the type of self we looked at in Principle No 1, which comes from trying to be the kind of person you think you should be) any decisions about your working life will never feel truly satisfying because they are coming from beliefs you have internalized about what it means to be successful that may not reflect your own. So, as you work through this chapter, make sure you are very honest with yourself about what you expect your working life to achieve for you, the extent to which you believe it defines who you are, and what you would be willing to sacrifice for creating a successful and rewarding career (such as free time, leisure pursuits, contact with family).

Exercise 30. Working out your priorities

To help you identify the role of career in your life, think about where you would place it on your list of priorities by rating each of the points below from 0–10, where 0 = of no importance and 10 = of vital importance. (Copy this into your learning log.

Remember, no one else needs to see this apart from you and you'll get more out of it if you are totally honest with yourself.)

1. Career or work life
   0   1   2   3   4   5   6   7   8   9   10

2. Relationship with spouse/partner
   0   1   2   3   4   5   6   7   8   9   10

3. Relationship with children
   0   1   2   3   4   5   6   7   8   9   10

4. Extended family and social life
   0   1   2   3   4   5   6   7   8   9   10

5. Plenty of free time
   0   1   2   3   4   5   6   7   8   9   10

6. Maintaining a healthy work–life balance
   0   1   2   3   4   5   6   7   8   9   10

7. Commitments to activities outside of work   (e.g., charity work, political activities, church)
   0   1   2   3   4   5   6   7   8   9   10

8. Leisure interests and pursuits
   0   1   2   3   4   5   6   7   8   9   10

Helpful hint. You might also find it helpful to review your Inspiration Inventory in Chapter One. Do your satisfaction ratings give you any clues about where your priorities lie in relation to work?

What do your answers tell you? Were they what you expected, or did you discover anything that surprised you? Were there any conflicting ideas between what you thought you should want and what you really want?

See also if your profile of results gives you any clues about the type of work you are likely to find rewarding, including whether you are most likely to feel fulfilled by having a single career focus, or a working life made up of multiple components. Listed below are some of the different ways in which you might choose to design your working life, depending on the role of career in your own life.

- Choosing to have a full-time, organization-based career.
- Choosing self-employment within a single industry.
- Choosing to start your own company.
- Developing a portfolio or peripatetic career in which you combine projects that relate to one, or several fields of expertise.
- Combining paid employment or self-employment with being a homemaker, parent or carer.
- Combining paid employment or self-employment with voluntary work, holding unpaid positions within charities, professional bodies, the church or the wider community.

In addition to these different ways of structuring employment, it is possible to play out a variety of roles at work – for example, having a generic role exercising a broad range of skills (typical of the expertise demonstrated in administrative and secretarial work) or becoming a technical specialist (such as a scientist). You might be a supervisor, trainer, or manager of others, and may combine these with other life roles such as parenting, being a carer, volunteer work, and holding positions within the wider community.

If you review your own working history, you may identify with several categories at different points in your life according to the choices you made or circumstances that were thrust upon you. You will probably find that your career has not been static but has evolved according to the professional climate, how you have chosen to use your skills and talents, your evolving Mission, and your responsibilities to self and others. In this sense, your professional self is an unfolding vision of who you are and who you might become that requires regular revisiting and updating.

Know your Attitude: discover your career orientation

It is possible that we have more influence over how our careers unfold than we often assume. I am not, of course, suggesting that success or lack of it is entirely of our own making, as there are many factors beyond our control that influence the outcome of our work-related efforts. But recognizing our own authority is a reminder that we live our working lives through the filter of beliefs we have inherited from our families, peer group, and society. If we peel away the layers of everything we have ever been taught about work, of all the beliefs we have inherited from our family, peer group, and society, we are better able to connect with our Mission and decide how we want to implement this in the world of work.

Peeling back the layers is both an opportunity and a challenge. When we start to engage with this process, we can see that there are multiple ways of creating a working life that might not fit comfortably with the received wisdom of our family or social group.

What ideas have you inherited about the place of work in a person's life? From whom? What have you been taught (directly or indirectly) about the relationship between career and identity? Career and self-worth? What beliefs do you have about the nature of 'important' work and 'less important' work? Record your answers in your learning log.

You may have been tempted to come up with 'politically correct' answers in which all types of work are of equal value and there is no relationship between career and worth. But I want you to delve more deeply than this in order to access that part of yourself that holds more hidden assumptions. Our culture bombards us with all kinds of pernicious messages about career that will have permeated your choices and beliefs at a subtle (or not so subtle) level. And as these are the attitudes that might tempt you into making unhelpful choices, I want you to get to know them well. So revisit your answers to the exercise above, until you are clear you know those attitudes that might help and hinder you.

If you start to tease apart those ideas you have inherited from those which come from your authentic self, some interesting possibilities start to emerge. For example, you might choose to alter your mindset (Principles 5–8) and, in doing so, become aware of opportunities that exist within your current work settings that you had previously overlooked. You might be able to recognize that your efforts make more of a contribution than you realized. Or you might become more open to learning new skills that can pave the way for finding a job elsewhere.

To help you consider your options, I want to introduce you to two models, drawn from career theory, that can alert you to your own career orientation. These models are not mutually exclusive, so each one might illuminate something special about you and the contribution you want to make in the workplace.

What is your career 'type'?

When considering what you want to get from your working life, it helps to have a good idea of your motivations, interests, strengths, and needs (you might want to refer back to your signature strengths in Principle No. 3).

According to career theorist J. L. Holland, we are most likely to be professionally fulfilled when we are doing work that is consistent with our interests and values. Holland proposes that each of us, as well as the settings in which we work, fall into six types or combination of types. The closer the match between what we have to offer and the context in which we offer it, the greater our satisfaction and chances of success. The six types Holland identifies are outlined below. See which ones relate to you.

1. *Realistic*: The realistic type sees themselves as practical and having manual and mechanical skills. They value material rewards for tangible accomplishments. They tend to prefer occupations involving the use of machines, tools, and objects.
2. *Investigative*: The investigative type sees themselves as analytical, intelligent, sceptical and academically talented. They value the development or acquisition of knowledge. They prefer occupations involving exploration and understanding, prediction or control of natural and social phenomena.
3. *Artistic*: The artistic type sees themselves as innovative and intellectual. They value the creative expression of ideas, emotions and sentiments and tend to prefer occupations involving literary, musical or artistic activities.
4. *Social*: The social type sees themselves as empathic, patient and having interpersonal skills. They value supporting the welfare of others and service to the community and/or society. They prefer occupations involving helping, teaching, treating or counselling.
5. *Enterprising*: The enterprising type sees themselves as having sales and persuasive ability. They value material accomplish-

ment and social status. They prefer activities and occupations that involve persuading, manipulating or directing others.

6. *Conventional*: The conventional type sees themselves as having technical skills in business or production. They value material or financial accomplishment and power in social, business or political arenas. They prefer activities and occupations that involve establishing or maintaining orderly routines, and the application of standards.

What stands out for you? Based on your Mission, what type are you and how does this fit with your work environment? Do you have a match or a mismatch? How does your type help explain choices you have made in relation to your professional life, to date? Write the answers to these questions in your learning log.

Another helpful model for thinking creatively about your career is Ed Schein's 'Anchors' theory. Anchors theory suggests that as a person's career and life unfolds, there is a gradual clarification of self-image in relation to interests, values, and talents. Schein sees this as a process of finding a 'career anchor'. The 'anchor' is that set of needs, values, and talents which the person is least willing to give up if forced to make a choice.

There are eight career anchors from which to choose. You may feel that several or even all of these anchors are relevant to you, but holding in mind your Mission, which one would you prioritize above all others?

1. *Technical/functional competence*: what you would not give up is the opportunity to apply, and continue to develop, skills and knowledge in your area of expertise. You derive your sense of identity from the exercise of your skills and are most happy when your work permits you to be challenged in your specialist area.

2. *General managerial competence*: what you would not give up is the opportunity to climb to a level high enough in an organization to enable you to integrate others' efforts across functions and to be responsible for the output of a particular unit of the organization.

3. *Autonomy/independence*: what you would not give up is the opportunity to define your own work in your own way. If you are in an organization, you want to remain in jobs that allow

215

you flexibility regarding when and how you work. You may even seek to have a business of your own in order to achieve a sense of autonomy.

4. *Security/stability*: what you would not give up is employment security or tenure in a job or organization. Your main concern is to achieve a sense of having succeeded so that you can relax.

5. Entrepreneurial creativity: what you would not give up is the opportunity to create an organization on your own initiative, built on your own abilities and your willingness to take risks and to overcome obstacles.

6. *Service/dedication to a cause*: what you would not give up is the opportunity to pursue work that achieves something of value, such as making the world a better place to live, solving environmental problems or helping others.

7. *Pure challenge*: what you would not give up is the opportunity to work on solutions to seemingly unsolvable problems, to win out over tough opponents, or to overcome difficult obstacles.

8. *Lifestyle integration*: what you would not give up is a situation that permits you to balance your personal needs, your family needs, and the requirements of your career. You need a career situation that provides enough flexibility to achieve such integration. [Schein, 1990, pp. 58–60]

What would you say is your main career anchor? To what extent does it fit with the different contexts in which you work? For example, if your 'career anchor' is security/stability but the organization in which you work emphasises entrepreneurial creativity, you might feel like a square peg in a round hole. Write your thoughts in your learning log.

Your career anchor may be different at various points in your life, but for the purposes of your self-coaching what matters most is where you are now. If you know your type and career anchor, you are in a stronger position to make wise and satisfying choices in relation to your career. Put your insights to the test by completing Exercise 31.

Exercise 31. What satisfies you?

Think of a time when you were most satisfied in your working life. Remember as many aspects of the situation as you can. What kind of work were you doing, and in what context? Think about the people, the setting, the skills and talents you were exercising, how success was rewarded, etc., and write these down in your learning log.

Now think of a time when you were least satisfied with your working life. Remember as many aspects of the situation as you can. What kind of work were you doing, and in what context? What made it feel so negative for you? Think about the people, the setting, the skills and talents you were exercising and not able to exercise, how success was rewarded and so on, and write these in your learning log.

Review your answers carefully – they provide an important clue about the kinds of work that will prove most satisfying. Are you someone, for example, who values a high level of autonomy? Or who values a steady, consistent workload? Do you thrive on using your technical expertise in a specialised setting, or need the challenge of variety? Do you enjoy managing others or prefer working alone? What do your answers tell you about your 'type', your career anchors, and your career orientation? How might you need to take account of your type and career anchor in the future (for example, through choice of work, combination of jobs and roles, continuing professional development and non-work roles and hobbies)?

Design your Process

By now you should have an emerging sense of what type of career context is likely to prove most rewarding for you. For example, your Mission (Principles 1–4) may lead you to suspect that an enterprising career will be the most rewarding career trajectory, offering high prestige roles in ways that enable you to develop your natural leadership and strong interpersonal skills. Alternatively, your career anchor may highlight a desire for autonomy and independence. The sense of reward that comes from selecting projects that stimulate your interest and the freedom to establish your own working patterns will perhaps point you towards seeking out networks of likeminded colleagues, rather than living your working life within a single organization.

Of course, knowing all this is not sufficient to create a working life that remains rewarding in the longer term. In order to turn your vision into a reality you have to design a Process that will get you from where you are now to where you want to be. You have to identify specific goals that will take you in the right direction, harness your creativity, and keep your motivation on track (particularly if your vision involves some big career changes that need to take place over months rather than weeks). You will also need to understand the social, political, economic, and global context in which you are immersed in order to make your particular skills attractive to potential employers or clients.

Turning preferences into choices: how will I get there?

To help you identify suitable goals, I want to invite you to complete two very detailed exercises with me (helpful hint: this can be quite a rich and detailed piece of work, so if you need some guidance contact a qualified occupational psychologist or coach. You will find a list of organizations at the end of this book).

The first exercise is called 'Constructing Your CV'. When we think about constructing a CV (a curriculum vitae in the traditional sense of the term), most of us think about the type of document we would send to a prospective employer, where we tailor what we reveal to meet what we imagine are the requirements. However, for the purpose of this exercise, it helps to take a fresh approach. Imagine that 'CV' stands for 'Creative Victory' and the record you compile reflects your skills, accomplishments, victories, talents, and character qualities – in other words, your own unique brand.

Julianne's story

At the start of our work together, I often invite my clients to obtain a notebook into which they can record summaries of our work together as well as any thoughts or insights they have. Most people buy one. However, Julianne decided to create a more personalized version. She obtained a plain scrapbook and then proceeded to decorate the cover with pictures and images cut out of magazines, each of which reflected some aspect of the journey she had embarked upon. As her journey continued, her scrapbook developed into a blaze of colour, photos, diagrams, and codes. It was a joy to see not only because it was an example of her highly developed creativity, but also because it was a hallmark of her authentic self.

So, when constructing your CV, feel free to adopt a method that honours your authentic style (or a style with which you would like to experiment). Type words into a PC by all means, if this is how you express yourself best. But also feel free to draw it, colour code it, write poems or stories about it, use photos, include quotations, insert copies of certificates, thank you cards, appraisals, or business plans – in fact anything that seems relevant to your Creative Victories over the years. Put your evidence in a diary or scrapbook, use electronic media, or put together a collage: whatever feels as though it is honouring the essence of you.

When you think about what to include in your CV, however, I do want to offer you some guidelines. In particular, make sure you give some space to the following.

- Your authentic self, the things that you are passionate about, your values, your signature strengths, and your capacity for courage (so you aren't tempted to censor your responses).
- Any beliefs, attitudes, and outlooks that have contributed to your successes so far.
- Your skills, accomplishments, and talents (whatever form these take).
- The different jobs and/or careers that have made up your working life so far.
- Your life journey so far, including the myriad experiences from which you have learnt.
- What you most want to contribute through your efforts.
- How you most want your work to impact on others.

This task may take you days, weeks or months, depending on what you want to gain from it. But as the project unfolds, see what you can learn. Although your CV will have a much more detailed summary of all of this, write any key themes in your learning log.

Identify your areas of learning[1]

When you have your CV, I want you to examine it thematically. What recurring themes do you notice that you can group into core areas? For example, you may discover that a recurring theme is you have learned how to resolve difficult situations. You may have found yourself being the person to whom members of your family turn to resolve conflicts; you may have found yourself arbitrating neighbours disputes, or effectively settling arguments between your children. You may have held a position as a mediator, advocate, or magistrate. On closer inspection, you discover that there is a theme in your life – that you keep a cool head in a crisis and are able to resolve conflicts and difficulties in a way that others cannot. This is an area of learning that you have accomplished.

Spend time sifting through your CV and identifying any core areas of learning. Write two column headings, 'Core area of learning', and 'Description of experiences relevant to this area of learning' in your learning log, and write in each column the relevant information from your background.

You will no doubt discover that you have developed a great deal of skill and knowledge over the years, and so have probably identified a number of critical themes. But, given that your areas of learning represent your personal brand of expertise, you need to pay particular attention to those that are relevant to where you want to go in the future, based on an understanding of your Mission and Attitude towards career. Consider, for example:

- what core areas of learning might form the basis of your working life?
- what forms of work – paid and unpaid – might allow you to use these areas to the full?
- how could you introduce them into different aspects of your working life? Can they be accommodated into your existing career or are more radical changes to your job or career path needed?
- what would you need to do to take these forward?

Keep pondering these questions and notice the answers that begin to emerge. They may come at once or take several months to crystallize.

Once you are clear about what these are, you can begin to design a way to get there. The final exercise in this chapter offers you a series of questions to guide you in your planning.

Exercise 32. Designing a way forward

Based on your Mission, Attitude and core areas of learning, what kind of Process do you want to design?

- What type of work would be most meaningful for you, given your current life stage? How would this fit with your own career 'type' and 'career anchor'?
- What specific steps do you now need to take to turn your preferences into a reality (think SMART)?
- What skills, knowledge, and abilities do you have already that you could draw upon to help you get there?
- What skills, knowledge, and abilities do you now need to acquire?
- What organizations, groups, or networks would support you? Who are the most significant people that can offer you guidance and advice (e.g., managers, mentors, partners, or social and professional contacts)?
- How might you find out about new job/work opportunities within your chosen field?
- What practical challenges do you anticipate pursuing your chosen direction will involve (e.g., potential loss of income if you change career direction)? How will you manage them?
- What motivational challenges do you anticipate pursuing this will involve (e.g., receiving rejection letters; losing out to the competition)? How will you manage them?

The take home message

In our rapidly changing professional, social, and economic world, where the notion of a job for life now seems like a quaint idea from the distant past, having a career will mean different things at different stages in our lives. It will also vary according to our fields of expertise, family responsibilities, and extra-curricular commitments.

221

However, if you take ownership of your working life, you can create the inner freedom to approach your career from different perspectives. This might lead you to re-evaluate the settings in which you work, appraising what is on offer rather than assuming you have no choice but to settle. You might find yourself contemplating how your learning and creativity are enabled and constrained by the different contexts in which you work. You might also widen your knowledge of potential career opportunities in similar or unrelated fields by talking to family, friends, and social contacts about the nature of their work.

As you contemplate your career options, you might also find it helpful to use the ideas in the Coaching Tool Box.

Coaching Tool Box. Reflective Career Planning: Suggestions to Guide your Thinking

1.   Have a long-term vision of how you want your career to look (it doesn't matter if it changes; having a long-term vision helps you make the right decisions for now).
2.   Define your career Mission and Attitude clearly before deciding on a plan of action (Process) to implement them.
3.   Challenge any outdated beliefs about what your career can help you accomplish (e.g., don't confuse career success with personal worth). Make decisions based on the values and priorities of the authentic self.
4.   Conduct a regular audit of your strengths, limits, and core areas of learning. Consider how to promote your learning (e.g., through acquiring new knowledge, new technology, joining new networks of colleagues, attending a course/conference).
5.   Be aware of how the different strands of your working life impact on you at all levels. In what ways do they facilitate and constrain your choices? How could you capitalize on the opportunities and manage any constraints?
6.   Build relationships with like-minded others who have made the kinds of career choices you find most appealing. Link up with them for ideas, feedback, and support.

As Professor Steven Rose, one of Britain's best known scientists, reminds us, we each have the ability to create our own futures, even if this is not always in circumstances of our own choosing. I hope that, by using the ideas and exercises in this chapter, you might be empowered to develop a personalized career plan that reflects a broader vision of yourself, your potential, and your contribution to the world in which you live.

Creating The Inspired Career

One idea I shall take away from this chapter is . . . (write the answer in your learning log).
One thing I will do differently to add value to my career is . . . (write the answer in your learning log).

Note

1. This exercise is based on original work by the Professional Development Foundation. It is adapted here with permission.

Bibliography

*Ferguson, A. (1999). *Lifeshift: Doing the Dream*. Moray: Breakthrough.

Holland, J. L. (1996). Exploring careers with a typology: what we have learned and some new directions. *American Psychologist*, *51*(4): 397–406.

PDF Net and Professional Development Foundation (2005). Further information and contact details online. Available at www.pdf.net.

Schein, E. H. (1990). *Career Anchors. Discovering your Real Values*. San Francisco, CA: Jossey-Bass Pfeiffer.

*Williams, N. (2004). *The Work We Were Born to Do. Find the Work You Love, Love the Work You Do*. London: Element.

CHAPTER TWENTY-TWO

Achieving an Optimum
Work–Life Balance

'A man who dares to waste one hour of life
has not discovered the value of life'

(Charles Darwin)

*In this chapter, we will examine one of modern life's biggest challenges:
how to achieve a healthy work–life balance. In helping you decide
what this means for you, we will explore:*

- *four golden rules of a great work-life balance;*
- *tools for enhancing your time management skills.*

Preparatory reading. To get the most out of this chapter, you will
need to have a clear idea of your Mission, so make sure you have
read Principle Nos. 1–4 of MAP. You will also need to know how
to set goals, so recap this now in Principle No. 9.

Do you often feel as though there simply aren't enough hours in
the day? Or that you are constantly running just to keep up? Does
free time seem like a far-distant memory or a luxury that you can't
afford? If so, then this chapter is for you.

In the fast-paced, pressure-generating gridlock of the twenty-
first century, we often think of material wealth as being the one
thing that everyone craves. But I think this is a myth. In my experience, the one thing of which most of us feel deprived is time.
We're preoccupied with it, crave more of it, buy time-saving
gadgets to help us acquire it, and plan our days around trying to

capitalize on it. And yet for all our efforts, our schedules often seem more tightly packed than ever.

Think about your typical week and notice how many timetables rule your life, whether it's catching the train to work, attending meetings, collecting the children from school or achieving project deadlines. Also notice how many time-saving devices you use – e-mails, mobile phones, and microwave ovens – all designed to enable you to do more and more in less and less time.

When I meet a client for the first time, I ask them about what their day looks like and where and how their time is spent. Given that time is so central to our lives, it is interesting that very few people can actually account for their precious hours, although most of them would acknowledge that achieving a healthy and rewarding work–life balance is very important.

The quality of our lives is closely related to how we manage our time. So before reading on, take a few moments to think about your own work–life balance using the exercise below:

Exercise 33. Your work–life balance

- How would you describe your current work–life balance?
- To what extent are you satisfied with the time you can devote to the different, core areas of your life?
- How do you try to manage your time to best advantage? What methods do you use?
  - In what ways are these methods effective?
  - In what ways are they ineffective?
- How often do you make time to relax and unwind?
- What would an optimum work-life balance look like for you, at this point in your life?

Write your responses to these questions in your learning log.

What is a good work–life balance?

Life today is a balancing act. Multiple demands are made upon us at home as well as work and we all have to manage diverse roles that often appear to conflict – to give more time to one means to detract time from another. Look at the grid in Figure 3 and see if

Relationships	*Work*
1. Partner/spouse	1. Career
2. Children	2. Professional development and promotion
3. Family	3. Working hours (official and unofficial)
4. Friends	4. Household chores
5. Community	5. Managing personal affairs
6. Contribution to the world around you (local or global)	6. Finances
Health and well-being	*Personal space*
1. Exercise	1. Personal development
2. Sleep	2. Free time
3. Diet	3. Leisure interests
4. Use of alcohol and caffeine	4. Entertainment and fun
5. Physical relaxation	5. Going out
6. Personal grooming	6. Quiet moments to reflect, pray, or simply be in the moment

Figure 3. The grid of life.

the different quadrants are equally proportioned in your life – or if one area tends to dominate the others.

If you have a healthy balance, there will be time for each of these different areas. Of course, some areas within each quadrant may be more central to your life than others. Or a particularly busy period in one area of your life (such as having to pull out all the stops to meet a project deadline) may cause you to neglect certain areas of your life for a limited period. A healthy work–life balance doesn't mean dogmatically assigning equal priority to all things all of the time, but rather ensuring that there is room for each broad domain in a way that is satisfying and sustaining.

There are many reasons why achieving a good work–life balance is so important. One is that it enables you to honour your Mission more completely. If you are wasting your precious time pursuing goals and activities that are not a reflection of what really matters to you, then your life will feel hollow. A good work–life balance also enables you to:

- enjoy and appreciate life more fully;
- have more time for the people who matter;
- have time for hobbies and leisure interests;
- respect your health by creating time for rest, exercise, healthy eating and good habits;
- have quiet time to yourself;
- pursue realistic and achievable goals in different areas of your life;
- enjoy each day, rather than putting your life on hold for some future date;
- remember that every day is precious and life is too short to squander.

The golden rules of balancing your work and your life

To an extent, living in the fast lane is the reality of living in the modern world. But we do have some choices. There are four golden rules that you need to know in order to achieve a work–life balance that works for you. These are as follows.

1. Knowing how you *actually* spend your time (rather than how you *think* you spend your time).
2. Being clear about your priorities.
3. Doing the most important things first.
4. Treating your time as your most precious resource.

1. Know how you actually spend your time

How do you spend your time? Do you know? Very often we get locked into patterns of thinking and behaving that we never stop to question. It is as though somewhere along the line we slipped into automatic pilot and have been following the same route ever since, without stopping to question whether or not we actually want to go there.

If your work–life balance needs improvement, then the first step is working out where exactly your time is going. Fortunately, you can do this quite easily with a tool called the 'Weekly Activity Diary'.

The Weekly Activity Diary gives you a bird's-eye view of exactly what you pack into each and every day. It tells you at a glance how much time is being devoted to work, extra-curricular activities, managing the practicalities of your life and mind-wasting activities (such as channel hopping when watching the television).

Have a look at the Weekly Activity Diary at the end of this chapter. You'll see that the day is split into hourly segments. All you need to do is write your main activity for that particular hour. For example, if you get up, shower, and dress between 7–8 a.m., write 'getting up' in that box. If you spend two hours commuting from 6–8 p.m., write 'travelling home from work'. Each box only needs the main activity for that particular hour. Remember to include everything you do – watching TV, shopping, travelling, organizing your paperwork, using the internet, eating and sleeping are all activities that make demands on your time.

Once you know exactly how your time is being spent, you can sift through your daily routine and decide which areas are being used productively and which are not. How much of your time is spent on meaningful activities? How much time is being wasted on 'empty activities' (that is, activities that aren't contributing something worthwhile or entertaining to your day)? To what extent does your use of time honour your Mission? What adjustments do you need to make?

Grace's story

Grace's story illustrates how you do not necessarily need to make huge changes to reap significant benefit.

When she first came to see me, Grace was exhausted. She worked full time for an insurance company in addition to running a home and raising two teenage children. She was also the main carer for her elderly parents, whom she would visit twice weekly after work and at the weekend. Time for her? Forget it! It was, she told me, a luxury she couldn't afford. 'When I can clone myself,' she laughed, '*then* we can talk about relaxation!'

And yet, Grace knew she could not continue at her current pace. With no time to refuel, she was burning out fast. Her health was suffering, and if she became unwell she would no longer be able to care for her parents.

Grace's story is a familiar one in that she had multiple responsibilities that seemed to pull her in conflicting directions. She needed to work, and indeed valued her career, but she also saw raising her children and caring for her parents as part of her Mission. The situation felt hopeless because she thought she knew exactly how she was spending her time. The most time-consuming aspect of her week was, she told me, visiting her parents, cooking for them, taking care of their paperwork, and chauffeuring them to various appointments.

However, after a week of keeping the Activity Diary, Grace discovered something surprising. Outside of work, the bulk of her time was not being spent caring for her parents, but running her own home – and in particular, cooking for and cleaning up after her two teenage children. The time that was spent juggling her work life and visiting her parents was less than she had assumed.

So Grace called a family meeting where she announced that some changes were needed. At first her children were resistant to the idea of having to contribute to the running of the household. But, armed with the results of her Activity Diary, Grace explained why things couldn't continue as they were. Her children admitted that they had been worried about her and this led to some positive discussions about how family life could be organized differently.

Both children accepted responsibility for tidying their rooms, Grace's daughter agreed to prepare dinner once a week and her son said he would visit his grandparents once a week instead of Grace. These changes may seem small, but they had a huge impact on Grace's quality of life. They also helped her children understand more about the responsibilities of adulthood.

However busy we are, our time is not necessarily used in the way we imagine. The results of her Weekly Activity Diary showed Grace that although her life was very busy, change was possible. True, her teenage children weren't initially delighted at the prospect of having to clear up after themselves, but they didn't want a mother who was under so much stress that she became ill.

2. Be clear about your priorities

If you have worked through Principles 1–4, then you should have no trouble being clear about your priorities. But do you honour them? This is the crunch. You need to sift through each new demand to work out exactly how it will contribute towards the vision you have for your life. If it does have something to offer, then it's a priority. If it doesn't, then it isn't, and you need to let it go. This will sometimes involve saying no to things that might have been fun or interesting because, if you are like most people, you do not have unlimited time. You need to select those tasks, projects, and opportunities that fit with the bigger picture. If they don't fit, then you need to move on. When you have a choice, choose to devote your time and energy *only* to those things that really matter.

Richard's story

Richard had recently started his own business. After years of working for someone else, he decided that he wanted the autonomy that came from being his own boss. He was an experienced management consultant who knew his field well and had a loyal client base.

But after three months, things weren't going to plan. He was not achieving the weekly goals he set himself and was slow at responding to business enquiries. Although he was working hard things were not getting done in a timely and productive fashion.

When Richard kept a Weekly Activity Diary, his suspicions were confirmed: he was indeed working hard, but he was getting sidetracked by other projects. For example, a former colleague had asked him to review a business plan, knowing Richard had expertise in the area, and he had devoted several hours to this project. He had also agreed to take on some extra work for his former employer to help out during a staffing crisis and he had spent a whole day helping a friend think about how to start her own company – all of which distracted Richard from his own business.

There was, of course, more to it than this. Because Richard felt anxious about setting up his own business, it was easy to spend time on projects that felt safe. Working on someone else's ideas for a business made Richard feel secure and validated because his friend was grateful for all his good ideas. And as long as he was focusing on someone else's needs he did not have to confront the discomfort that came from testing out his talents in a new arena. But the Weekly Activity Diary helped Richard see how this strategy had backfired. Once he understood this, he was free to devise a new strategy – which meant saying no to what didn't really matter.

3. Do the most important things first

Typically we stop doing the most important things first when we anticipate that those things will stir up some uncomfortable feelings or force us to examine some part of our lives that we don't want to face. Procrastinating or avoiding those things that really need doing might feel like a way of escaping certain uncomfortable feelings but it is a trap. Sooner or later you have to face what it is you have been avoiding.

When I was studying for my exams as a psychology student, I had a friend who had this strategy down to a fine art. Whenever it came to revising, she would experience an uncontrollable urge to do the housework. Every piece of clothing would be washed and ironed, the whole house would be dusted and vacuumed until – whoops! Another day had passed and she still hadn't opened her books.

My friend persuaded herself that once she had all the cleaning, dusting, vacuuming, and ironing out of the way, she would then get down to her revision. Her family had never known the place so clean! But deep down she knew that it was a way of trying to avoid the discomfort of exam preparation. It was an attempt to avoid the inevitable.

I learnt a lot from my friend's story. Now, if there is something I find myself resisting, something that really gets my stomach in knots, I commit myself to doing it first. If this is not humanly possible, then I work out exactly when I am going to tackle it and make a note of the date and time in my diary. If the task is tough, I know I only make myself feel worse by putting it off and getting it done gives my confidence a boost – at least it's one less thing to do. You can save a great deal of time and energy just by tackling the important things first.

Exercise 34. Tackle the big things first

Have you ever been in a situation where you knew you had to do something really important but just couldn't bring yourself to do it? Is this a problem for you right now? If it is, write a brief description in your learning log of what it is you are avoiding.

What if you committed yourself to doing whatever it is you are avoiding – regardless of how you feel? What if, just on this occasion, you chose to overrule procrastination and just do it? Why not treat this as an experiment to find out what really happens (rather than living life based on what you think will happen)?

Identify what it is that you need to tackle and then rate your level of anxiety or discomfort, where 0 = no discomfort and 10 = maximum discomfort. Then re-rate your level of anxiety or discomfort after you have done it. Are there any changes? Was the task any more enjoyable for putting it off? Or did you feel more energized and empowered simply by having tackled it?

4. Treat your time as your most precious resource

Let's do the maths. There are only 24 hours in a day and 168 hours in a week. A year consists of 8,760 hours. If you live to the age of 70, you will have 613,200 hours available to you. If you are 40 now, that leaves you with only 262,800 hours to live. That's all. The clock is ticking, so please use these precious hours wisely. They are all you have.

Signs that you are not respecting your time include the following.

- Over-committing. You take on too many things, and know you are taking on too many things but tell yourself you'll find the time somehow.
- Finding it hard to say 'no' to requests (even though every cell in your body is screaming at you to give yourself a break).
- Feeling guilty about taking a day off.
- Neglecting your needs for rest and relaxation.
- Failing to make quality time for family and friends.

Being busy is a contemporary addiction and behind this addiction lies an equally sinister and pervasive theme. Best-selling author Stephen Covey reminds us of a pervasive and dangerous myth operating in our culture: that being busy means we are important. As a result, filling our time from morning to night gives us a sense of security. It can also be a great way of avoiding other areas of our life that need some attention (such as health matters or a relationship issue).

If you find it difficult to respect your time, see if there is something deeper going on. It may be that you find it hard to say no for fear of upsetting people (notice the link with some of the ideas we talked about in the authenticity chapter). Or you may have nagging doubts about your sense of self-worth without the trappings of your accomplishments (if so, you'll benefit from Chapter Twenty-three on building self-esteem); your over-striving is an attempt to compensate for doubts about your competency or worth.

So, if this is true of you, try to work out what is missing. What don't you trust within yourself that leads you to believe you can never take your foot off the accelerator? Whose formula of success are you attempting to follow by throwing yourself into something that will undermine your emotional well-being and your physical health? Whatever the reason, remember that you cannot be all things to all people, nor should you attempt to be.

Improve your productivity – some additional pointers

Being busy is not the same thing as being productive. Great productivity is the result of knowing the right thing to do, at the right time and with just the right amount of effort. If you are clear about your priorities, attend to the most pressing tasks first, respect your time and honour your emotional and physical needs, you have a healthy formula for achieving a great work–life balance – not to mention a greatly enhanced productivity.

A good weekly routine will include space for:

- eating well (including making time to prepare healthy and nourishing meals);
- sleeping well (including having a 'wind down' routine at the end of the day);
- regular exercise;

- breaks during the working day;
- time for fun;
- time for being with the people who matter;
- 'quiet time' for prayer (if this is important to you) and/or time to be alone.

Exercise 35. Your work–life health check

Look over the results from your Weekly Activity Diary.

- Which areas need more time?
- Which areas need less?
- Are there any areas of your life that feel like time wasted? (This doesn't mean you have to be busy all the time but refers to those areas that don't feel rewarding, relaxing, or meaningful for you.) How could you reduce these to create space for more meaningful pursuits?
- Which obligations no longer bring joy to your life, or bring you unnecessary stress?
- How could you incorporate more of the things that really matter to you?

Remember, the aim is not to make your life more hectic but to identify those spaces that are not being used wisely and self-respectfully.

Don't compartmentalize – synthesize!

Achieving an effective work–life balance relies on your ability to streamline your life. The most effective way to do this is to ensure that your tasks, projects, and responsibilities are synthesized. Everything should be singing to the same tune, working towards the same purpose, and honouring your signature strengths.

Rachel, a minister of a local Christian church who also works in secular employment, once told me that she had complained to her spiritual director how difficult she found juggling so many different elements of life. 'No,' he said to her. 'Not juggling, but weaving together.'

Personal development author Steve Pavlina agrees. As he explains,

> When you view your life as a series of different compartments, each with different rules, then life gets pretty complicated. Trying to achieve balance is very difficult because you constantly feel the need to task switch. My relationship needs attention. Oh no, I've been neglecting my health. I need to work harder. I've got to stop thinking so much and take more action. The different 'bins' of your life are all fighting for your time. And the longer you neglect one of those bins, the louder it gets and the harder it will fight for attention.

He poses the all-important question, 'What if your life had only one bin, one ball to juggle, one plate to spin?' If the different areas of our lives are consistent, then there is co-operation between them. Everything becomes interdependent and then our values, choices, and actions can become aligned. This, he suggests, is how different parts of our lives can be synthesized so that we can start to achieve congruence. We no longer need to balance work and life because they are not independent of each other but contribute to a whole.

How does each of your goals contribute to the overall fabric of your life? Is there alignment or are you spinning too many plates? Write your thoughts in your learning log – including any thoughts on what might need to change.

To do lists

Assuming you now know where you need to make changes, let's look at one very useful way of handling the practicalities.

One practice I recommend is to end each day by identifying and writing down your priorities for the next day. Five minutes is all you need to identify your priorities. (Remember that your list needs to include what matters most – not what feels most pleasant to do!) Include everything – chores as well as actions relating to your Mission – but whatever you put down, make sure it is realistic and manageable. It's no good including fifteen things if each one takes half an hour or more. See if you can do any preparation the night before, as well: for example, putting files out on your desk, locating relevant telephone numbers, or tidying up can all be time-savers for the following day.

If you are unfamiliar with list-making as a way of managing your time, set yourself only one or two goals per day to begin with. You can always increase the number later on. Work out how you are going to organize this. Will a note in your diary be sufficient or will you need a separate notebook? How about a sticky label on your fridge door? Find a system that works for you. Alternatively, you could use the form below.

Date		
Priority task	Task	Achieved? (tick)
1.		
2.		
3.		
4.		
5.		

At the end of each day, review your list and check what has been accomplished. Cross things off as you go to give you a sense of achievement. If there are any items you haven't completed, see what you can learn from this. Did you have too many tasks on your list? Get side-tracked by non-essential tasks? Was it really that important to begin with? (If it is, put it on tomorrow's list.)

Finally, set limits around your time. Work on something for a set period and then take a break. You do not need to do anything perfectly – good enough will be fine. And if there are things that need particularly high quality of attention, tackle it when you are at your most alert and creative, saving more routine jobs for when you are getting tired.

If you need some additional points to ponder, try the tips in the Coaching Tool Box below.

Coaching Tool Box: Top Tips for Achieving a Great Work–Life Balance

1. Keep your Mission at the forefront of your mind. Select only those opportunities that contribute to your sense of purpose.
2. Prioritize. Devote time and energy to what needs doing that day – tomorrow can take care of itself.
3. Do the most important things first (especially when you feel some resistance!).
4. Beware worrying about how much you have to do, as this drains your energy and prevents productive action. Deal with the negative thoughts first as you learnt to do in Principle No. 10.
5. Take short, regular breaks to prevent burnout.
6. Take regular holidays. Use up your holiday allowance if you are employed. Plan your annual breaks if self-employed. Regular breaks improve both productivity and sense of well-being.

Take home message

The solution to having a great work–life balance is knowing what really matters to you and prioritizing your efforts accordingly. This will be easier to accomplish if you recognize that your time on this earth is limited and the hours in the day are all you have. In the same way that you plan your finances, your holiday, or your career, plan how you want to use your time using tools such as the Weekly Activity Diary, attending to what matters first and using 'to do' lists. You owe it to yourself to use your precious hours wisely.

As the author Thomas Merton points out, to give in to too many demands and commit ourselves to too many tasks is to surrender to one of the main pressures of the modern world. Ultimately, it comes down to knowing who you are and what you stand for and gently challenging any sense of needing to be busy for unhealthy reasons. If you can give yourself permission to be true to yourself, your life will always be in balance.

Enjoying an Optimum Work–Life Balance

One thing I will take away from this chapter is . . . (write the answer in your learning log).
One thing I will try differently as a result of this chapter is . . . (write the answer in your learning log).

The Weekly Activity Diary

Time	Mon	Tues	Wed	Thurs	Fri	Sat	Sun
6–7 a.m.							
7–8 a.m.							
8–9 a.m.							
9–10 a.m.							
10–11 a.m.							
11 a.m.–12 noon							
12–1 p.m.							
1–2 p.m.							
2–3 p.m.							
3–4 p.m.							
4–5 p.m.							
5–6 p.m.							
6–7 p.m.							
7–8 p.m.							
8–9 p.m.							
9–10 p.m.							
10–11 p.m.							
11–12 p.m.							
12–1 a.m.							
1–2 a.m.							
2–3 a.m.							
3–4 a.m.							
4–5 a.m.							
5–6 a.m.							

Bibliography

*Covey, S. R. (1989). *The Seven Habits of Highly Effective People*. New York: Simon and Shuster.

CHAPTER TWENTY-THREE

Building Healthy Self-Esteem

'Let your own nature be proclaimed'

(Native American proverb)

In this chapter, we look at one of the essential components of inspired living: healthy self-esteem. Together we will explore:

- *the true nature of healthy self-esteem;*
- *how to manage the internal critic that prevents you from fulfilling your potential;*
- *ways of developing robust and enduring self-esteem.*

Preparatory reading. To get the most out of this chapter, you will need to have worked through the exercises in Authenticity (Principle No. 1), Signature Strengths (Principle No. 3), Compassion (Principle No. 8), and Thinking Skills (Principle No. 10).

Helpful hint. If self-esteem is a personal stumbling block, you may feel resistant to some of the ideas in this chapter. But don't be put off; objections may well indicate that the ideas are highly relevant to you.

Are you your strongest supporter or silent saboteur? Do you encourage yourself to think big or play at being small? When life is at its toughest, do you give yourself the encouragement and strength to continue or undermine your efforts with self-criticism and personal condemnation? When all is said and done, do you like the person that you are?

There's a famous Woody Allen joke about how his only regret in life is that he wasn't somebody else. In my work I often meet people who seem to have signed up to the Woody Allen philosophy of life. Stephan was one.

Stephan's story

Stephan wanted a partner more than anything else. But when he first came to see me, he had no doubt that he would remain single forever. The reason for this, he told me, was that anyone who got close to him would eventually find out the truth: that he was bad. Stephan had not actually committed any acts that he judged as bad. Rather, his badness related to a feeling deep inside of him, something he 'knew' to be true at the core of his being.

It was not difficult to understand how Stephan had reached such a devastating conclusion about himself. Raised in an environment where love was scarce, violence was frequent, and punishments were inflicted at random, he concluded early on in life that his parents reacted this way because they didn't love him. Because he knew that parents are 'supposed' to love their children, the fact that his didn't could mean only one thing: he was essentially bad.

Stephan's 'badness' felt very real to him. However, I saw a courageous, caring and gifted man – someone who was prepared to put himself through the pain of telling me his story and who, against all odds had been very successful. But Stephan struggled to see any of this. Unfortunately, because he had such a negative view of himself, he had always avoided meeting new people. However, he had now reached a stage where his desire for a relationship was so strong that hiding was no longer an option.

Justin's story

On the surface, Justin couldn't have been more different. He oozed confidence and self-assurance and announced proudly that his sales record at work was yet to be beaten. He had read extensive amounts of personal development books and from his research had concluded that he could 'be, do, and have anything he wanted, as long as he believed in himself enough'. For Justin, being, having, and doing anything he wanted meant having an outstanding career, the perfect relationship, and a life of financial freedom and luxury.

Justin did indeed, have a thriving career, a relationship with a woman who loved him, and a good salary that enabled him to enjoy a very comfortable lifestyle. But there was a problem. His belief that he could 'be, have, and do anything he wanted' led him to bulldoze his way to success. He didn't see any problem with his strategy, but his wife and colleagues did. His workaholic tendencies were undermining his marriage and his wife was threatening to leave him. Moreover, Justin's 'straight talking' approach was experienced by others as intimidating and he was now facing a disciplinary action at work because of his conduct. For the first time, Justin was forced to confront facts: his wife found him emotionally unavailable and his colleagues saw him as a bully.

Stephan and Justin may seem very different, but they were both struggling with fragile self-esteem. Stephan's sense of his own badness limited his life choices and prevented him from seeking out a partner with whom he could share his life. Justin's sense of inadequacy led him to over-compensate; the veneer of confidence papered over the cracks of a very shaky sense of self-worth.

The true nature of healthy self-esteem: taking a closer look

Healthy self-esteem enables us to live with purpose and confidence, but its qualities can be difficult to pin down. What would you see as the key ingredients? Use the next exercise to guide you.

Exercise 36. The ingredients of healthy self-esteem

Think of someone you know personally, whom you would regard as having high self-esteem, then answer the following questions in your learning log.

- What leads you to believe they have high self-esteem?
- How do they behave towards themselves and others?
- How do they conduct themselves in their daily lives?

- How do you feel when you spend time with them?
- Based on your assessment of that person, what would you see as being the key ingredients of robust self-esteem?

Now think of someone you know personally, whom you would judge as having low self-esteem, and answer the following questions.

- What leads you to believe they have low self-esteem?
- How do they behave towards themselves and others?
- How do they conduct themselves in their daily lives?
- How do you feel when you spend time with them?
- Based on your assessment of that person, what would you see as being the warning signs of low self-esteem?

There is a growing interest in self-esteem and a flourishing literature on how to build it. Much of this literature is very helpful, but it can sometimes be easy to come away with the idea that the higher your self-esteem, the happier and more successful you will be. Or even that if you believe in yourself enough you can conquer the world . . .

While positive self-belief is a wonderful, empowering quality, there is a serious problem with buying into a belief that our limitations exist solely inside our own heads and that with enough self-belief we can achieve anything, as Justin found out to his cost.

Healthy self-esteem is not about acquiring unshakable self-belief that will lead us to giddy heights of success. Nor is it about becoming so self-absorbed that we become self-satisfied and smug (we've all met people who are so convinced of their own self-importance that they are unbearable to be around – remember the mythical god Narcissus, who fell in love with his own reflection).

As psychologists Roy Baumeister and Kathleen Vohs suggest, healthy self-esteem consists of two key elements: (1) a sense of self-efficacy – that is, a faith in our abilities, competencies, and skills; trusting ourselves to handle life's challenges and a belief that our efforts can make a difference to the world and (2) a sense of self-worth – a positive, yet flexible and realistic self-evaluation, a deep-felt sense that we are essentially decent and appreciating our worth while acknowledging our limitations.

In a world where we are constantly confronted with new opportunities and challenges, it is helpful to see healthy self-esteem not so much as a static entity, but as a dynamic and ever-changing part of ourselves. In essence, self-esteem reflects the ongoing relationship we have with ourselves. In the same way that we learn to like or dislike other people through talking and listening to them, and by observing how they act, so we observe our own thoughts, feelings, and actions and decide whether or not we fundamentally respect and value the person that we are.

Our relationship with ourselves is a uniquely intimate one. It is, after all, only we who have access to the whole picture – the image we present to the world as well as the most private selves we daren't reveal to anyone. But, as with all relationships, it pays to review it objectively every now and then. Does your relationship with your own self nurture and support you, or has it become a stale or even destructive force in your life? Record your reactions in your learning log.

Healthy (and unhealthy) self-esteem: know the critical signs

Self-esteem affects how we feel, think, act, and experience the world. It influences our choice of partner and friends, whether or not we feel secure in our relationships and whether or not we choose to develop our potential. In this sense, our self-esteem – whether robust or fragile – triggers a chain reaction of physiological, emotional, and behavioural changes that reinforce our beliefs about who we are and what we can do. See if you can identify any potential chain reactions in the signs of healthy self-esteem listed below.

- You are generally positive and optimistic.
- You feel at peace with yourself most of the time.
- You have confidence in yourself, your competencies and skills.
- You are self-reliant.
- You feel energized and excited by life's opportunities.
- You take care of your physical and emotional needs.
- You appreciate others' strengths and talents without feeling threatened by them.

245

- You are appropriately open and honest with others.
- You are considerate towards others in your dealings with them.
- You tend to put others at their ease and bring out the best in them.

Now see if you can identify any potential chain reactions in the signs of fragile self-esteem.

- You rarely feel at peace with yourself or, alternatively, dislike the person that you are.
- You worry constantly about whether you are good enough in key areas of your life.
- You struggle to be self-reliant.
- You neglect your physical and emotional needs.
- You rarely give yourself time for relaxation and fun.
- You tend to burn yourself out with overwork.
- You feel tense and wound up most of the time.
- You feel threatened by others' successes and accomplishments.
- You try to be what you think others want you to be.
- You are so focused on yourself and your weaknesses that you tend to neglect your relationships and/or the needs of those around you.

> Health check. If any of these warning signs are so true for you that, on occasion, you feel the need to punish or harm yourself, please seek the support of someone who is professionally qualified to work with low self-esteem, such as a psychologist, psychotherapist or counsellor.

If you review the signs of healthy and unhealthy self-esteem, which ones feel relevant for you? Write your thoughts in your learning log.

Get to know who's running the show: competing voices, multiple selves

In the same way that unshakable self-belief can be problematic, so too can self-aversion. Both are extreme ways of viewing oneself that represent a shaky foundation for inspired living.

A teacher once told me that self-aversion is one of the biggest problems in our society today. This may sound extreme, but in a world that seems to demand so much and that is often so unforgiving of mistakes, it is all too easy to feel as though we are falling short.

But a lot of our self-aversion comes from within ourselves, rather than without. Author Jack Kornfield highlights how we typically relate to ourselves through our self-image rather than through an objective appraisal of our strengths and needs. This leads to highly distorted images of ourselves that, if our self-esteem is fragile, become toxic in their own right.

This was true for Stephan. As part of his early judgement about himself as bad, he recalled a belief that no one had liked him. But when we looked back at his early history through the eyes of the compassionate adult, he began to appreciate that some people had cared for and appreciated him. He had had a few friends at school; there was a teacher who seemed to show particular interest in his artistic abilities and the mother of a friend always seemed pleased to see him when Stephan came round to play. Moreover, he began to see how his parents' actions were in fact those of desperate people whose own difficulties prevented them from understanding and responding appropriately to the needs of a small child. Until this time, Stephan's choices had been determined by an image of himself that existed inside his head. But his 'badness' was not the truth of who he was.

A curious thing about self-esteem, as a function of the relationship we have with ourselves, is that we seem to have many different selves, each one with its own agenda. Who, for example, is not familiar with that part of ourselves that seems bent on self-sabotage – the one that has dark and uncharitable thoughts, who holds the invitation to be destructive. Similarly, I have not yet encountered anyone who isn't intimately acquainted with the inner critic – that small self who does such a good job of pointing out our short-comings, limitations, and failings. And who doesn't know the small, insecure, and frightened self, who feels vulnerable and bullied by the inner critic and fearful of what lurks in the deep recesses of our mind?

These parts of our selves are in constant dialogue and jostle for supremacy in the context of any decision we need to make or goal we try to achieve. The outcome of all this jostling has a powerful affect on how we decide to act. Which 'small self' wins? And what is the price we pay?

In his research on self-to-self relating, Professor Paul Gilbert identifies two types of self-relating that are critical to understanding the true nature of self-esteem: (1) a hostile dominant self leading to the fearful, subordinated self, and (2) a caring empathic self leading to a sense of being respected and cared for. The relationship between these different parts of ourselves gets played out in our inner dialogue and the impact of this dialogue on our emotions, choices and actions.

The style of self-relating is critical to understand because, as Paul Gilbert explains, it actually triggers physiological changes in the brain. When your inner critic bullies you, the effect on the brain is the same as if someone was literally bullying you: it stimulates neural pathways that create bodily tension (remember the fight-or-flight response?), fear, and self-doubt. But for all its drawbacks, self-criticism isn't necessarily what it seems. In order to build healthy self-esteem, we first need to understand what our internal critic is trying to tell us.

What is your self-criticism trying to tell you?

Many self-esteem programmes recommend trying to ignore the internal critic, or even conquering it into submission. But if we do this, we are in danger of overlooking something important. First, having negative beliefs about ourselves or our competencies is not necessarily a bad thing. It can, if we know how to use it, lead us to self-correct, make us work harder, or try alternative (and more beneficial) strategies. Second, even when it is clearly unhelpful, your inner critic is actually working hard on your behalf. True, its efforts may be counterproductive but its intention is none the less a noble one.

Very often, when we take a closer look at the inner critic, we find that it is fighting a battle that was over a long time ago. This may be a battle from childhood, adolescence, or even sometime during your adulthood. Like the Japanese soldiers who were discovered marooned on an island and could not accept that the

Second World War had ended, so, too, the inner critic is determined to continue fighting a battle that is over.

Recognizing this was the key to helping Justin make changes to how he lived his life. When we looked beneath the veneer of his false confidence we discovered that his inner critic believed that Justin simply wasn't good enough. His internal critic was issuing a dire warning: "Bully or be bullied. Pull the wool over everyone's eyes or be exposed as a fraud."

Justin had been badly bullied at school, and when he had attempted to confide in his parents, his father had accused him of being weak for not fighting back. It seemed to Justin that he had lost both the respect of his peers and his parents, and that to show vulnerability was a sign of intolerable weakness. He vowed that from then on, however much he was hurting, he would never let on. The world would see him as strong and capable. The internal critic that led him to bully others was in fact trying to protect him from the most terrible catastrophe: the shame that would come from failing and having others ridicule him for his inadequacy.

Recognizing this battle helped Justin make sense of how he behaved towards his wife and his colleagues, as well as his workaholism. He kept himself emotionally distant from his wife for fear that if she got too close she would encounter his more vulnerable side and reject him. Similarly, bullying others at work was an attempt to prove his strength. And in terms of his work patterns, he explained that, 'If I work fewer hours, I just won't get the sales, and then I won't be any different from anyone else.' It was as though he needed to work twice as hard and achieve twice as much to be recognized as just as good as everyone else.

If you have a very active inner critic, see if you can identify the life experiences that taught you to feel this way. What is its crusade? Table 8 shows some examples that I commonly encounter in my work with clients. See if any of them apply to you.

As you get to know your inner critic, you'll discover that it is actually rather anxious and over-burdened, trying to offer protection from the catastrophes it believes will befall you if you stretch yourself beyond your capabilities or ask for too much. Like all anxious and over-burdened aspects of ourselves, the best way to respond is by working *with* it rather than *against* it, understanding

Table 8. The functions of self-criticism.

Category of self-criticism	Translation
'You'll never succeed so why bother trying.'	'You were so badly hurt last time things didn't work out – I don't want you to get hurt again.'
'You're pathetic; why don't you stand up for yourself?'	'I'm scared people will walk all over you.'
'It's selfish and wrong to ask for what you want.'	'Be good or else others will get angry and reject you and then you'll be alone and humiliated.'
'You never give anything all of your effort.'	'Because you're not clever, talented or accomplished, you have to work harder than everyone else just to keep up. You don't want everyone to see how inadequate you are.'
'Don't get carried away by your successes.'	'No one will like you if you become a bighead!'
'You're so lazy.'	'Without me nagging you constantly, you'd never do anything.'
'You can't do that.'	'Don't set yourself up for disappointment and failure.'
'Despite what they say, people don't really like or care about you.'	'If you let people get too close they will discover the truth about you and reject you.'
'You must be a terrible person to have acted in that way (or let someone else behave towards you in that way).'	'I'll punish you so you don't have to carry the burden of feeling guilty.'
'You don't deserve to be successful.'	'If you ask for more than you deserve, you'll be punished one way or another.'

its perspective, acknowledging its efforts, and then gently working to correct its misconceptions.

Your inner critic may not be as well-developed as Justin's or Stephan's, but you are probably familiar with your own personal variety. So ask your inner critic what's on its mind. Use Exercise 37 to guide you.

Exercise 37. Get to know your inner critic

- What does your inner critic tell you about the kind of person that you are?
- What is the battle that your internal critic is still fighting?
- When and how did the battle begin?
- From what is your internal critic trying to protect you now?
- What does your inner critic fear would happen if you had faith in yourself and trusted your competencies?

Spend some time studying your answers. What do they tell you? Is your internal critic helping you get the most out of life? If not, what would be a more compassionate and balanced perspective that might create new possibilities for a more self-respectful attitude?

Your inner critic may be trying to help you, but, as we've seen, it has problems discriminating between current challenges and past battles. And let's face it, if its dire warnings were accurate, you'd probably have life sorted by now! The problem with self-criticism is, as self-esteem expert Dr Melanie Fennell explains, that it doesn't give you any clues on what you need to do differently. However, it is possible to get the benefits the internal critic promises you without getting caught up in all its negativity.

Towards robust self-esteem: getting to know yourself anew

Healthy self-esteem is an ongoing project, not something that you achieve once and for all. Building self-esteem involves having a realistic, flexible, respectful relationship with yourself that recognizes your human frailties and your shadow sides as well as your talents, strengths, and resourcefulness. Note that the aim is not to endorse yourself regardless of how you behave, but to nurture a mature self-awareness in which you honour your feelings and behave with respect towards yourself and others. Healthy self-esteem also requires us to take full responsibility for all the different parts of ourselves, including those parts we find less appealing or from which we might otherwise seek to flee. Any parts of ourselves we do not trust or that hurt us (including the inner critic)

251

need to be invited back into our lives with kindly concern and gentle, but firm, handling.

Exercise 38. Imagine the future

How would your life be different if you had optimally healthy self-esteem? (Remember we are talking here about healthy self-acceptance, not believing you're invincible.)

- How would you live differently?
- How would you implement your Mission?
- What Attitudes would you have?
- What goals would you set yourself?
- How would your relationships change?
- What sort of work–life balance would you have?
- How you would you take care of your health?

Pay careful attention to the impact of your answers. Do you feel excited and energized, or anxious and doubtful? Is your internal critic threatened by the prospect of you developing a new relationship with yourself, or does this feel like an intriguing possibility? Observe any of the internal critic's objections gently but objectively. Do they contain any exaggerations or distortions in thinking? Is it possible that these objections are themselves built upon a house of cards? Reframe them as you learnt to do in Principle No. 10, while being sure to thank your inner critic for its valiant (if misguided) efforts on your behalf.

One of the keys to healthy self-esteem is to learn to be true to our sense of who we are, rather than trying to live up to someone else's version of you. Trainer and author Nick Williams points out that so much of our struggle in life is based on trying to secure the approval of others and to measure up to some idealized view of how we should be – imposed on us by others or ourselves. Jack Kornfield agrees. In order to build truly respectful and self-respectful self-esteem, he advocates the value of the Buddhist practice of 'inquiring into who we think we are'. The purpose, he reminds us, is not to get us locked into self-interrogation but rather to help us let go of old beliefs that no longer serve us. Once released from the burdens of these old stories, we can allow ourselves to 'become eccentric' – that is, to revel in our uniqueness.

If you rewrote your criteria at this point in your life, on what would you base your self-esteem?

- Whose formula of being a worthwhile person have you followed so far?
- What have been the results – good and bad?
- What drives you to conform to it now?
- What would happen if you replaced it with a formula of your own choosing? What if you tried to stop being the perfect employee, spouse, parent, friend, professional and made a commitment to being your own, unique, 'eccentric' self?

Another key to robust self-esteem is to avoid the trap of basing your self-esteem on something outside of your control. This might include achieving a particular position or job title at work (you could be made redundant or someone may be promoted over you); the amount of money you have (you could become unemployed, get sick, or the stock market could crash); your physical appearance (bodies age, health status varies, and appearances change) or being in a relationship (relationships break down and separations are inevitable). Of course, there is nothing wrong with taking pride in these things, and when they go well they can enrich our lives immeasurably. But when you base your sense of worth upon having them, you are vulnerable. Try instead basing your self-esteem on your authenticity and uniqueness, your signature strengths, your sense of meaning or your courage, a cause you believe in or your faith in a higher power – in other words something that puts you on a much surer footing.

Behaving your way to healthy self-esteem

Imagine you had a coach mentoring you on your self-esteem from the moment you got up in the morning until the moment you went to bed. What would your coach say? What specific advice would they give you for managing events throughout the day?

A good coach combines total commitment to your goals with an appreciation of your strengths and talents, suggestions for action and honest feedback. Becoming this type of self-coach is a great formula for enhancing self-esteem, as it combines a type of self-to-self relating that is honest (which means facing yourself and your life squarely in the face; eliminating thinking errors, and separating your accomplishments from your worth); commitment to your goals (setting appropriate targets; pursuing them with motivation while being compassionate towards setbacks and learning from the experience); and behaviour changes (putting your plans into action and learning new skills where necessary). How could you put this formula into practice to enhance your self-esteem, as of today?

Melanie Fennell suggests keeping a record of information, experiences, and events that directly contradict your worst fears about yourself. This can be any event, experience, or outcome, but you may want to focus this particularly around the way in which your self-esteem manifests. For example, Stephan's fragile self-esteem manifested in beliefs about his badness, and so his record of strengths focused mainly on any experiences or events that directly contradicted this idea: kind acts towards others, thoughtful gestures, and occasions when others gave him positive feedback about how much they valued his contribution to their lives.

For Justin, however, the Record of Strengths adopted a slightly different focus. As his fear was about being exposed as a failure or fraud, his self-esteem fears centred on beliefs of incompetence, so he kept a record of accomplishments and successes throughout his life that could act as reminders that his inner critic was not an accurate assessor of his strengths. What would be the focus of your Record of Strengths? Start one now and add to it day by day – the evidence is there, so use it.

At the beginning of this book, I also suggested you create a system for recording your gains. This is vital to any form of coaching (otherwise how can you keep track of how your life is changing?), but can be particularly beneficial for working with low self-esteem. In psychology, learning theory highlights how we are more likely to achieve our goals and accomplish more when we notice our successes. The problem with low self-esteem is that the gains are typically overlooked. So, if you haven't done so already, create a system now.

Remember, though, that nothing influences self-esteem quite like how we behave towards ourselves. A robust sense of self-worth needs a maintenance programme in which you attend to your emotional and physical needs, make sufficient time for fun and free time, allow space for the relationships that empower you and avoid the trap of overwork (or under-work for that matter!).

How you behave towards yourself gives you important messages. In the same way that if you treated someone else badly, if you ignored their needs, overworked them and constantly criticized them, they would start to feel unhappy and abused, so the same is true in relation to how you treat yourself. Behave towards yourself *as though* you genuinely respected and valued yourself and, even if it feels strange to begin with, you will soon start to notice the difference. Your efforts will be more effective if you work from the outside in, as well as the inside out.

Exercise 39. Seeing yourself through the eyes of the valuing other

To get the most out of this exercise, you need to have had some practice at keeping a 'Record of Strengths' diary, to be familiar with your own version of the inner critic and be able to disarm it using the methods you learnt in Principle No. 10.

Think of someone who loves, values or appreciates you. The more intimately this person knows you the better, but you could also identify a friend, colleague, or acquaintance – in fact, anyone who has a good opinion of you. This person is not so infatuated with you that they see you through rose-tinted glasses; they genuinely appreciate you while knowing that you have strengths and weaknesses, good points and bad. See yourself through their eyes for a moment. What do they see? Write your answers in your learning log.

Keep looking at yourself through the eyes of the valuing other and see if you can identify specific aspects of you that they value. What exactly does this other person value? How do they view your strengths of character? Your accomplishments? Your ability to relate to others? The way you contribute to the world?

Now think about how this image differs from any existing, unhelpful images you have had of yourself – the ones that have contributed to fragile self-esteem. What would it be like to live as though this other, more balanced and empowering image of you were in fact, true? How would you behave differently? Dress differently? Organize your time differently? Respond to others' requests differently? Write your responses in your learning log.

Now, here comes the challenge! Just as an experiment, take one day in the next week and treat yourself in the way that you would if you truly saw yourself in the way that this other person sees you. This may feel like a real stretch but don't be tempted to avoid this part of the exercise. After all, you are not committing yourself to a life of change; you are just undertaking an experiment to notice the impact of seeing yourself through a different lens. And, ultimately, that's what improving self-esteem is all about . . .

The take home message

Healthy self-esteem is not about having unshakable confidence in yourself or your abilities. It is about developing a mature self-awareness that allows you to better co-ordinate the many mini-selves that make up your relationship with yourself.

However you see yourself today will be the outcome of all the experiences, knowledge, assumptions, and ideas you have built up over a lifetime. As we have seen, self-esteem is not a static state; it can never be a definitive judgement about your worth, but represents a platform for viewing yourself and your potential that allows for the creation of new possibilities in your life.

If your self-esteem rests on shaky foundations, like Stephan or Justin, it will need to be a special focus of your coaching journey and it may take months of steady, committed work before you notice a difference. But be persistent: your efforts will pay off and the rewards are well worthwhile.

Ultimately, there is nothing and no one that can make you feel complete. That task has been assigned to you and you alone. But, by reclaiming this quest, you may discover that you no longer need to be constrained by the person whom you think you are. If, however, you need some additional support while you embark upon your quest of discovery, try the suggestions in the coaching tool box.

A life well lived involves encountering many disappointments as well as many successes. If you become ensnared in the trap of fear,

Coaching Tool Box: Top Tips for Boosting Self-Esteem

1.   Learn to view global evaluations about yourself with suspicion. A human being can never be summed up by a single label.
2.   Forgive yourself for your limitations. You were never meant to be perfect.
3.   Differentiate your actions from your worth. If you behave in a way you are not happy with, accept responsibility and change it. But don't confuse this with your value as a human being.
4.   Remind yourself of why you are valuable and worthy.
5.   Reassure the inner critic: its intentions are good, but its perception is flawed.
6.   Write yourself a reminder of why you deserve self-belief and read it every day.
7.   Draw on your council for advice on how to view yourself through more impartial eyes (remember the exercise at the end of the Attitude section of MAP?).

shame, pride, or grandiosity, you limit your options. Having a positive, yet realistic view of yourself isn't just a palliative, it's a responsibility. You do not honour anyone by ignoring your Mission, or keeping your talents and strengths hidden. Nor do you honour anyone by having an inflated sense of your potential. As author and teacher Jack Kornfield warns us, sometimes the struggle to be someone different actually prevents us from finding our own true nature. Healthy self-esteem is about straddling that tension between working out what is ours to nurture and what is ours to accept – with grace, humility, and gratitude.

Building Healthy Self-Esteem

One idea I shall take away from this chapter is . . . (write your answer in your learning log).
One thing I shall do differently/more gratefully is . . . (write your answer in your learning log).

Bibliography

*Fennell, M. J. V. (1999). *Overcoming Low Self-Esteem*. London: Constable Robinson.

*Gilbert, P. (1997). *Overcoming Depression. A Self-Help Guide using Cognitive-Behavioural Techniques*. London: Robinson. (Also contains some excellent ideas and exercises that relate to self-esteem.)
*McKay, M., & Fanning, P. (1992). *Self-Esteem: A Proven Program of Cognitive Techniques for Assessing, Improving and Maintaining Your Self-esteem*. Oakland, CA: New Harbinger.

CHAPTER TWENTY-FOUR

How to Have a Happy and Healthy Relationship with Your Body

'There is more wisdom in your body than
in your deepest philosophy'

(Friedrich Nietzsche)

'To keep the body in good health is a duty. Otherwise we
shall not be able to keep our mind strong and clear'

(Buddha)

In this chapter, we look at ways of developing and sustaining a positive relationship with your body. Together we will explore:

- *how to improve your relationship with your physical appearance;*
- *a model of well-being that can help you identify any areas that need improving;*
- *ways of discovering your true image.*

Preparatory reading. To get the most out of this chapter, you will need to be familiar with the ideas we explored in the Principles on Gratitude (No. 7); Compassion (No. 8); Thinking Skills (No. 10); and Motivation (Principle No. 12).

So far in this book we have focused on ways of living, being, and doing that can sustain you emotionally and psychologically. But you are also a physical being, born into a body that carries you through life and enables you to act on the world. This chapter is dedicated to that part of you that can easily get overlooked: your physical self and the needs of the body.

Good health is often something we take for granted until it is taken from us, or someone we love falls sick. How often, for example, do you stop what you are doing and check in with your body to see how it feels? How often do you ask it what it needs? And how often do you take the trouble to say thank you for everything it enables you to accomplish? If you're like most people, probably not too often.

We live in the age of the mind. In the Western world, the intellect rules the heart, rationality is favoured over romance, and we no longer see the body as a source of wisdom in its own right. These priorities make it easy to view the body as little more than an instrument that carries out our instructions, or as an undisciplined part of ourselves that needs to be dieted, exercised, or otherwise controlled into submission. Both perspectives create difficulties: the first leads us to neglect our physical well-being; the second causes us to be at war with our bodies.

Many people with whom I work have developed a distorted relationship with their physical selves such that their bodies have become a battleground. They may live in a state of constant fear that they are about to develop a serious illness; their bodies may finally be rebelling against years of neglect, or they may simply dislike what they see when they look in the mirror.

Briony's story

Briony was typical of too many young women I see. A beautiful, vivacious, and highly intelligent young woman, Briony could not bear to look at herself in the mirror because what she saw appalled her. I tried to imagine what she must be seeing, struggling to unite her self-perception with the striking woman who sat opposite me.

'I'm just so fat and ugly,' she told me. She was neither of these things, but I knew that my pointing this out wouldn't help her right then.

'Is there anything about yourself you *do* like?' I asked, looking for exceptions to her global self-condemnation. 'No,' she said, without a moment's hesitation.

'Tell me more about what you see when you look at yourself in the mirror,' I asked her. And so we began, with Briony going to some lengths to convince me of all the imperfections with which her reflection confronted her . . .

Wayne's story

Wayne had no problem with how he looked. But he was terrified of what is going on inside his body. His worries about his health had come and gone for years, but just recently he had begun experiencing unexplained physical sensations that he feared were signs of cancer. All the doctors (and he had seen many) have told him that there was nothing wrong with him and the multiple test results appeared to confirm this. But Wayne was still worried.

I asked him why he has come to see a psychologist. He paused. 'Deep down I know I've become obsessed with my health,' he told me. 'It's the first thing I think about every morning and the last thing I think about at night. I'm not sure I believe the doctors when they tell me nothing is wrong, but I do know that every new symptom shoots my anxiety into orbit. I can't go on like this.' Wayne saw his body as a walking time-bomb and each day felt compelled to check himself for signs of disease, whether it was looking for lumps, checking the colour of his tongue, or taking his pulse. The problem was, the more carefully he looked for bodily changes, the more he tended to find . . .

How do you feel about your body?

Many of us have a difficult relationship with our bodies at some point in our lives. We would like to be taller or shorter, slimmer or more curvy, leaner or more muscular. Or, if we are dealing with illness, we would like a healthier body or perhaps a different body altogether. Our lists of dissatisfactions are endless. Indeed, entire industries have been built around the conflicted relationships we have with our physical selves: from beauty salons to Botox injections, slimming clubs to plastic surgery, we are prepared to sacrifice time, money – even our health – to iron out our physical flaws.

But we all know that this preoccupation can go too far. High profile cases reported in the media remind us how people can become caricatures of their former selves through undergoing too many 'self-improvement' procedures. And this is no longer solely the prerogative of the celebrities who adorn our magazines. Recently, I read an article in a local newspaper that reported an alarming increase in people doing DIY plastic surgery. When we get to the stage where we think it is acceptable to carve into our own bodies, something has gone terribly wrong.

I do not know what your health status is. Nor do I know what you see when you look in the mirror. But, whatever your circumstances, if you are unhappy with your physical self your journey in life will always be hampered by this extra burden. In this chapter, I want to help you make peace with your physical self and appreciate your body for the extraordinary phenomenon that it is.

Exercise 40. How do you feel about your body?

Begin by reflecting on how you feel about your body right now. Do you like it or loathe it? See it as friend or foe? Respect it or misuse it? Write your reactions in your learning log.

Now copy the statements listed on the facing page into your learning log, and tick the appropriate column for each statement.

If you ticked 'Mostly true of me' for the majority of the questions in Exercise 40, then you have a happy, healthy relationship with your body that is based on self-respect. If, however, you found yourself drawn to the 'Rarely' or 'Never true of me' responses, your relationship with your body needs some fine-tuning.

Reconnecting with the physical self

In our society, we have a very strange relationship to the body. By turns, we worship it, make a fetish out of it, attempt to control it and condemn it. But rarely do we listen to it, attend to it, experience it, and honour it.

When it comes to having a happy, healthy relationship with your physical self, you need to be able to inhabit and experience what is, rather than relating to the body through the filter of your

---

Exercise 40.   *Your relationship with your physical self.*

	Mostly true of me	Rarely true of me	Never true of me
You are comfortable in your own skin.	☐	☐	☐
You feel a genuine appreciation for your body and everything it does for you.	☐	☐	☐
When you look in the mirror you feel OK about the person looking back at you.	☐	☐	☐
Overall, you feel comfortable with your physical appearance.	☐	☐	☐
You are not embarrassed by your body's shape or weight.	☐	☐	☐
You do not experience self-loathing towards your physical self.	☐	☐	☐
You take good care of your physical health and appearance.	☐	☐	☐
You are not interested in comparing your physical appearance to that of others.	☐	☐	☐
Despite the imperfections that come with being human, you have a positive self-image.	☐	☐	☐

---

perceptions and judgements. Most of the time, however, we relate to our bodies through an image we hold of them, rather than being truly conscious of our embodied experience.

In Principle No. 10, we identified a number of common thinking traps, or filters, that prevent you from thinking clearly, impartially and constructively about your life (if you can't remember them, recap now). These were very relevant to Briony and Wayne. Briony, for example, related to her body through a filter of 'I am ugly'. She would over-generalize imperfections, discount positive information and exaggerate the negatives. It was the operation of her filters that enabled she and I to arrive at totally different conclusions about her attractiveness.

Wayne, in contrast, saw his body through the filter of a story about his vulnerability to disease. He would catastrophise physical sensations in the absence of supporting evidence, fortune-tell himself into a future that had him dying and had an inability to disconfirm his worst fears (hence the fact he took no comfort in the medical tests that repeatedly concluded he was a fit and healthy man).

Take a moment to reflect on your own filters as reflected in your fundamental assumptions and beliefs about physical well-being. Use the questions in Exercise 41 to guide you, and write the answers in your learning log.

Exercise 41. Identify your assumptions about health and well-being

- What assumptions and beliefs do you have about your body, health, and illness?
    - To what extent do you see your health as being under your own control or due to factors over which you can exert little or no control?
    - How do you imagine the inside of your body looks?
    - What image do you have of your external appearance?
- Where do your assumptions and beliefs come from? What experiences, people, and events have helped shape these ideas?
- How do these assumptions and beliefs empower you? In what ways do they nurture your relationship with your body?
- How do these assumptions and beliefs disempower you? In what ways do they undermine your relationship with your body?

The purpose of identifying your assumptions and beliefs is not to determine whether or not they are correct. It is to help you understand that your beliefs shape your reality through creating the filters by which you come to experience your body. Looking at your answers to the questions in Exercise 41, can you see any assumptions or beliefs that it would now be helpful to discard? Any beliefs that involve global judgements that are examples of toxic thinking? Write any thoughts in your learning log.

It is probably impossible to see ourselves without any filters at all; the power of thought is too advanced in our culture for us to be entirely free of our perceptions. But if you are willing to look beyond the filters that cause you to judge the different parts of your body, you will start to appreciate how extraordinary your physical being really is. It comprises a highly sophisticated network of systems, transports messages from one part of the body to another with remarkable efficiency, alerts us when something needs attending to, and has a capacity to regenerate and heal. Being open to these extraordinary qualities you will find yourself better able to make peace with what is – even when it falls short of some idealized version inside your own head.

The wheel of well-being: the dimensions of a healthy you

Achieving a positive relationship with our bodies is not just a matter of keeping ourselves healthy. Certainly, this can help but a truly harmonious relationship involves a holistic approach in which we attend to our perceptions, feelings, sensations, and beliefs about our bodies just as well as our habits, lifestyle, and behaviour.

When I am working with clients who have come to see their bodies as a battleground, I have found it helpful to explore what I call the Wheel of Well-Being. The Wheel of Well-Being comprises two dimensions: (1) The dimension of Acceptance–Change and (2) The dimension of Internal Experience–External Appearance. Have a look at Figure 4 to see how these dimensions relate to one another.

At the centre of the diagram lies what you are aiming for: a peaceful and harmonious relationship with your body. Each spoke of the wheel leads back to this central axis. Notice, though, that the central axis is not describing optimum health or beauty. This is because there will always be elements of our physical selves that are beyond our direct control. Health status varies, as does physical attractiveness, and to assume that we should somehow gain control of what our bodies do and how they look creates the very same traps that cause our distress in the first place.

You'll see that the two dimensions are placed on intersecting axes: one axis relates to a dimension I call Acceptance–Change; the

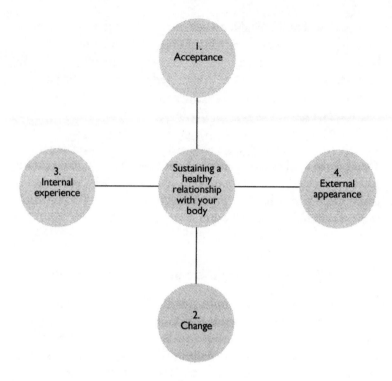

Figure 4. The wheel of well-being.

other relates to the dimension of Internal Experience–External Appearance. Each one, when attended to and held in balance with the others, provides a route back to a healthy relationship with your body.

The dimension of acceptance–change

This dimension is concerned with managing the tension between accepting what is not amenable to change, and changing those areas that you can. For example, if you have a large bone structure, assuming that you can slim yourself into a size zero is confusing what is and isn't in your sphere of control. Alternatively, if you are managing chronic pain, to keep searching for a 'cure' merely accentuates the discrepancy between where you are and where you want to be and creates more distress in the process.

Learning to accept what is

Acceptance – a willingness to embrace what is – offers a route to greater peace and contentment with our physical selves. It allows us to enjoy sensory experience and relish the opportunities (and limitations) that come from embodying physical form, without distorting the body by attaching undue significance to its functions or appearance.

When it comes to our physical selves, so much distress comes from having a fixed view of how our bodies should look. These 'shoulds' may come from trying to live up to idealized images we encounter through the media; ideas we may have been taught about how male and female bodies need to look in order to be acceptable, or having had an experience of being bullied for our physical appearance at some point in our lives.

'Shoulds' create distress because they highlight the discrepancy between how we actually are and how we would like to be. They are also a form of cognitive distortion because in the real world, there are no shoulds about the body. True, there may be states of feeling and functioning that are more desirable than others, but to collapse these subtle distinctions into a single judgement is faulty reasoning.

But what if you were to change the game plan? What if, instead of continuing to relate to your body through the image you hold of it, you began to relate to it based on your experience of it? Your body has its own style, rhythm, language, and seasons. It tells you when you are tired, overly stressed, or need to eat. In this sense, it has its own form of expression that reflects a wisdom of its own. As the great American poet, Walt Whitman, said '. . . your very flesh shall be a great poem'. The body is the crucible for our hopes and dreams: we can achieve nothing without its participation. But it is more than this; it is a source of imagination and invention in its own right.

Exercise 42. Getting to know the body on its own terms

Identify a part of the body that feels fairly neutral to you. It may be a forearm, foot, or lower leg – any part of you that generally does not stir up uncomfortable feelings or judgements.

Spend a moment studying this part of your body, as though you are seeing it for the first time. As best you can, suspend any judgements in favour of what is actually there. Examine it from all angles until you feel you really know this part of your body – its colour and tone, its texture, shape, and size. Now gently begin to move that part of your body so you can observe it in action. How does it move? What can it do? What sensations accompany its movements? As best you can, connect with the body's experience of movement, without piling on the judgement.

When you have had some experience of this exercise, move on to a more emotive part of your body – a part of you that stirs up some degree of uneasiness or criticism. Can you observe this part of you with the same impartiality? Notice its colour, texture and movement as though encountering it for the first time. Can you really get to know this part of your body without resorting to judgements about good and bad?

Gradually build your skills in impartial observation until you can look at all of you in a full-length mirror. See if you can observe the whole of your body now with the same impartiality. Can you welcome all of you, just as you are? See if you can visually scan the body noticing the different shades and textures, curves and straight areas that make up your body. Notice any judgements that get in the way and see if you can gently put them to one side so you can observe what is really present – not what your mind tells you is present.

Helpful hint. This can be quite an emotive exercise to begin with, but with practice it will get easier – and help you grow towards a more peaceful and harmonious relationship with your physical self.

Changing what no longer works

At the opposite end of the dimension from acceptance, is change. If you can free yourself from the tyranny of critical judgement, you can see the body through fresh eyes. Instead of good and bad or right or wrong, you are free to tune into your body's wisdom to discover any areas that might need some attention. If you listen closely, your body will tell you the ways in which it is thriving, ways in which it is struggling, and the role you have played in bringing about these outcomes. Without judgement and condemnation, you are able to start working with your body and able to think about its needs sensitively and creatively.

Exercise 43. Dialoguing with the body

Close your eyes and take a few gentle, slow breaths. When you are ready, think about all the demands you place upon your body every day.

If your body could talk, what would it say? Thank you for taking care of me? I need a break? I'm breaking down? Are there any messages that your body is trying to give you at the moment, through experiences of pressure, pain, fatigue, or a general feeling of uneasiness? Would your body alert you to anything it needs more or less of? Would it recommend a change of lifestyle? An alteration to your diet? Would any particular part of your body want to draw your attention to misuse or neglect? (It may feel strange to think about entering into a dialogue with your physical self, but do your best to override any intellectual objections). Write any advice in your learning log.

If you were able to engage with the process, Exercise 43 probably alerted you to some areas that require your attention. Changes may include letting go of old habits around use of alcohol and caffeine, overworking, or even biting your nails. They might involve shedding stories about your body that you have now outgrown, or revising your self-care routines. They may even mean re-committing yourself to following medical advice for a particular condition.

What changes would it be most helpful to implement right now? Are they big changes or small ones? Would they require major upheavals to your life or minor adjustments? Letting go of bad habits or acquiring new ones? Can you imagine what it would be like having achieved these? (When it comes to making changes and identifying suitable goals, watch out for any toxic thinking that tells you change is impossible, or idealized assumptions that changing this one area will transform your life). Write your thoughts in your learning log.

> **Helpful hint**. For great tips on enhancing your motivation, try re-reading Principle No. 12, particularly if you have found it difficult to make changes in the past.

Internal experience–external appearance

It is one thing to know that something needs to change, but quite another to know where to pitch your efforts: is it the inside that needs attending to, or the outside?

The dimension of Internal Experience–External Appearance is concerned with achieving a balance between taking care of the inside and creating a positive image on the outside. For example, it is no good attempting to manipulate your external appearance if something on the inside is screaming for attention. Similarly, neglecting the image you present to the world is to miss out on an important opportunity for expressing your uniqueness and your imaginative potential.

In the Wheel of Well-Being, Internal Experience refers to anything that has an impact on the inside of the body, including what you choose to eat and drink, how you protect yourself from pollution, taking medication, and seeking medical advice when you know something is wrong. Attending to Internal Experience is about listening to your body and, in this sense, involves the two of you working in genuine partnership. External Appearance, in contrast, is concerned with elements of our behaviour that support or undermine the body's expression as well as how we present our body to the world through the way we dress.

Tuning into internal experience

In Chapter Twenty-two, I introduced you to a tool called the Weekly Activity Diary. To recap, the Weekly Activity Diary gives you a bird's-/eye view of exactly what you are doing and when. This tool will help you identify exactly what you are putting into your body so that you can decide whether any changes are needed.

Have a look at the diary sheet at the end of this chapter. To work out if you need to make any changes to your Internal Experience, I'd like you to keep a record of everything that goes in to your body over the next week. You'll see that the day is split into hourly segments. When you eat or drink something, when you exercise, go for a massage, take medication or supplements, or do anything else designed to have an internal impact, write it down in the allotted space. For example, if you had two slices of toast between 7 and 8 a.m., write them in the relevant box. If you had a coffee at 9 a.m. and again at 11 a.m., write these in also. A cigarette break at 2 p.m. should go in the relevant box, and so on. Anything you do that has an impact on the inside of your body needs to be included.

Once you know exactly what is going into the body, you're in a stronger position to revise those areas that need to be changed.

Exercise 44. Your weekly inputs health check

Keep your diary for a week and see what you notice. How many 'inputs' to your body preserve or enhance your physical well-being? How many do not enhance your well-being? Notice what is present and absent in your record: episodes of over-eating or meals skipped and replaced with coffee, cigarettes, or alcohol? Too little sleep or too much? Lack of exercise or a forceful physical regime?

Once you have a clear picture, answer the following questions.

- What does your body need more of?
- What does your body need less of?
- Are there any habits you want to introduce into your life?
- Are there any habits it's time to let go of?

Remember, the purpose of this exercise is not necessarily to instruct you in the principles of good dietary habits or to advise you to reduce your alcohol. The aim is to look across your inputs as a whole and decide how you can develop a happier, more respectful relationship with your physical self. If there are any areas relating to your Internal Experience that you would like to change, see if you can identify some SMART goals, as you learned in Principle No. 9.

Taking care of the outside

As people change how they relate to and care for their bodies, it's not uncommon to find that changes in image or self-presentation

271

follow. Today, the whole of idea of external appearance has become fraught with complications. When we think about changing our external appearance, we often think about ideal images of the body conveyed through the media, which highlight the discrepancy between how we actually look and how we would like to look. In this way, our desire to look good can easily become distorted and disconnected from our authentic selves. We assume that managing the outward impression can replace the work we need to do on the inside and, like Briony, worry constantly about our appearance. Or we simply never pay enough attention to how we look because it's too far down our list of priorities.

But, used wisely, self-image – including fashion, accessories, and cosmetics – can engage our imagination, our creativity, and our sense of possibility in new and exciting ways. Our external appearance provides a means of cultivating a personal style that is every inch an expression of the authentic self and that enhances our relationship with our bodies.

I have a friend who feels beautiful whenever she wears baby blue. It is not that she has an intellectual sense of this colour suiting her complexion. She actually experiences her body differently. She feels more energized and more beautiful – not in a superficial sense but at a deep and authentic level. Wearing baby blue resonates with some part of her that needs and enjoys expression. In the same way, your body is a canvas on which you can express aspects of your Mission, through which you convey your Attitude and around which you can design a Process for optimum effectiveness.

I came across a wonderful example of this a couple of years ago, when I visited a Museum called the 'World of WearableArt' in New Zealand. The museum houses the most extraordinary exhibitions that pushed my understanding of fashion to the limit. The designers' innovative combinations of colours, textures, and materials (including surprising artefacts such as common household items) were so obviously a celebration of the human body. But their designs were also a challenge to see the body in a new way. Through defying conventional ideas about style, the exhibits engaged the imagination of its visitors, encouraging us to see the body as a canvas upon which to represent, experiment and invent.

There was something about the spirit of the collection that captures the essence of what you are aiming for. Creating personalized images are far from becoming a slave to fashion – they are about honouring what is on the inside by giving it expression on the outside.

You, too, have a personal style that, if given space for expression, can allow you to deepen your relationship with your body. It may be something as simple as wearing baby blue, like my friend. Or it may be choosing particular textures over others. If you are a woman, it may be through wearing make-up or no make-up. If you are a man, it might involve reviewing and revising the colours or style of clothing you've always worn in the past.

Of course, there may be times when you want to create a specific image for strategic purposes: for example, dressing a certain way for a job interview, 'power dressing' in order to boost your confidence during a presentation or meeting, or looking your best in order to impress someone you are dating. There is nothing wrong with cultivating a particular image, or subtly changing that image for a particular purpose. Indeed, adjusting one's style of dress is often interpreted by others as a sign of respect, such as when we follow a dress code for a formal dinner, or wear black at a funeral. However, what matters is keeping your choices consistent with who you are and what you want to express.

Exercise 45. Designing your new image

Think about the Mission, Attitude, and Process that have emerged from all the work you have done in the previous chapters. If you were to express these through your external appearance, how would you look? What sort of style would you want to cultivate, as an expression of your authenticity? Specifically:

- how would you dress?
- would your approach to personal grooming change?
- how would your new style allow your body more expression in your life?
- if you were living your Mission, what would optimum physical attractiveness look like for you (e.g., casual or cultured? Slim or well-built)?

Spend some time thinking this through and then see what images emerge. Elaborate your image in detail in your learning log.

Helpful hint. if this feels like a real challenge, spend some time gathering images from magazines and observing the images that other people have created for themselves. Identify any people who have a sense of style that you admire. The aim is not to copy someone else's image, of course, but to open up a channel for your own creative thinking.

Once you have created an image, spend a few weeks reflecting on and refining it before implementing any changes. You want to avoid any sudden dramatic changes and aim for something that will help you to feel more comfortable in your own skin. Think about how it will actually feel to present yourself to the world in this way. Are there any concerns or objections? If so, see if you can identify what these are before proceeding. And remember, this is all about experimentation – your image will evolve over the years as a function of your changing self.

Take home message

You only have one body so it makes sense to make peace with it. But achieving a balance between acceptance and change, internal experience and external appearance is often harder than it seems. Our bodies are in a constant state of flux, and so creating an optimum relationship with our physical selves is an ongoing project rather than a finite goal.

Changing aspects of your physical appearance or body-related behaviour is great, but only if it comes from a place of self-respect. Attempting to make changes on a 'blame and shame' basis rarely pays dividends in the long-term (as many dieters will tell you). Change is most accessible to us when we can recognize and shed the influence of concepts we hold about the body and learn what it feels like when it is hungry and when it is full, when it is tense and when it is relaxed, when it is tired and when it is alert. Keeping a clear perception of what is and isn't possible frees you to make any necessary changes without the added burden of judgement and condemnation.

If your physical appearance is a personal stumbling block, I hope there are quite a few ideas in this chapter that can get you thinking creatively about making changes. But please remember that this is not a substitute for professional advice. If you have a health issue that concerns you or a self-image that is proving emotionally damaging, please seek the support of someone qualified to help, such as your doctor or a psychologist.

That said, if you use the Wheel of Well-Being to guide you, my hope is that you'll be better able to navigate the tides of acceptance and change, internal experience and external appearance, because one thing is certain: in the years to come, your body will change and your health status will vary. Bodies age and alter; it is just what they do. What matters is how you respond to change, how you attend to and nurture the body in all its different stages and ultimately how you stay with the experience of the physical self without retreating into a world where you only know your body through the perceptions you have of it.

Coaching Tool Box. Top Tips for Honouring the Body

1.   Practise being in your body as it is – not as you would like it to be.
2.   If you have any persistent, unhelpful images of your body, use the work sheet from Principle No. 10 to help you reframe your toxic thoughts.
3.   Make an appointment to see a personal shopper. Many operate on a no-obligation, no-charge basis and it's a great way to start experimenting with a new image.
4.   Every night before you go to sleep, think of all the things your body has helped you accomplish that day. Thank it for the miraculous things it does for you.
5.   Check any self-esteem (inner critic) issues that get in the way by whispering unhelpful comments (see Chapter 23).
6.   As with every other principle we have examined in this book, aim for a balanced perspective. Extreme thinking and behaviour rarely come from a wise place within us.

Honouring the body

One idea I shall take away from this chapter is . . . (write your answer in your learning log).
One thing I shall do differently is . . . (write your answer in your learning log).

Your Weekly Inputs Diary							
Time	Mon	Tues	Wed	Thurs	Fri	Sat	Sun
6–7 a.m.							
7–8 a.m.							
8–9 a.m.							
9–10 a.m.							
10–11 a.m.							
11 a.m.–12 noon							
12–1 p.m.							
1–2 p.m.							
2–3 p.m.							
3–4 p.m.							
4–5 p.m.							
5–6 p.m.							
6–7 p.m.							
7–8 p.m.							
8–9 p.m.							
9–10 p.m.							
10–11 p.m.							
11–12 p.m.							
12–1 a.m.							
1–2 a.m.							
2–3 a.m.							
3–4 a.m.							
4–5 a.m.							
5–6 a.m.							

CHAPTER TWENTY-FIVE

Building Positive Relationships

'Of all the things which wisdom provides to make life entirely
happy, much the greatest is the possession of friendship'

(Epicurus)

*In this final chapter in Part III, we will look at one of the most
rewarding yet complex aspects of our lives: our relationships. In this
chapter you will:*

- *discover what drives your relationship choices;*
- *learn how to form wise relationships;*
- *identify the secret to having successful relationships.*

*Preparatory reading. To get the most out of this chapter, you will need
to be familiar with the 'MAP' coaching model; Principle No. 7:
Gratitude; Principle No. 10: Essential Thinking Skills; and Chapter
Twenty-three on Self-esteem.*

Our happiness does not occur in a vacuum. It is intimately bound
up with those around us – our family, friends, colleagues, and
acquaintances.

As a species, we are primed to form relationships. It is through
our relationships that we give and receive the emotional nurturing
that fosters our development and increases our chances of survival.
There is good evidence that the capacity to form relationships is
hard-wired into our brains and from an evolutionary perspective,
many of our emotions such as love, shame, and guilt have a strong

social component, keeping us bonded to our social groups and enabling us to achieve more through cooperative effort.

In addition, much of what brings meaning and direction to our lives can only be made sense of in the context of relationships. If you think about your Mission, Attitude, and Process, you will probably notice how it is almost impossible to carry them through without the participation of others, at some level. Indeed, psychologist Susan Harter goes as far as suggesting that discovering our true selves is inseparable from our growth within relationships.

Intimate connections

In his book, *The Dark Nights of the Soul,* author Thomas Moore reminds us how, in the era of individualism, we may not think deeply enough about the network of relationships that help define who we are. However much we work on our individual selves, our individual potential, and pursue our individual goals, we are each part of an intricate web of relationships through which we both influence and are influenced.

Some cultures are very comfortable with the idea of our interconnectedness. Aboriginal people, for example, see themselves as part of others, and every other person as part of them. Their world is conceptualized in terms of patterns; everything has its place within the pattern and belongs within it. Nothing truly exists apart from anything else.

Even some of the great Western minds would seem to agree with this principle. Albert Einstein, for example, believed that attempting to see ourselves as separate becomes a conceptual prison that prevents us from achieving a full connection not just with others, but also with the world around us.

Think about the web of relationships in which you are immersed. It is easy to remember those who affect your life directly and intimately – your family, your partner, your children, your close friends. But what of your colleagues, acquaintances, and others who touch your life briefly and then are gone forever? Then there are those who know you, but whom you have never met – the faceless people employed by banks, insurance companies, and pension schemes who have access to your personal details. And what about those who produce the food you eat and who train the doctors that know how to treat you when you are ill? The web gets larger and larger the more you look until you come to the inevitable conclusion that everyone is connected with everyone else. And this is before you even begin to think about how you touch the lives of others . . .

Yet, for all that they can add to our well-being, our relationships are one of the most complex parts of our lives. They demand time, attention, and emotional energy, but offer no guarantee of a return. We have all been in situations where someone we saw as a good friend behaves in a way that leaves us wondering whether we ever knew them at all. Or someone we saw as a distant acquaintance proves themselves to be a true friend at a time of adversity. Even when our relationships seem to be going smoothly, there is an in-built element of unpredictability. At times we feel totally at one with those we love; there is passion in our connection and a closeness that feels strong enough to move mountains. At other times, the relationship can feel mundane or even stale.

Relationships are organic. They cannot (and should not) remain static but are highly sensitive to the tides of life and the individual as well as shared journeys we undertake. Shortly before I got married, I remember asking a colleague for any last minute advice. He thought long and hard before replying. 'Marriage is a bit like the owl and pussycat,' he said. 'You get into your little boat and sail away. Sometimes it's all plain sailing and things are just great. But at other times it can get pretty choppy and then you find yourselves gripping on to the sides of the boat for dear life. But you stay in the boat and keeping sailing, none the less, because that's what it's all about.'

Over the years, his words have stayed with me, because he summed up something important about the essence of good relationships. They are not about plain sailing. They are about sticking together through thick and thin – at least until you know for certain that it's time to abandon ship. It can be all too easy to want to stay with those feelings that are comfortable and easy. But that is not where the substance really lies. The true substance of relationships comprises much tougher stuff and is to be found within the deep and uncomfortable process of discovering one another's vulnerabilities.

The three stages of building positive relationships

There are three stages involved in developing and maintaining healthy relationships. These are listed below.

1. Know your implicit model of relationships – that is, the beliefs and assumptions that guide your interactions with others.
2. Make wise relationship choices.
3. Develop skills for achieving and enhancing intimacy.

1. What is your implicit model of relationships?

Just as you have learned to examine your beliefs in other areas of your life, so you have a series of beliefs about relationships and how they work. We all carry an implicit model of relationships, which is the product of previous experiences and cultural ideals. It is important to know what your personal model is, because this will greatly influence the expectations, hopes, and fears you bring to all new relationships. Use the following exercise to help you.

Exercise 46. What is your implicit model of relationships?

For this exercise, you will need to dig deeper than the sensible, rational part of yourself that comes up with well-reasoned responses. Our implicit ideas about other people can be accessed only through connecting with a deeper 'gut feeling'. Take a moment to connect with that gut feeling about other people and then copy the continua below into your learning log. Place an 'X' on the line according to your views. The central mark denotes a neutral response (try to avoid this where possible).

Others are trustworthy	Others are untrustworthy
People are generally reliable	People generally let you down
Others are accepting	Others are judgemental
People are safe	People are dangerous
People basically like to help each other	People are basically self-serving

People are essentially good	People are essentially bad
Others are stronger than me	Others are weaker than me
I can rely on others to meet my needs	The only one I can rely on is myself
I am superior to others	I am inferior to others
Others think I am better than they are	Others look down on me
Close relationships are forever	Close relationships are for as long as they work

Look over your answers. What clues do they give you concerning your fundamental beliefs about other people? How might they inform your choice of, and behaviour in, relationships – intimate, social, and professional? Can you think of ways in which your implicit model of relationships might help or hinder you in your own coaching journey, or quality of life more generally? Write your thoughts in your learning log.

The more you are aware of your implicit assumptions about relationships, the better placed you are to develop relationships that will nurture you. For example, you might like to think about where these ideas came from and whether they are still relevant for your life today. Or you might want to think about how these assumptions support or negate wise choice, such as might be the case if you have an implicit belief that others cannot be relied upon and then find yourself sabotaging your relationships.

2. Making wise relationship choices

Making wise judgements about whom you want in your life is no small matter. Good relationships enhance our quality of life beyond measure; bad ones erode our confidence and well-being. You need to be able to identify the signs – good and bad – from the outset.

Here are some questions I suggest you hold in mind when deciding whether someone new in your life is someone with whom you might want to form a deeper relationship. Remember, these questions apply regardless of whether the relationship is a potential intimate relationship, a new friendship, or a business partnership.

- Do you know what draws you to this person?
  - Are you clear about your agenda for this relationship?
  - Does your wish to get to know them better come from a healthy or unhealthy part of you (for example, a genuine desire to know them, or a sense that they can fix some part of you that you've never truly been happy with)?
- What do you need to know about this person to feel safe and comfortable about taking it to the next level?
  - How much information do you need to make an informed decision?
  - What areas do you need to know about?
- Do you have some sense of this person's 'MAP' (do you know what they stand for, their sense of meaning and authenticity? Do you know the attitudes and beliefs that drive what they do? Do you know the methods they tend to use to achieve their goals)? Is their 'MAP' sufficiently similar to yours to allow you to proceed in this relationship or are there signs that your values and approaches might be incompatible?

Mark's story

Mark had set up a successful business that he had been running single-handedly for the past three years. He wanted to expand the company as he saw abundant opportunities to expand his range of services and increase his income. But to do so, Mark would need to hire extra help – someone who knew the business as well as he did, and whom he could trust to share his vision for the future of his company.

When he was approached by Sam, it seemed as if fate were intervening. Sharing a mutual acquaintance, Sam seemed to tick all the right boxes. His CV was the best Mark had ever seen and boasted extensive experience in the areas in which Mark wanted to specialise. He also had impressive credentials – not to mention a long list of business contacts. True, he had had rather a lot of jobs in the last five years, but he was an entrepreneur and Mark respected that. Sam's charm, confidence, and strong personality left Mark feeling a little daunted but, being eager to get things under way and not having hired anyone before, Mark swallowed his doubts and offered Sam a contract.

After the first two months, Mark began to get an uneasy feeling about the partnership. Sam's list of business contacts had evaporated and he seemed to lack knowledge of areas that Mark saw as fundamental to the business. Mark began to wonder how much of Sam's CV was actually true and berated himself for not looking into Sam's employment history and credentials more carefully . . .

Tina's story

When she first came to see me, Tina's self-esteem was shaky, to say the least. Several months of hard work had improved her relationship with herself beyond all recognition. However, there was a stumbling block: her closest friend, Alison. Tina spent a lot of time with Alison and would consult her before making any major decision. Alison was equally forthcoming with her views on how Tina should improve her life and would often criticize Tina for falling short.

Alison professed to 'only be concerned' for Tina's well-being. But her 'concern' came with a high price tag. In order to remain close to her, Tina had to subject herself her to constant put-downs. As Tina's self-belief became more robust, the relationship was starting to look less attractive.

I asked Tina to focus on how she felt when she was with Alison. 'Small inside, like I am shrinking,' she said. I asked her where she felt it in her body. She replied, 'I get a sinking feeling in my stomach. My mind feels all fuzzy, as though my brain has seized up.' Tina had assumed that these signs were proof that she was inadequate in some way. But when I encouraged her to listen to them more carefully, she began to appreciate that her feelings were telling her something important.

These two stories are very different, but they highlight a key point: very often, when things aren't right, deep down we know it. The same may be true for you, too. If you stop trying to rationalise away your doubts and fears, do you experience any uncomfortable feelings in the body in the presence of certain people that may be a warning sign?

When you meet someone for the first time, and get to know them in the weeks to come, check out how you feel when you are with them. Be particularly alert to any extreme emotions, sensations, or beliefs about them. Look out for any tell-tale signs of uneasiness, anxiety, or sense of inadequacy in yourself or a tendency to view the other person as wonderful, superior, or as someone whom you should try to impress.

For some good indicators of whether a relationship is good or bad for you, use Exercise 47 below.

Exercise 47. Key signs of a good relationship

Think about a current relationship: intimate, social, or professional. It can be one you are thinking about developing or one you have already. Copy the following questions into your learning log and answer them by ticking the response that feels most true of this relationship for you.

	Yes, definitely	Not sure	No
1. Do I feel respected by this person? (Or are there subtle put-downs in the form of supposed 'advice' or 'concern'?)	☐	☐	☐
2. Does this person value me for who I am? (Or are they constantly trying to change me?)	☐	☐	☐
3. Can I be myself with this person? (Or am I constantly trying to be someone I am not, in order to impress them?)	☐	☐	☐
4. Can I express my wishes and opinions openly? (Or do I constantly sacrifice my own views and preferences to please them, when this is not true of me generally?)	☐	☐	☐
5. Is our relationship reciprocal? (Or is one of us working much harder than the other?)	☐	☐	☐
6. Do I feel as if I have something to offer this relationship? (Or does the other person give the impression that they are doing me a big favour by spending time with me?)	☐	☐	☐

	Yes, definitely	Not sure	No
7. Do I feel emotionally safe with this person? (Or does something inside of me feel uncomfortable when I am with them?)	☐	☐	☐
8. Do I have a strong sense of myself in this relationship? (Or do I feel swept along with, or so highly impressed by, this person that I often lose a sense of myself?)	☐	☐	☐
9. Do I feel good with this person: happy, contented, and generally relaxed? (Or do I tend to feel tense and anxious?)	☐	☐	☐
10. Is this person open and honest about themselves and their life? (Or are certain key areas concealed?)	☐	☐	☐
11. Based on my experience, is this person capable of sharing themselves in a way appropriate to our relationship? (Or is there something inaccessible or overly intrusive about them?)	☐	☐	☐
12. In my experience, does this person keep their promises? (Or are there often excuses, broken agreements, or even lies?)	☐	☐	☐

What you are aiming for is a sense that it is safe to be yourself with this person. You feel free to express your thoughts, views and feelings (albeit gradually, if you are just getting to know one another) without feeling criticized, inferior, or over-awed.

In addition to strong negative feelings, it also helps to be wary of very strong, positive feelings early on in a relationship. Extreme attraction is so intoxicating that it causes us to accelerate the development of intimacy and makes it easier to override objections that may be coming from a wise part of ourselves. Of course, your instant attraction may prove to have some substance in the longer term, but don't place too much faith in it to begin with.

Another useful exercise, which can also help you navigate the ebb and flow of relationships, is what I call 'The Golden Rules' exercise.

What are your 'golden rules'?

When I am working with someone who suspects they are caught up in a negative relationship pattern, I always ask about their 'golden rules'.

Golden rules are about expressing, in very clear terms, the circumstances in which the relationship between you and the other person would have to end. This decision might be based on a single, major incident, or an accumulation of small incidents over a much longer period of time. For example, I have one friend who cannot bear lies. Once she becomes aware that she has been lied to, the relationship ends. This may sound harsh, but honesty is so central to her sense of integrity that she knows from experience she cannot sustain a meaningful relationship without it. Someone else I know has golden rules around criticisms and put-downs: if, in the first three months of a new relationship, intimate, social, or professional, the other person makes critical comments about her on a particular number of occasions, she knows it's time to move on.

This may sound excessive, but I would argue that having golden rules is something that all people in happy, healthy, mutually satisfying relationships know to be true. Golden rules are not about demanding perfection of a partner. Nor are they meant to be a decision-making straitjacket. They are about equipping yourself with a compass to navigate more effectively the changing landscape that is the world of other people.

The major benefits of having golden rules are:

- they enable you to establish self-protective boundaries around relationships;
- they help you decide what is nurturing for you, so you don't waste valuable emotional energy on relationships that are doomed to fail;
- they save heartache by preventing you from entering harmful relationships;

- they help you identify (and end) bad relationships more quickly;
- because they are based on a person's behaviour, rather than their character (we'll talk about this more below), they help you depersonalize what the person is doing and take appropriate action without condemning yourself or them.

And, in case you are wondering, it is always better to have golden rules based on criteria for ending the relationship, rather than criteria for keep it going. This is because devising a list of positive criteria can easily turn into a wish list that no one can ever match (for example, 'the person must always be loving and caring'). Far from being negative, knowing the terms and conditions in which you would end a relationship gives you greater flexibility around relationship decision-making, while also giving others permission to be human.

Please remember that when it comes to golden rules, there are no definitive rights and wrongs (although I would argue that any form of physical, sexual, or emotional cruelty would constitute grounds for ending a relationship). But there will be rights and wrongs that work for you.

Exercise 48. Defining your 'Golden Rules'

What are your Golden Rules for relationships? What would be the standards which, if broken, would mean that the relationship was beyond repair? Spend some time thinking about these very carefully – they are, after all, an investment in your future. Once you think you know your relationship rules, write them in your learning log.

Helpful hint. Remember to make your Golden Rules very specific (e.g., not 'Being treated disrespectfully', but 'Having critical comments made about my physical appearance in front of other people, on five occasions, after I have asked them explicitly not to do this').

3. Specific skills for achieving and enhancing intimacy

As we have already seen, a relationship is created and recreated over
its entire lifespan, not something that is achieved for all time. As a
result, there can be no universal definition of a good relationship
– what works for one person, couple, or group will be different for
another. However, many good relationships seem to have certain
characteristics. Think about your own relationships as you look at
the list below. How many of your relationships meet these criteria?

- Mutual respect.
- Equal rights and responsibilities.
- Acceptance of one another's limitations (note: this does not
  mean subjecting yourself to others' unacceptable or abusive
  behaviour).
- More frequent positive interactions than negative inter-
  actions.
- Solving relationship ruptures swiftly and effectively.
- The ability to compromise around the practicalities of living.
- Never having to compromise your core values.
- Achieving a satisfying balance between time together and time
  apart.

Attaining these criteria requires a working knowledge of the 12
Principles we have covered in this book. For example, you need to
know and respect the other person's Mission (their authenticity,
meaning, signature strengths) and to harness your Courage to per-
severe with the relationship through tricky times. You need to
appreciate the Attitude they bring to their relationship with you
(while bringing to the partnership your own optimism, curiosity,
gratitude for they are and what they do, and compassion for them
and the dilemmas they face). You also need to understand something of the Process through which the other person engages with
life (their goals, thinking habits, brand of creativity, and motivation).

In addition, there are a number of essential relationship skills
which, if mastered, can enhance the survival changes of all your
relationships. As you read these skills, you may find it helpful to
hold in mind a specific relationship, or think about themes within
your relationships more broadly.

Skill No. 1: Be responsible

Being responsible means knowing the kind of person you want to be in your relationships. Your signature strengths (Principle No. 3) might give you a clue here. Be clear what it is you have to give and what you expect in return, and make sure the other person knows this, too. It is your responsibility to know and let others know what matters most.

Being responsible also means taking ownership of your part in the relationship – including any difficulties you are having. If you have made a mistake or caused the other person pain, hold your hands up and ask for feedback on what you can do differently next time (far from being weak, you convey the courage to be honest, which has a reparative quality in its own right). If you're behaving in a way you're not entirely happy with, identify what you need to do differently and do it. Prove yourself reliable and trustworthy through your actions – this always deepens the bond between people. Of course, this is easier to achieve if you are honest with yourself from the start about what you want to give and receive in the relationship. But the more open you can be with each other, the easier it will be to negotiate areas of difference and work towards a shared vision for your future.

Skill No. 2: Get your thinking straight

In Principle No. 10 we looked at the damage that can be inflicted by toxic thinking and the need to develop a thinking style that allows for balanced and reasonable decision-making. In no area is this more important than the arena of relationships.

It is so easy to be wrong about other people's feelings, intentions, and actions – to assume we know when in fact we do not. A great deal of pain in our relationships is caused simply by misinterpreting others' intentions.

When I was training to be a psychologist, I was taught a simple exercise that I still use. After meeting with someone, I was encouraged to write down three different lists: one list for what I had observed, one list for what I had heard, and one list for what I had inferred. If the first two lists were very short and the third list was very long, I knew that my attentiveness to the person had probably gone astray: I had got caught in the trap of seeing the other person through my own filters and had to learn to look and listen afresh next time. I would certainly recommend you use this same approach – particularly when you are dealing with a challenging situation.

Skill No. 3: Listen to each other

Listening is not as easy as it sounds. Particularly in longer-term relationships, it is very easy to listen to each other on 'automatic pilot', allowing the person to chat away while our minds wander elsewhere. Effective listening is an extremely powerful tool and one that you can learn, even though it takes time and practice to perfect. To help you develop your listening skills, try the following exercise.

Choose someone with whom you would like to deepen your relationship (they also have to agree to this for the exercise to proceed). One of you needs to talk about something for three minutes. It can be about your day, a particular concern, or something good that has happened. Generally though, it's best to start with a fairly neutral topic rather than anything that might cause conflict between you. After three minutes, the person who did the talking stops and the other person feeds back what they have heard. Be sure to steer clear of offering advice or coming up with a counter-argument: the task is simply to feed back what has been heard. After giving feedback, the other person says how accurate they felt this was and corrects any listening errors, without criticism or judgement. You then change roles and repeat the exercise.

This may sound like a strange idea, but you'll be surprised how you can start to get to know each other at a much deeper level just by learning to listen. And because we all love to feel heard, it can make each of you feel truly valued. Of course, this exercise also requires you to talk! As you build up your listening skills, begin to extend your communication time into new areas, such as telling your partner or friend what it is that you need from them and why this matters to you. This way it becomes easier to make changes without getting stuck in the 'Yes, but . . .' dialogues that are typical of most conflicts.

Skill No. 4: Express your appreciation

In Principle No. 7 we looked at the power of gratitude. Learning to express gratitude in your relationships has the capacity to transform them. Tell your partner, friends, and colleagues when they do something you appreciate, or something that makes a positive difference to your life – especially the small things (it is often small gestures that have the greatest impact). Positive feedback shapes behaviour far more effectively than negative feedback and also has the effect of allowing the other person to feel valued, validated in their efforts, and supported.

Giving positive feedback does not mean coming up with sentimental expressions of undying admiration or love. If you're not sure where to start, think of one thing the other person does for you every day, every week or every month (depending on how often you have contact). And then another . . . Find a way to say thank you, whether it's over the dinner table or via an e-mail, text message, or card. Occasionally, it might involve splashing out on a special treat, such as a present or dinner date, but most of the time it is what you say that will make all the difference. Not only does this bring you closer together, but if you are used to giving and receiving positive feedback it also makes it easier to raise sensitive and challenging topics when the need arises.

Skill No. 5: Deal with difficulties

The ability to manage dissatisfactions in a relationship is vital to its continued success. The most rewarding relationships are not those that are conflict-free, but those where both partners are able to resolve differences swiftly and effectively.

In Skill No. 2, we looked at how easy it can be to misconstrue the other's intention by engaging in toxic thinking. In situations of conflict where emotions run high this is even more likely and tends to result in accusatory statements such as 'You *always* do (something negative)' or 'You *never* do (what I want you to)'. These are ineffective ways of resolving conflict because they are based on a criticism of the person rather than explaining what you would like them to do differently. They are also examples of over-generalization.

Psychologist John Gottman tells us that when we are faced with difficulties in relationships it is vital to differentiate criticism and complaints. Complaints involve a description of the behaviour that you don't like, whereas criticism is an attack on the other's character. Generally, personalities don't change but behaviour can, so avoid criticizing the person for who they are and focus on what they can do differently. Make it specific so the other person has a clear idea of what is required of them as this also helps depersonalize difficulties.

Tina used this strategy to challenge Alison's behaviour. Initially very angry with Alison, Tina wanted to tell her how she '*always* criticized her in front of others and that she wasn't going to stand for her cruel behaviour any longer'. But, through role-play, she realized that Alison was probably trying to be a decent friend (even if the strategy misfired) and talking to her in this way would simply hurt Alison's feelings and jeopardize the relationship. Instead, Tina chose another strategy, in which she explained to Alison the effect of her criticisms and why this needed to change. She also fed this back using a lot of positive feedback, which included telling Alison how much she valued their friendship and wanted it to continue. In fact, their relationship was strong enough to survive the needed changes and Tina learned something important in the process: that voicing a complaint paves the way for solution-finding, whereas criticism does not.

Skill No. 6: Make quality time for the relationship

The fastest route to relationship failure I know of is complacency. Complacency erodes everything that is special in a partnership and eventually leads to disillusionment, disappointment and even contempt. Whatever other priorities you have in life, make your relationships one of them by ensuring that there is some quality time for the two of you – whether this is an intimate relationship or an important social one.

Quality time will mean different things in different relationships. For example, the quality time you devote to a new business relationship will differ from the kind of quality time needed to allow an intimate relationship to blossom. Think about the range of relationships in your life and the kind of attention that each significant one might need. It may mean meeting up once a week or once a month. It may be going out together or staying at home together. It may involve an additional activity or a lack of additional activities. Work out what would make the difference and then stick to it. And it often helps to diarize your time together, giving it the same level of importance that you would a business appointment.

Quality time reminds you not to take the other person for granted and also provides an opportunity for listening to each other, learning about each other, and sharing fun experiences that help cement your bond.

Take home message

We spend our entire lives in relationships with other people. Yet most of us are never given the opportunity to learn the rules of good relating.

Relationships are always a work in progress and will require commitment, perseverance, and constant renewal. The best relationships are not those that avoid conflict, but those that give each other room for growth and change. This involves mutual respect, attentiveness to the needs of the other, and a willingness to take full responsibility for the inevitable ups and downs that will occur as a function of your continuing development.

There are many actions you can take to enrich your relationships, but skills are not enough. We each bring to our relationships implicit ideas about ourselves and others and need to understand the impact of these implicit ideas (and the implicit ideas of others) if our relationships are to yield the rich harvest that their potential promises.

Relationships add a unique dimension to our growth because through them we both lose and find ourselves. They invite us to be both more of who we are, and yet to transcend who we are by merging with something bigger than our individual selves. By engaging in relationships, we encounter possibilities of an altogether different kind. It is through our relationship with others, through our willingness to know and be known, that the best of us can ultimately find a home for its self-expression.

Coaching Tool Box. Top Tips for Creating and Sustaining Enriching Relationships

1.   Be clear about what you want from, and what you have to offer, a relationship. Check that your hopes and expectations fit with the other person's agenda.
2.   Be wary of the well-intentioned friend for whom you somehow never quite fit the bill. These people are not your real friends.
3.   Never compromise your authenticity to be with another person. If you are, something is wrong.
4.   Know your 'Golden Rules' for relationships. If appropriate, share them with the other person.
5.   Practise the six relationship skills described in this chapter. Personalize them according to your relationships and lifestyle and you will soon notice the difference.

Honouring your Relationships

One idea I shall take away from this chapter is . . . (write the answer in your learning log).
One thing I shall do differently is . . . (write the answer in your learning log).

In Need of Further Guidance?

If you have relationship difficulties that you are struggling to sort out by yourself, or if you are putting yourself or someone else at risk by your behaviour, please seek professional advice that can help you work things out. A list of organizations can be found at the end of this book.

Bibliography

*Alberti, R., & Emmons, M. (1981). *Your Perfect Right. A Guide to Assertive Living*. San Luis Obispo, CA: Impact.

*De Angelis, B. (1992). *Are You the One for Me?* London: Element.

*Gottman, J., & Silver, N. (1999). *The Seven Principles for Making Marriage Work*. New York: Three Rivers Press.

*Moore, T. (1992). *Care of the Soul: A Guide for Cultivating Depth and Sacredness in Everyday Life*. New York: Harper Perennial.

*Moore, T. (2004). *Dark Nights of the Soul: A Guide to Finding Your Way through Life's Ordeals*. London: Piatkus.

*Quilliam, S. (1995). *Staying Together. From Crisis to Deeper Commitment*. London: Vermilion.

PART IV

CHAPTER TWENTY-SIX

The Art of Inspired Living: Building Inspiration to Last a Lifetime

'Not I – not anyone else, can travel that road for you; you must travel it for yourself'

(Walt Whitman)

'Life is the greatest bargain – we get it for nothing'

(Yiddish Proverb)

Congratulations on completing this book. Undertaking a journey of this kind is no small achievement; if you genuinely engage with the opportunities and challenges it presents, personal development is guaranteed to bring you face to face with yourself – who you are, what you have to offer and what lies within you as latent potential. This can lead to revelations that are both liberating and challenging. Self-coaching involves having the courage to look – and keep looking – even when you have some doubts about how to use what you are discovering.

By now, having worked through the different chapters and applied the ideas thoughtfully to your own life, you should have a rich collection of insights, ideas, personal knowledge, frameworks, and tools to help you capitalize on your talents, enhance your motivation, and fulfil your potential. But you will probably have questions, doubts, and areas of uncertainty, too. If you do, then let me assure you that this is perfectly normal.

As you complete this book, you are facing both an ending and a beginning. Your journey is ending in the sense that we have almost finished our work together. But it is also beginning in that you must now decide how you want to apply what you have learnt to the next stage of your life. Where are you headed? What will this next stage of your journey look like? Author Thomas Moore describes the sense of uncertainty that comes with this stage of the process when he reminds us that there can be no single end point, definitive conclusion, or clear set of instructions on what to do next. This is down to you.

Before you can turn your attention to what you might want to do next, it is important to mark the end of this phase of your journey. You have achieved a great deal, and acknowledging your successes is an important part of honouring who you are as well as a major motivator for the future.

Review the entries recorded in your gains diary and the notes you have been keeping in your Learning Log. You might also want to repeat the Inspiration Inventory in Part I, to give you a more objective indication of what has and hasn't changed (it is repeated at the end of this book so that you can take a clean copy). Once you have a clear picture of all that you have achieved, consider how you want to acknowledge yourself for your efforts. How do you want to celebrate your gains? With whom do you want to share them? Copy the next exercise into your learning log and use it to help you.

Exercise 49. The celebration exercise

1. What are three of the most important things you have learned from 'The Art of Inspired Living'?
2. What are your three most important gains from working through this book?
3. What do you most want to celebrate about yourself and your life?
4. How would you most like to celebrate your successes and gains?
5. How will your learning and gains shape the way you *view* yourself and your life from now on?
6. How will your learning and gains shape the way you *live* your life from now on?

Take a moment to reflect on your responses. You may be tempted to overlook this aspect of inspired living, but please don't! Your efforts deserve acknowledgement because they reflect the coming together of your talents and resourcefulness in a way that says something important about the kind of person you are. And this holds a vital clue to your future . . .

Coaching, 'MAP', and the principles of inspired living

As we have seen, good coaching is about a lot more than good outcomes. It is about creating possibilities for your life and facilitating transitions that might lead to new destinations. Outcomes, once achieved, give us no basis for further growth. But the learning required to get there offers an unlimited supply of opportunities for the expression of our values, our creativity, our courage, and our potential.

Psychologist and author Jack Kornfield describes our growth as 'richly organic' and this, I think, speaks to the very best of what coaching has to offer. You comprise a complex terrain of experiences, circumstances, stories, strengths, habits, hopes, and plans. Coaching can help you navigate this terrain more effectively in order to enrich your life and the lives of others.

Of course, life will continue to do what it always does – present challenges and opportunities, serve up demands and expectations. And it will, at times, force you to revise your sense of who you are and what you can do. However much you try to influence the route you take, your journey will ultimately be determined by many factors, some of which are beyond your control. The best you can do is set your compass in the desired direction and immerse yourself fully in the prevailing conditions – while wearing the psychological armour with which your self-coaching work has equipped you. I do hope, however, that this book has helped you set your compass more accurately. It is not enough to change your behaviour and acquire new skills. To make the most of who you are and who you might become, you also need to attend to those broader frameworks that underpin your choices: your authenticity, your values, and the essence of what brings meaning to your life.

In this book, I have introduced you to a simple yet powerful coaching model called 'MAP'. Now that you know what MAP is all about, you can use it whenever you want to design a method of change: big or small. We have looked at five areas in which MAP can be applied: career choices, work-life balance, self-esteem, physical well-being, and relationships, but this is only a starting point. There are as many potential destinations and goals as there are individual people, so feel free to be creative with MAP and use it in ways that make sense to you and your life.

I have also introduced you to 12 Principles that I believe have the power to inspire you and help you appreciate your life for the gift that it is. Remember, there is always a balance to be struck between accepting ourselves as we are, and opening ourselves up to change. Our culture's preoccupation with results and outcomes can sometimes lead us astray, helping us become addicted to the pursuit of change when, in fact, nothing may need changing.

Moreover, if your journey does involve deciding to change certain areas, don't assume that this must involve the pursuit of big results that will require major upheavals to your lifestyle, work, or relationships. Small changes are often more desirable than big ones, because they are more likely to be sustained in the longer term and lead slowly but surely in directions you may not have anticipated. So, don't stifle yourself with burdensome expectations that detract from getting to know the unique rhythm and subtle nuances of you. Your life is your ongoing creative project, and if you tune in to what is going on around you it will be the best source of feedback you could ever hope for. As author Thomas Moore advises, aim for a full life, not a perfect one!

Taking the next steps

It is my belief that personal development work, sincerely and thoughtfully undertaken, contributes to the well-being of others as well as ourselves, and pays dividends for the world around us. There are many ways in which the work you have done can shape your world and many doors that it might open, if you are prepared to look.

So give some thought to where you now wish to be headed. What does the next stage look like for you? What priority, medium-term, and long-term goals make sense for you, having come this far? Plan the next stage of your journey now, with the help of the following exercise. Copy it into your learning log, and answer the questions as fully as possible.

Exercise 50. Planning your journey

1(a) What are your goals for the immediate future (the next six months)?

1(b) How can you enhance your chances of achieving these goals? (What do you need to know or learn to do to bring this about? What resources and opportunities are required?)

1(c) How will your life change as a result of achieving these goals? Will you be happy with these changes?

1(d) What could get in the way of achieving these goals? How will you manage these obstacles?

2(a) What are your medium-term goals (the next six to twelve months)?

2(b) How can you enhance your chances of achieving these goals? (What do you need to know or learn to do to bring this about? What resources and opportunities are required?)

2(c) How will your life change as a result of achieving these goals? Will you be happy with these changes?

2(d) What could get in the way of achieving your medium-term goals? How will you manage these obstacles?

3(a) What are your long-term goals (the next five years)?

3(b) How can you enhance your chances of achieving these goals? (What do you need to know or learn to do to bring this about? What resources and opportunities are required?)

3(c) How will your life change as a result of achieving these goals? Will you be happy with these changes?

3(d) What could get in the way of achieving your long-term goals? How will you manage these obstacles?

If you have goals with which you feel you need some help, or your answers to any of the questions in Exercise 50 left you feeling doubtful about how to proceed, you might like to consider contacting a professional coach. This can be a very valuable investment in your future as well as helping you capitalize on the self-coaching work you have done already. If this is something you are interested in, please refer to the list of organizations I have provided at the end of this book.

A parting wish from me to you

When I start working with a client, I recognize it for the privilege that it is. Very often, I have no idea where the work will lead us. It doesn't matter how carefully we develop a suitable plan of action or how much thought I give to methods that might be of benefit, what emerges will be unique to that person. Their individual style, character strengths, creativity, and brand of courage – as well as the relationship that forms between us – will be indelibly stamped on the journey we undertake.

My experience of writing this book, and the sense of privilege that has come with it, has been no different. My initial ideas have come and gone, been developed or discarded as new insights and inspirations have emerged. As is always the case with any journey, the end result is not what I had originally anticipated, but it has remained true to the vision of what I most wanted to offer you.

I do not know what life has in store for you. But I do hope that by reading this book, you are clearer about what inspires you and what makes your life worth living. To quote Seneca, 'As long as you live, keep learning how to live'. I hope you will consider doing just this – learn how to live over and over again, through setting out on a course of action that will help you appreciate more fully who you are and what you might achieve. As the famous author George Eliot once said, it is never too late to be the person you might have become. I wish you a life that is full of meaning – wherever your journey leads you.

Appendix 1: Gains Diary

Brief description of the gain	Date of gain

Appendix 2: The Inspiration Inventory

The Inspiration Inventory

1 **Overall happiness and emotional well-being:**

   0   1   2   3   4   5   6   7   8   9   10

   Prompt questions: Do you enjoy your life? Are you glad just to be alive? Does your life inspire you or are you often anxious, disillusioned, or unhappy?

2 **Relationship to self:**

   0   1   2   3   4   5   6   7   8   9   10

   Prompt questions: Do you respect the person that you are? Are you at peace with yourself, confident in your abilities or do you worry about coming up to scratch?

3 **Intimate relationships:**

   0   1   2   3   4   5   6   7   8   9   10

   Prompt questions: Do you feel loved, appreciated and supported by those that matter to you? Can you express emotional and physical intimacy easily? Can you give and receive love freely?

4 **Friendships and social life:**

   0   1   2   3   4   5   6   7   8   9   10

   Prompt questions: Do you have good friendships based on mutual respect and trust? Can you be yourself in your friendships or do you feel pressured to be someone you are not?

5 **Health:**

   0   1   2   3   4   5   6   7   8   9   10

   Prompt questions: Do you have abundant energy? Do you respect and nurture your body? Do you nourish yourself with healthy foods, sufficient sleep, and time to relax and unwind?

6 **Lifestyle and work–life balance:**

   0   1   2   3   4   5   6   7   8   9   10

Prompt questions: Does your lifestyle reflect and honour your priorities? Do you have a good work–life balance or often feel exhausted or 'burnt out'?

7 Career and work:

0   1   2   3   4   5   6   7   8   9   10

Prompt questions: Do you enjoy your work? Does it inspire you and enrich your life? Does it allow you to express your talents and abilities? Does your work sustain or undermine you?

8 Money and finances:

0   1   2   3   4   5   6   7   8   9   10

Prompt questions: Do you have sufficient money to meet your needs? Are you satisfied with your income? Do you have a system for organizing your finances, including outgoings, savings, and pension?

9 Hobbies and leisure interests:

0   1   2   3   4   5   6   7   8   9   10

Prompt questions: Do you have fulfilling hobbies and interests separate from your work? Do you have sufficient time for this part of your life or is it often eroded by work or other pressures?

10 Values and principles:

0   1   2   3   4   5   6   7   8   9   10

Prompt questions: Are you clear about what you stand for? Are you living life according to your core values? Are there any areas of your life in which you compromise your values?

11 Community and contribution:

0   1   2   3   4   5   6   7   8   9   10

Do you feel you make a difference to the world, even in a small way? Do others benefit from your talents and gifts?

12 Spiritual life:

0   1   2   3   4   5   6   7   8   9   10

Prompt questions: Is there space in your life to develop your potential, your expanded self, and your spiritual self? Do you feel the need to belong to a religious or spiritual community? If so, is this need being met?

13 Any other areas important to you (name them in the space below).

0   1   2   3   4   5   6   7   8   9   10

Prompt questions: What other areas of your life really matter to you that are not included in the above?

Appendix 3: Organizations

If you feel you need any additional help to achieve your goals, the following organizations will be of interest to you.

British Association for Behavioural & Cognitive Psychotherapies: for a list of accredited cognitive–behaviour therapists and information about how CBT can help. Information available online at www.babcp.com, or telephone +44 (0)161 797 4484.

British Association for Counselling and Psychotherapy: for a list of accredited counsellors and psychotherapists. Information available online at www.bacp.co.uk, or telephone +44 (0)870 443 5252.

British Psychological Society: for information on how psychology can help, a list of different groups and divisions within the society (including a Special Group in Coaching Psychology) and a list of Chartered Psychologists. Information available online at www.bps.org.uk, or telephone + 44 (0)116 254 9568.

Gaia House Meditation Retreat Centre: for information on mindfulness and other meditation retreats. Available online at www.gaiahouse.co.uk, or telephone +44 (0)1626 333613.

The Professional Development Foundation: a professional development network providing evidence based consultancy, research, coaching and accreditation services to individuals, professional bodies and organizations. Information available on line at www.pdf.net, or telephone +44 (0) 20 7987 2805.

Relate: for counselling for relationship difficulties. Information available online at www.relate.org.uk, or telephone +44 (0)300 100 1234 (Central Office).

UK Council of Psychotherapy: for a list of registered psychotherapists. Available online at www.psychotherapy.org.uk, or telephone
+44 (0)20 7014 9955.